THE
GREATEST
SPORTS
Trivia
THROWDOWN
OF ALL TIME

BY
GARY GUTHRIE

ISBN-13: 978-1523253593
ISBN-10: 1523253592

Dedication

To my alphabetical order of trivia kin:
Jane Duncan, Sarah Horton, and Gary Moore.
Thank you for keeping my quest for trivialities alive
and my life anything but trivial.

Contents

Foreword

If you're reading this book, I don't have to tell you that trivia can be one addictive mofo – that constant itch to find a little info bit that no one else knows. One you can tuck away for the perfect moment when you want to make someone drop their jaw just a little.

For me, trivia answers can be beautiful rabbit holes lined with interesting backstories and tangents. And, that's a component of my trivia book series that I hope makes them unique and gives the reader a deeper, richer experience.

These sports questions aren't for the "What's the name of Boston's NBA team" novices, mind you. They're designed for sports junkies who thirst for meaty, big-league minutiae. And, I have to issue a fair warning: while most of the questions are from "major" sports (baseball, basketball, football, etc.), there is an occasional question from lesser-known sports (like cricket or billiards). Just sayin'.

Now, let's play ball!

(Ladies and) Gentlemen,
start your engines

Alright, folks – here's the trivia questions, all 500 of 'em! They're all multiple choice and you'll find the answers starting on page 119.

If you're interested in turning the book into a game, there's a little how-to on page 339.

Good luck...

1. Prior to relocating to Los Angeles (the *first* time back in 1946), the pro football Rams called what city their home?
    a. Milwaukee
    b. Toledo
    c. Buffalo
    d. Cleveland

2. Which of these National Basketball Association draft picks was *not* a #1 pick?
    a. Tim Duncan
    b. Allen Iverson
    c. Bob McAdoo
    d. LaRue Martin

3. Of these well-known University of Cincinnati basketball players that made it to the pros, which one played the most games in the NBA?
   a. Kenyon Martin
   b. Jim Ard
   c. Jack Twyman
   d. Oscar Robertson

4. Which of these former NFL coaches also played in the National Basketball Association?
   a. Bud Grant
   b. George Allen
   c. Tom Flores
   d. Chuck Knox

5. This NFL team has retired the jerseys of Don Maynard, Curtis Martin, Joe Klecko, and Dennis Byrd.
   a. Jets
   b. Bills
   c. Eagles
   d. Dolphins

6. Billy Martin played for all of these baseball teams except one. Which one?
   a. New York Yankees
   b. Washington Senators
   c. Detroit Tigers
   d. Cincinnati Reds

7. This NBA player missed only 24 games in 15 seasons, earning him the moniker "The Horse."
   a. Dan Issel
   b. Tommy Heinsohn
   c. Bill Bradley
   d. Bill Laimbeer

8. Who's considered the creator of the Ultimate
    Fighting Championship, and the father of mixed
    martial arts (MMA)?
    a. Jake Hooker
    b. Terry Luttrell
    c. Rich Williams
    d. Art Davie

9. These two matches represent the very first and
    very last opponent for Muhammad Ali.
    a. Tunney Hunsaker & Trevor Berbick
    b. Herb Siler & Alfredo Evangelista
    c. LaMar Clark & Larry Holmes
    d. Tony Esperti & Larry Holmes

10. These sports were once discontinued in the Olympics
    but returned in 1972 and 1988 respectively.
    a. Baseball & curling
    b. Skeleton & polo
    c. Archery & tennis
    d. Tug of war & rhythmic gymnastics

11. The first pair of brothers to become World
    Champions in boxing was...
    a. Joe and Vince Dundee
    b. Noel and Terry McGee
    c. Sid and Fitz Vanderpool
    d. Christophe and Fabrice Tiozzo

12. The modern version of this game's "court" owes its
    design to Major Walter Clopton Wingfield.
    a. Basketball
    b. Tennis
    c. Lawn Bowling
    d. Jai Alai

13. Which of these Lakers has captured the most NBA Finals MVPs?
    a. Kareem Abdul-Jabbar
    b. Wilt Chamberlain
    c. Kobe Bryant
    d. Magic Johnson

14. In a normal Jai Alai match, the first team to score how many points wins?
    a. 5
    b. 8
    c. 10
    d. 7

15. In 1941, this became the first football league to play a double round-robin schedule (5 home/5 away games).
    a. American Football League
    b. National Football League
    c. All-America Football Conference
    d. Atlantic Coast Football League

16. This horse race has been termed "The Run for the Black-Eyed Susans".
    a. Kentucky Derby
    b. The Preakness
    c. The Belmont
    d. Santa Anita Derby

17. The laws of rugby league state that the hooker wears this number.
    a. 9
    b. 5
    c. 6
    d. 8

18. In 1995, the Belgian Ministry of Health mandated drug testing in order to protect the welfare of the participants in this sport.
    a. Motocross
    b. Tennis
    c. Pigeon racing
    d. Cross-country skiing

19. He and his son Damon are the only dad-son pair to have both won the Formula One world title.
    a. Graham Hill
    b. Jim Clark
    c. Henri Pescarolo
    d. Dan Gurney

20. The youngest player in AL history to reach 100 career home runs was...
    a. Tony Conigliaro
    b. Mel Ott
    c. Rogers Hornsby
    d. Harmon Killebrew

21. The Big Ten Conference has only one *former* member. Who?
    a. Ohio University
    b. Loyola of Chicago
    c. Drake University
    d. University of Chicago

22. Kenneth Michael "Ken" Stabler, aka The Snake, played his college ball at this school.
    a. Texas A&M
    b. Alabama
    c. Louisiana State
    d. University of Houston

23. The term "innings" can be applied to these sports.
    a. Baseball and bossaball
    b. Baseball and cricket
    c. Bicycle kick and baseball
    d. Baseball and basta

24. The only driver to win the Indianapolis 500, Daytona 500, the 24 Hours of Daytona, and the 24 Hours of Le Mans is...
    a. Jackie Stewart
    b. Al Unser
    c. Bobby Unser
    d. A.J. Foyt

25. This player was key to the Los Angeles Rams' 1951 championship season, with a record 1,495 yards receiving, a record that stood for 19 years.
    a. Elroy Hirsch
    b. Lamar Lundy
    c. Jack Snow
    d. Tom Fears

26. At any one time, there are how many batsmen in the playing area in cricket?
    a. One
    b. Three
    c. Four
    d. Two

27. Trainer D. Wayne Lukas can lay claim to being the trainer for these two Kentucky Derby winners.
    a. Grindstone and Thunder Gulch
    b. Sunday Silence and Alysheba
    c. Real Quiet and Silver Charm
    d. Go for Gin and Spectacular Bid

28. This baseball franchise moved twice, once becoming the Minnesota Twins and, the other time, becoming the Texas Rangers.
    a. Milwaukee Braves
    b. Louisville Colonels
    c. Washington Senators
    d. Seattle Mariners

29. Hall of Fame coach George Allen finished his coaching career here.
    a. Arizona Wranglers
    b. Washington Redskins
    c. Pepperdine University
    d. Long Beach State

30. To honor the Apollo 11 crew, this university retired the number "11" jersey.
    a. Marquette
    b. Purdue
    c. Houston
    d. Central Florida

31. In the inaugural season of the XFL, San Francisco's team was called what?
    a. Demons
    b. Thunderbolts
    c. Enforcers
    d. Bay

32. What sport is also known as "Borden ball"?
    a. Sepak takraw
    b. Handball
    c. Lacrosse
    d. Bocce

33. Alright, pigskin'ers, let's see how well you know your game. This route run by a receiver in football, where the receiver runs straight upfield towards the end zone, is also called a seam route, streak route or go route.
    a. Flag route
    b. Flare Route
    c. Steak Route
    d. Fly Pattern

34. In bowling, getting four strikes in a row is sometimes referred to as a "llama," but many TV announcers refer to it as a...
    a. Hambone
    b. Punt
    c. Wham
    d. Turkey

35. Let's see how much you know about Bruce (now Caitlyn) Jenner's collegiate career. Look over these Jenner-related factoids and pick out the one that's accurate...
    a. Bruce was on the wrestling team at Augustana College, but didn't do any track and field events until his senior year.
    b. Jenner went to Graceland University on a football scholarship, but injured his knee and switched to the decathlon.
    c. Bruce won back-to-back NCAA decathlon crowns while he was at the University of Oregon.
    d. Jenner was on the track team at the University of Connecticut (UConn) where he was on the relay team that won the Penn Relays in 1972.

36. The Old Brass Spittoon is given to the winner of the annual football match 'tween these schools.
    a. Indiana–Michigan State
    b. Boston College-Boston University
    c. South Carolina-Clemson
    d. Fresno State-UC Irvine

37. The Los Angeles Clippers franchise had its beginning in 1970 when they were what?
    a. Miami Floridians
    b. Oakland Oaks
    c. Buffalo Braves
    d. Pittsburgh Pipers

38. Identical twins Tom and Dick Van Arsdale played their college ball where?
    a. Purdue
    b. Michigan State
    c. Ohio State
    d. Indiana University

39. At the behest of James Naismith, this company was the first to produce a basketball for official use.
    a. Voit
    b. Spalding
    c. Reach
    d. Rawlings

40. The 1960 television show *Home Run Derby* was held at this park.
    a. Crosley Field
    b. Shibe Park
    c. Baker Bowl
    d. Wrigley Field

41. The Women's heptathlon consists of 100-meter hurdles, high jump, shot put, 200-meter (sprint), long jump, javelin throw, and...
    a. Discus throw
    b. Triple jump
    c. 40-yard dash
    d. 800 meters

42. Who were the first surfers? It goes back to the 1700s if that helps any.
    a. The Kardashians
    b. Spanish Colonists (in California)
    c. Ancient Polynesians
    d. The Vikings

43. The first-ever British female to win Olympic Gold in a track & field event...
    a. Mary Rand
    b. Willye White
    c. Anne Leyman
    d. Sue Hearnshaw

44. This 6'5" center, is the first player to dunk in a WNBA game.
    a. Diana Taurasi
    b. Lisa Leslie
    c. Cappie Pondexter
    d. Penny Taylor

45. Prior to his career at Alabama, Bear Bryant coached at Kentucky, Texas A&M and...
    a. Rice
    b. Georgia Tech
    c. Missouri
    d. Maryland

46. This MLB "Rookie of the Year" was drafted as the last player in the 1988 draft and only then 'coz his old man asked the team's manager for a favor.
    a. Robin Ventura
    b. Andy Benes
    c. Mike Piazza
    d. Chuck Knoblauch

47. He was the quarterback on Notre Dame's 1966 National Champion football team.
    a. Joe Theismann
    b. Terry Hanratty
    c. John Huarte
    d. Tom Clements

48. In the Tour de France, the rider with the lowest aggregate time is the leader of the race and gets to wear what color jersey?
    a. Red
    b. Yellow
    c. Green
    d. Pink

49. Since 1950, the College World Series has been in Omaha. What city hosted it directly prior to that?
    a. Wichita
    b. Kalamazoo
    c. Evansville
    d. Lubbock

50. This Olympic event was an actual event... once.
    a. Men's synchronized swimming
    b. Speedwalk snowshoeing
    c. 3-on-3 basketball
    d. Plunge for distance

51. In the Rodeo event of Bull Riding, the ride is scored how?
    a. from 0–100 points
    b. from 0-20 points
    c. from 1-25 points
    d. from 1-10 points

52. The 1904 Summer Olympics were held in St. Louis at what is now known as Francis Field on the campus of this university.
    a. St. Louis University
    b. Washington University in St. Louis
    c. Fontbonne
    d. Creighton

53. Dawn Fraser and Ian Thorpe are two Aussie athletes who compete in this sport.
    a. Tennis
    b. Cycling
    c. Skiing
    d. Swimming

54. Prior to managing the NY Yankees, Casey Stengel was an assistant coach for this SEC baseball team.
    a. Vanderbilt
    b. Tennessee
    c. Ole Miss
    d. Auburn

55. What was the name of the John Wayne movie where he plays a hockey player?
    a. Seeing Stars
    b. That's My Boy
    c. The Sweater
    d. Idol of the Crowds

56. A multi-rotational 1-ft. turn is called what in the sport of figure skating?
    a. Mohawk
    b. Rocker
    c. Twizzle
    d. Contour

57. This hockey player played on more Stanley Cup champion teams than any other player.
    a. Henri Richard
    b. Jean Béliveau
    c. L'École Saint-David
    d. Red Kelly

58. A typical major league curveball rotates at an average of how many revolutions per minute?
    a. 2400
    b. 1400
    c. 400
    d. 3400

59. Where did famed Olympic swimmer Mark Spitz go to college?
    a. Cornell
    b. USC
    c. Florida
    d. Indiana University

60. Since '73-74 when the NBA started recording this stat, who blocked 10 or more shots in a game more times than anyone else in NBA history?
    a. Manute Bol
    b. Mark Eaton
    c. Kareem Abdul-Jabbar
    d. Hakeem Olajuwon

61. The oldest swimmer to win an Olympic medal is...
    a. Dara Torres
    b. Pablo Morales
    c. Matt Biondi
    d. Andy Jameson

62. In golf, what qualifies as an albatross?
    a. 2 strokes under par on a hole
    b. 5 strokes under par on a hole
    c. 4 strokes under par on a hole
    d. 3 strokes under par on a hole

63. As of January 1, 2016, who was the oldest active player in the NFL?
    a. Jay Feely
    b. Charles Woodson
    c. Matt Hasselbeck
    d. Adam Vinatieri

64. Who's the "Joan" that won the Boston Marathon twice and the Summer Olympics once?
    a. Kristiansen
    b. Benoit
    c. Furniss
    d. Gilder

65. When North Carolina State beat Houston in the 1983 NCAA Men's Basketball championship, the game was decided on a last-second dunk by which Wolfpack forward?
    a. Dereck Whittenburg
    b. Thurl Bailey
    c. Sidney Lowe
    d. Lorenzo Charles

66. In 1992, what player became the first-ever third generation MLB player in history?
    a. Bret Boone
    b. Mike Bell
    c. Scott Hairston
    d. Brian Bannister

67. A soccer player is being (what) when we see a ref writing their name down in a notebook?
    a. booked
    b. signposted
    c. carded
    d. presaged

68. Of these college basketball coaches who moved on to the NBA, which has the best regular season W-L % in their NBA coaching tenure (as of 2016)?
    a. Frank Layden
    b. John Calipari
    c. Flip Saunders
    d. Rick Pitino

69. Janet Guthrie was the first woman driver to race in the Indy 500 as well as this other major race.
    a. Bristol 500
    b. Firecracker 500
    c. 24 Hours of LeMans
    d. Daytona 500

70. The terms "drivers" and "irons" are used in which of the following sports?
    a. Hockey and golf
    b. Cricket and hockey
    c. Horse racing and golf
    d. Auto racing and javelin

71. What Olympic medal did heavyweight champion Floyd Patterson win at the 1952 Helsinki games?
    a. Bronze medal - middleweight boxing
    b. Silver medal - heavyweight boxing
    c. Gold medal - middleweight boxing
    d. None

72. What player hit over 50 home runs in 1955 and 1965, representing the longest time span between 50-plus home run seasons for any player in Major League Baseball history.?
    a. Willie Mays
    b. Ted Williams
    c. Mickey Mantle
    d. Stan Musial

73. What position did David Beckham play in soccer?
    a. Goalie
    b. Defender
    c. Forward
    d. Midfielder

74. This driver started the tradition of drinking milk (buttermilk) in victory lane at the Indy 500...
    a. Wilbur Shaw
    b. Lester Spangler
    c. Louis Meyer
    d. Claude Virden

75. Besides his career in the NBA, Danny Ainge spent part of three seasons with this MLB team.
    a. Pittsburgh Pirates
    b. Tampa Bay Devil Rays
    c. Texas Rangers
    d. Toronto Blue Jays

76. Led by this player/coach, the Dallas Chaparrals were one of 11 teams to take the floor in the inaugural season of the ABA.
    a. Cliff Hagan
    b. Rick Mount
    c. Larry Jones
    d. Jerry Lucas

77. He set 80 world records and 81 Soviet records in weightlifting, plus won Gold medals at the 1972 Olympics in Munich and the '76 Montreal Olympics...
    a. Aleksandr Kurlovich
    b. Boris Badenov
    c. Andrei Chemerkin
    d. Vasily Alekseyev

78. Before his pro wrestling days, Dwayne Johnson (The Rock) played college football at this college.
    a. Florida State
    b. University of Florida
    c. Miami
    d. South Florida

79. In 1993, the Canadian Football League admitted this team as its first United States-based franchise.
    a. Sacramento Gold Miners
    b. Birmingham Barracudas
    c. Memphis Mad Dogs
    d. Las Vegas Posse

80. Tennis star Maria Sharapova hails from what country?
    a. Czech Republic
    b. Hungary
    c. Serbia
    d. Russia

81. What professional team was the first to field players in white shoes?
    a. Seattle Seahawks
    b. Baltimore Orioles
    c. Kansas City A's
    d. Oakland Raiders

82. This future baseball superstar began his pro career with the semi-pro Baxter Springs Whiz Kids.
    a. Henry Aaron
    b. Stan Musial
    c. Barry Bonds
    d. Mickey Mantle

83. The shot clock in basketball came into being when the owner of this team experimented with a 24-second version during a scrimmage.
    a. Minn.-St. Paul Lakers
    b. Cincinnati Royals
    c. Baltimore Bullets
    d. Syracuse Nationals

84. Who was the only player to win the Heisman Trophy as a player for a losing team?
    a. Terry Baker (Oregon State)
    b. John David Crow (Texas A&M)
    c. Paul Hornung (Notre Dame)
    d. Ernie Davis (Syracuse)

85. In 2004, Ichiro Suzuki of the Mariners' 262 hits broke this player's record of 257.
    a. George Sisler
    b. Walter Johnson
    c. Ty Cobb
    d. Pete Rose

86. Who makes the official ball of the NFL?
    a. Spalding
    b. Wilson
    c. Nike
    d. Adidas

87. Prior to MLB's Colorado franchise using the nickname "Rockies," another Colorado team used the same nickname but in this sport.
    a. Soccer (MISL)
    b. Arena football
    c. Hockey
    d. World Team Tennis

88. Which of these college team nicknames does not in the letter "s"?
    a. University of Memphis
    b. University of North Carolina
    c. University of Georgia
    d. Stanford University

89. Of these second basemen, who won the most Gold Gloves?
    a. Ryne Sandberg
    b. Bobby Richardson
    c. Frank White
    d. Lou Whitaker

90. In 1976, this MLB team's new uniforms featured collars and jerseys designed to be worn un-tucked.
    a. Kansas City Royals
    b. Chicago White Sox
    c. Toronto Blue Jays
    d. Montreal Expos

91. What was the only horse to ever beat Man o' War?
It happened at the Sanford Stakes at Saratoga way
back in 1919.
   a. War Admiral
   b. Sir Barton
   c. Exterminator
   d. Upset

92. I tried to resist asking a question about croquet,
but I have failed. So, asking your indulgence, can
you tell me what a "bisque" is in croquet?
   a. A fault when the mallet pushes the striker's
      ball, rather than making a clean strike
   b. An imaginary line one yard from the
      boundary
   c. A free turn in a handicap match
   d. An imaginary line on which a ball is placed
      for its first shot in the game

93. One of the differences between fast pitch softball
and baseball is that, in fast pitch softball, there is
no (what)?
   a. "leading off"
   b. helmet required
   c. wooden bats allowed
   d. second base

94. Each team consists of how many mounted players
in the sport of polo?
   a. 6
   b. 5
   c. 3
   d. 4

THE GREATEST SPORTS TRIVIA THROWDOWN OF ALL-TIME

95. There have been only about a dozen athletes who played in both Major League Baseball and the National Basketball Association (or its predecessor the Basketball Association of America). Of the following, which one didn't?
    a. Dave DeBusschere
    b. Bobby Shantz
    c. Cotton Nash
    d. Chuck Connors

96. Which of these major golf tournaments has the smallest "field"? (meaning the number of participants).
    a. Masters
    b. U.S. Open
    c. PGA Championship
    d. British Open

97. What Rams defensive lineman, variety show host, and future minister authored a book called *Needlepoint for Men*?
    a. Rosey Grier
    b. Merlin Olsen
    c. Jack Youngblood
    d. Deacon Jones

98. In archery, what do you call the aerodynamic stabilization of arrows or darts with materials such as feathers?
    a. Fletching or flight
    b. Nock
    c. Venials
    d. Anabs or Anabials

99. Which division of the NCAA has the largest number of colleges fielding a men's lacrosse team?
   a. Division 1
   b. Division 2
   c. Division 4
   d. Division 3

100. Until 2014, this college's basketball team went by one nickname and the baseball team by another.
   a. Texas Tech
   b. Murray State
   c. Rice
   d. University of Idaho

101. Daunte Culpepper, Ray Lewis, Michael Vick, Brett Favre and others have been "cursed" after appearing on the cover of this "product."
   a. A box of Wheaties
   b. Sports Illustrated
   c. ESPN – The Magazine
   d. Madden NFL game

102. This professional sports league has teams like the Rochester Rattlers and Florida Launch.
   a. Major League Lacrosse
   b. Roller Hockey International
   c. Women's Prof. Football Association
   d. World Indoor Soccer League

103. The most used name for a U.S. college mascot is...
   a. Ace
   b. Blaze
   c. Sammy (or Sammie)
   d. Victor E. (e.g. Victor E. Lion)

104. The origins of this particular National Basketball
Association franchise can be traced back to 1946
and the establishment of the Buffalo Bisons as a
member of the National Basketball League.
a. Detroit Pistons
b. Washington Wizards
c. Atlanta Hawks
d. Chicago Bulls

105. Going back to the 2010-11 season in this sport,
Maria Riesch of Germany won the "Women's
Overall Title". What's the sport?
a. Alpine Skiing
b. Fencing
c. Handball
d. Kickboxing

106. Henry Armstrong holds the record for the most
consecutive title defenses at this weight division in
professional boxing. Not that it'll help you figure
out the answer, but Henry was 5' 5 ½" tall and
had a 67" reach.
a. Heavyweight
b. Lightweight
c. Catch Weight
d. Welterweight

107. When Joe Montana arrived at Notre Dame and
donned the blue and gold in the fall of 1974, the
Fighting Irish' varsity football program was
coached by whom?
a. Ara Parseghian
b. Dan Devine
c. Lou Holtz
d. Terry Brennan

108. All of these NBA players played for this college –
Jeff Hornacek, Marcus Fizer, and Jamaal Tinsley.
   a. Gonzaga
   b. Bradley
   c. San Jose State
   d. Iowa State

109. Football fans may remember a play called "Ghost
to the Post" as part of NFL lore – something that
happened in a double-overtime game in 1977 and
one that marked the last appearance of the
Baltimore-based Colts. Who was the Colts'
opponent in the "Ghost to the Post" game?
   a. Oakland Raiders
   b. Denver Broncos
   c. Kansas City Chiefs
   d. NY Giants

110. Which of these colleges has the most NCAA
Men's Basketball Tournament appearances
without ever reaching a Final Four?
   a. Missouri
   b. Xavier
   c. BYU
   d. Western Kentucky

111. Which of these superstars graced the cover of
Sports Illustrated more often than anyone else
from 1954-2015?
   a. Michael Jordan
   b. Magic Johnson
   c. Tom Brady
   d. Tiger Woods

112. The Albuquerque Isotopes, Rancho Cucamonga Quakes, Ogden Raptors, Great Lakes Loons, and the Chattanooga Lookouts are minor league affiliates of this professional team.
    a. Los Angeles Lakers
    b. San Francisco Giants
    c. Sacramento Kings
    d. Los Angeles Dodgers

113. The "Curse of Jeffrey Maier" (originally coined in the book *The Worst of Sports*) is a curse belonging to what pro sports franchise?
    a. Milwaukee Bucks
    b. Buffalo Bills
    c. Baltimore Orioles
    d. Toronto Argonauts

114. What pro sports team do celebrities Jennifer Lopez, Gloria Estefan, Serena and Venus Williams, and Fergie of the Black Eyed Peas own a piece of?
    a. Miami Dolphins
    b. Brooklyn Nets
    c. Tampa Bay Bucs
    d. California Angels

115. In what sport does the hitter/server/batter have to hit the ball within eight seconds after the first referee whistles for service/play/action?
    a. Volleyball
    b. Cricket
    c. Football (American)
    d. Dodgeball

116. Which of these players was *not* picked first in the NBA draft?
    a. Austin Carr
    b. Shaquille O'Neal
    c. Marcus Camby
    d. Glenn Robinson

117. Who was the first major league baseball player to officially endorse a bat via a deal struck with Hillerich & Bradsby (Louisville Slugger)?
    a. Honus Wagner
    b. Rogers Hornsby
    c. Ty Cobb
    d. Babe Ruth

118. When coach Fritz Crisler arrived from Princeton to begin a new era in this team's football heritage, he brought his famous "winged" helmet with him.
    a. University of Michigan
    b. Philadelphia Eagles
    c. University of Oregon
    d. St. Louis Cardinals

119. Which of these "courts" is the longest in length?
    a. Volleyball
    b. Tennis
    c. Badminton
    d. Basketball (U.S. college/pro version)

120. When it comes to golf equipment, which one of these clubs has the lowest loft?
    a. 1-wood
    b. 2-wood
    c. 3-wood
    d. 4-wood

121. This NBA HOF'er spent most of his life in New York but ended his career in Orlando.
    a. Bernard King
    b. Patrick Ewing
    c. Drazen Petrovic
    d. Alonzo Mourning

122. What number car does Jeff Gordon drive?
    a. 34
    b. 54
    c. 42
    d. 24

123. In what sport would you find these types of matches or game variants: Luchas de Apuestas, Lumberjack, Taipei Deathmatch, and Pig Pen?
    a. Interprovincial hurling
    b. Professional wrestling
    c. Snooker
    d. Streetluge

124. Liz Heaston was the first woman ever to score in a college football game. Who did she play for?
    a. William Jewell College
    b. William & Mary
    c. Willamette University
    d. Willem Defoe State

125. Which of these players received the longest non-drug-related suspension in NBA history?
    a. Gilbert Arenas
    b. Kermit Washington
    c. Latrell Sprewell
    d. Ron Artest

126. Who is Ab Smith and why should we care?
    a. He's the guy who first promoted bodybuilding as a competitive sport
    b. He coined the golf term "birdie"
    c. He's the guy who came up with the idea to have solid color and striped billiard balls
    d. Ab is short for "Abigail" and she coached the very first women's collegiate basketball team at Sophie Newcomb College

127. In the ancient sport of chariot racing, how many horses pulled each chariot?
    a. 4
    b. 2
    c. 6
    d. 1

128. The Pac-12 conference's roots date back to 1915 when it was the Pacific Coast Conference. All of two of the schools that were in that original conference are still in the Pac-12 today. What two teams were uninvited or jumped ship along the way as the conference evolved?
    a. Univ. of Idaho, Univ. of Montana
    b. Portland State, Utah State
    c. Cal State Fullerton, UC Davis
    d. Univ. of Nevada, Univ. of Wyoming

129. What title would all these gents share – Raymond Beadle, Don Prudhomme, and John Force?
    a. British Open champions
    b. Boston Marathon champions
    c. Olympics Discus Gold Medal winners
    d. NHRA Top Fuel Funny Car champions

130. Who is the only male in tennis history to have won six consecutive Grand Slam singles titles?
    a. Bjorn Borg
    b. Rod Laver
    c. Don Budge
    d. Pete Sampras

131. What sport uses the term "pike"?
    a. Diving
    b. Sorority ex-boyfriend hurling
    c. Polo
    d. Archery

132. In his last season at Oregon, this coach led the school to its first outright Pac-10 championship and first Rose Bowl appearance in 37 years.
    a. Monte Kiffin
    b. Rich Brooks
    c. Ray Greene
    d. Dennis Erickson

133. In 1972, he became the first Cowboy running back to have a 1,000-yard rushing season. Who is he?
    a. Lance Alworth
    b. Herb Adderly
    c. Emmitt Smith
    d. Calvin Hill

134. If a headline read, "Nairo Quintana wins Giro d'Italia," what sport would it be referring to?
    a. Cycling
    b. Tennis
    c. Marathon
    d. Iron Man

135. Well, it's assumed – and true – that the first *indoor* major use "Astroturf" was at the Astrodome in Houston, but where was the first *outdoor* use of Astroturf at the college or pro level?
   a. Memorial Stadium at Indiana State University in Terre Haute
   b. Rice Stadium in Houston
   c. Riverfront Stadium in Cincinnati
   d. Ralph Wilson Stadium in Buffalo

136. Before he became a front office exec, Billy Beane, the character behind *Moneyball*, played this position for the Mets, Twins, et al.
   a. Shortstop
   b. Third base
   c. Catcher
   d. Outfield

137. Which of these notable players from the 1980 Olympics "Miracle on Ice" did not participate in any high-level ice hockey afterward?
   a. Ken Morrow
   b. Jim Craig
   c. Mike Eruzione
   d. Mark Johnson

138. After being fired by the Lakers, he won the Coach of the Year award with Indiana, leading the Pacers to the playoffs for the first time since the ABA-NBA merger in '76.
   a. Dick Versace
   b. Jack Ramsay
   c. Jack McKinney
   d. Slick Leonard

139. When the Milwaukee Bucks traded Kareem Abdul-Jabbar to the Lakers, they got Junior Bridgeman, Brian Winters, Elmore Smith, and this guy in return.
    a. Jim Price
    b. Dave Meyers
    c. Happy Hairston
    d. Kermit Washington

140. What baseball pitcher has given up more walks (base on balls) than any other pitcher?
    a. Nolan Ryan
    b. Steve Carlton
    c. Roger Clemons
    d. Tom Glavine

141. Who is the only player to have played in both a World Series *and* a Super Bowl?
    a. Deion Sanders
    b. Jim Thorpe
    c. Bo Jackson
    d. Lou Gross

142. What college did these NFL players attend: Byron Leftwich, Chad Pennington, and Randy Moss?
    a. Southern Mississippi
    b. Florida State
    c. East Carolina
    d. Marshall

143. The first professional American football team to put a logo on their helmets was...
    a. Los Angeles Rams
    b. Dallas Cowboys
    c. San Francisco 49ers
    d. NY Giants

144. Who or what is (or are) the "Mormon Meteor(s)"?
  a. Creed Haymond, NCAA 100-yard dash'er
  b. A speed racing car
  c. Ted Kozlowski, WR, Chicago Bears
  d. The 1989 BYU Cougar football team

145. Which one of these College Bowl games has been around the longest?
  a. Sugar Bowl
  b. Cotton Bowl
  c. Rose Bowl
  d. Fiesta Bowl

146. What era in MLB would we be talking about where Johnny Bench and Boog Powell were named MVPs, Jim Perry and Bob Gibson as Cy Young Award winners, and Thurman Munson and Carl Morton as Rookies of the Year?
  a. Sixties
  b. Seventies
  c. Eighties
  d. Fifties

147. Only once in the history of the NHL has a father played with his sons, and that was when...
  a. Gordie Howe played with sons Mark and Marty for one season with the Hartford Whalers.
  b. Greg Johnson played two seasons with his son, Ryan, for the Chicago Blackhawks.
  c. Billy Taylor, Sr. played 14 games with his son, Billy Taylor, Jr. with the NY Rangers.
  d. Ray Bourque came out of retirement to play one game with his son, Chris, for the Boston Bruins.

148. The rules for this event stipulate that at least three drivers must drive each car.
    a. Daytona 500
    b. Gumball Rally
    c. Cannonball Run
    d. 24 Hours of LeMans

149. Despite a career that earned each of these players a place in their respective sport's hall of fame, only one of these players got to play for a professional-level title. Who?
    a. Ralph Sampson (basketball)
    b. Barry Sanders (football)
    c. Dominique Wilkins (basketball)
    d. Ernie Banks (baseball)

150. What Major League Baseball stadium was the very first to eliminate the dirt infield in favor of a) painted lines on the artificial turf and, b) sliding pits?
    a. Coors Field (Denver)
    b. Riverfront Stadium (Cincinnati)
    c. Candlestick Park (San Francisco)
    d. Comiskey Park (Chicago

151. A "piste" is a what?
    a. A marked ski run/path down a mountain for snow skiers, snowboarders, et al
    b. The net part of a lacrosse stick
    c. The original term for one lap in Olympic swimming events
    d. The French term for the clay used in clay tennis courts

152. The first "NCAA College Division" (now "Division 2") coach inducted into the Naismith Basketball Hall of Fame was...
    a. Clarence Gaines/Winston-Salem State
    b. John Chaney/Cheyney State
    c. Arad McCutchan/University of Evansville
    d. Herb Magee/Philadelphia University

153. For seven years or so, the chequered flag that's used in auto racing was also used in game situations by a major franchise in a different sport. Know which one?
    a. Baseball
    b. Hockey
    c. Football
    d. Basketball

154. Which of these NY Jets quarterbacks rang up more than 25,000 yards in his career... led the NFL with the lowest interception rate for three years... and the first QB to pass for more than 400+ yards in a game?
    a. Joe Namath
    b. Richard Todd
    c. Pat Ryan
    d. Ken O'Brien

155. This former major league player is listed as the very first one from the Dominican Republic to play pro baseball...
    a. Francisco Liriano
    b. Ozzie Virgil, Sr.
    c. Juan Marichal
    d. Robinson Cano

156. Which of these NASCAR drivers can claim they won the Daytona 500 a record seven times?
    a. Dale Earnhardt, Sr.
    b. Bobby Allison
    c. Wayne Newton
    d. Richard Petty

157. In what sport would you find these "patterns": viper, chameleon, cheetah, and scorpion?
    a. Yacht racing
    b. Water skiing
    c. Bowling
    d. Racquetball

158. After Jackie Robinson, who was the *second* African-American to play Major League Baseball?
    a. Hank Thompson
    b. Sam Jethroe
    c. Monte Irvin
    d. Larry Doby

159. The basic ideas of the "triangle offense" were initially established by this coach at what respective college?
    a. Tex Winter/Kansas State
    b. Sam Barry/Southern California
    c. Leon Barmore/Louisiana Tech
    d. Larry Brown/Kansas

160. When William G. Morgan invented volleyball in 1895, he used this name for the game.
    a. Netball
    b. Netapult
    c. Salvo
    d. Mintonette

161. Not all head football coaches played the game.
As a matter of fact, this well-known coach never
played a lick of college or pro ball.
    a. Lou Holtz
    b. Charlie Weis
    c. Joe Glbbs
    d. Jon Gruden

162. What's the nickname for the right field foul pole at
Fenway Park?
    a. Pesky's Pole
    b. Ted's Tower
    c. Cotton Candy
    d. Golden Rod

163. Which of these events happened first?
    a. David Robinson was the first pick in the
       NBA draft
    b. Michael Jordan signed a minor league
       contract with the Chicago White Sox
    c. Tiger Woods won his first Masters
    d. Joe Torre replaced Bobby Cox as the
       manager of the Atlanta Braves

164. If you happened upon this guy on the street and
asked him for his résumé, he might say, "*I was a
two-time All-American at Providence, then played
for the St. Louis Hawks, and coached the Cavs,
the Knicks, and the Sonics.*" So, who would you
think he was?
    a. Bill Sharman
    b. Bob Hopkins
    c. Lenny Wilkens
    d. Bernie Bickerstaff

165. Vancouver became home to a professional ice hockey team for the first time in 1911 when Frank & Lester Patrick established this team...
    a. Senators
    b. Canucks
    c. Cyclones
    d. Millionaires

166. The Univ. of Tennessee's official "fight song" is...
    a. "Rocky Top"
    b. "Get Up & Go You Mighty Huskies"
    c. "Down the Field"
    d. "Scotland the Brave"

167. Who does the "William Harridge Trophy" go to every year?
    a. The NHL player who scores the most points in a season
    b. The winner of the University of Washington vs. Washington State football game
    c. Top NHL rookie
    d. Baseball's American League champ

168. How do the foul poles at Citi Field differ from other ballparks' foul poles?
    a. They're orange
    b. They have an "L" shape 10 ft. from the top
    c. They're 4 ft. shorter
    d. They're not different. Trick question.

169. The medical term for "Tommy John surgery" is...
    a. Thoracic Transverse Process
    b. Triangular Cartilage Renewal
    c. New Dang Elbow
    d. Ulnar Collateral Ligament Reconstruction

170. Which of the three Triple Crown races did California Chrome lose?
    a. Louisiana Hayride
    b. Kentucky Derby
    c. Belmont
    d. Preakness

171. Of these sets of players who were among the first 11 players picked in the 2001 NBA draft, which set did not attend college?
    a. Jason Richardson, Eddie Griffin
    b. Shane Battier, Kedrick Brown
    c. Tyson Chandler, Eddy Curry
    d. Rodney White, Joe Johnson

172. This famous Cleveland Indian has as one of his nicknames, "Mr. Freeze".
    a. Mel Harder
    b. Chris Perez
    c. Mike Hargrove
    d. Albert Belle

173. The first Canadian-born QB to start in the NFL and first foreign-born to win Super Bowl MVP was...
    a. Kurt Warner
    b. Mark Rypien
    c. Steve Young
    d. Drew Brees

174. Which of these "Ivy League" schools' home football stadiums has the largest capacity?
    a. Penn
    b. Cornell
    c. Columbia
    d. Yale

175. This tourney is a series of men's Golf matches between a team from the USA and an International team representing the rest of the world (sans Europe)...
    a. Ryder Cup
    b. The Grey Cup
    c. The Eisenhower Cup
    d. The President's Cup

176. Calling all Bucky Badgers! The University of Wisconsin fight song "On, Wisconsin" was originally written for this other Big Ten school.
    a. Minnesota
    b. Purdue
    c. Michigan
    d. Illinois

177. On 8/21/70, this ABA team was sold to P. W. Blake. Ten days later, he moved the team to Memphis and changed its name to the Pros.
    a. The Floridians
    b. Pittsburgh Pipers
    c. Virginia Squires
    d. New Orleans Buccaneers

178. Who is Harry Statham?
    a. He's one of six MLB players who've struck out more than 2,000 times
    b. He's one of a handful of college basketball coaches with 1,000 or more wins at a four-year school
    c. He was the first NBA player to score 1,000 points in a single season
    d. He's one of a handful of NHL coaches with 1,000 or more wins

179. The winter version of a biathlon combines what two events?
   a. Cross-country skiing and rifle shooting
   b. Cross-country running and archery
   c. Sledding and snowshoe racing
   d. Archery and cross-country skiing

180. Kim Duk-koo was a South Korean boxer who died following a boxing match against who?
   a. Sugar Ray Leonard
   b. Leon Spinks
   c. Ray Mancini
   d. Roberto Duran

181. Which of these schools has won the most NCAA titles in Men's Volleyball?
   a. Pepperdine
   b. Ohio State
   c. BYU
   d. UCLA

182. In 1964, Cassius Clay (now Muhammad Ali) released a single on Columbia Records – a cover version of this classic.
   a. Papa's Got a Brand New Bag
   b. Don't Be Cruel
   c. Try a Little Tenderness
   d. Stand by Me

183. In the classic poem "Casey at the Bat," who was on base when Casey stepped to the plate?
   a. Blake and Flynn
   b. Cooney and Barrows
   c. Rote and Phineas
   d. Curle and Cassidy

184. According to NCAA men's basketball rule book (2013), the only hand contact that is legal by the defense is what?
    a. The defender contacts the ball-handler/dribbler ANYTIME with 2 hands.
    b. The defender places a hand (front or back of the hand) on the ball-handler/dribbler and keeps it on (aka "Soft Hands")
    c. A one hand "measure up" by the defense (aka "hot stove")
    d. The defender contacts the ball-handler/dribbler with an arm-bar

185. Besides Walter Johnson, who's the only other pitcher that has 300 wins, 3,000 strikeouts, and a career ERA less than 3.00?
    a. Bob Gibson
    b. Jim Palmer
    c. Gaylord Perry
    d. Tom Seaver

186. What position do these current or former New England Patriots play: Eric Alexander, Tully Banta-Cain, Matt Chatham, and Tedy Bruschi?
    a. Halfback
    b. Fullback
    c. Guard
    d. Linebacker

187. The "cutter" is one of this pitcher's signature pitches, and his "intro music" is "Enter Sandman".
    a. Trevor Hoffman
    b. Dan Quisenberry
    c. Mariano Rivera
    d. Randy Myers

188. Most people connect David Ortiz with the Boston Red Sox but, before Boston, he played for this team from 1997-2002.
    a. Chicago White Sox
    b. Texas Rangers
    c. California Angels
    d. Minnesota Twins

189. According to NCAA rules, which of these jersey numbers is not legal in basketball?
    a. 6
    b. 3
    c. 32
    d. 15

190. Texas A&M can claim which of these College Football Hall of Famers as one of their alums?
    a. Gene Stallings
    b. Duffy Daugherty
    c. Barry Alvarez
    d. Vince Dooley

191. On November 6, 1869, these two teams competed in the first intercollegiate football game.
    a. Dartmouth & Yale
    b. Rutgers & Princeton
    c. Johns Hopkins & Washington College
    d. University of Maryland & Towson

192. At the age 25, he became the youngest man to broadcast a World Series game.
    a. Harry Caray
    b. Vin Scully
    c. Red Barber
    d. Joe Pignatano

193. This team's colors are blue, black, silver, and white; its first head coach was Terry Crisp; its first home court was at Expo Hall; and one of its minor league affiliates is the Brampton Beast. Who is it?
       a. Orlando Magic
       b. Nashville Predators
       c. Manchester United
       d. Tampa Bay Lightning

194. One of Reggie Jackson's crowning achievements came with a three-home-run performance in a World Series-clinching Game Six where the Yankees were playing who?
       a. Giants
       b. Cardinals
       c. Dodgers
       d. Philadelphia

195. Which of these gents would have "ESPN NASCAR analyst" and "retired American basketball player" on their résumé?
       a. Matt Doherty
       b. Denny Doherty
       c. Pat Daugherty
       d. Brad Daugherty

196. The Philadelphia Big 5 (Penn, St. Joseph's, Temple, La Salle, Villanova) originally played all its games at this gym.
       a. The Palestra
       b. Philadelphia Ice Palace
       c. T.M. Elmore Gymnasium
       d. Acmonia Fieldhouse

197. What's the name of the rating system that's been used in soccer (futbol), as part of the Bowl Championship Series, and major league baseball?
    a. Swensen
    b. Elo
    c. Stratten
    d. Arbitron

198. What MLB player has the most intentional walks in baseball history?
    a. Hank Aaron
    b. Albert Pujols
    c. Mark McGwire
    d. Barry Bonds

199. Which of these college basketball arenas has the largest capacity?
    a. Lloyd Noble Center (Oklahoma)
    b. John Paul Jones Arena (U. Va.)
    c. Matthew Knight Arena (Oregon)
    d. Hofheinz Pavilion (U. Houston)

200. Regulation dartboards are made of what?
    a. Sisal fibers
    b. Rolled cardboard
    c. Cellulose acetate fiber
    d. Charcoal

201. How many players to a side in water polo (in the senior ranks – games played by the International Swimming Federation)?
    a. 8
    b. 6
    c. 9
    d. 7

202. Johnny Unitas, Lance Alworth, Don Nelson, and Bob Feller all wore this jersey number.
    a. 19
    b. 17
    c. 6
    d. 8

203. Which of these basketball coaches would *not* be found on Larry Brown's "coaching tree," either as an assistant or volunteer assistant?
    a. John Calipari
    b. Bill Self
    c. Frank Vogel
    d. Gregg Popovich

204. Besides Villanova, Kansas State, et al, this college's team name is also "Wildcats."
    a. New Hampshire
    b. Norfolk State
    c. Northern Colorado
    d. Niagara

205. In 2015, a major controversy arose in the sport of curling. What was the controversy?
    a. BalancePlus created a broom that had directional fabric making redirecting the stone too easy
    b. Some players were freezing the stones to make them go further
    c. Some players were using shoes that had Norwex soles which allowed them to slide at about the same speed of the stone
    d. Sweep Sports started making stones that had tapered handles which allowed a smoother release

206. Hubie Brown (Hubert Jude to his ma and pa) has coached four professional basketball teams – the Kentucky Colonels, Atlanta Hawks, New York Knicks, and who else?
    a. Philadelphia 76ers
    b. Sacramento Kings
    c. New Jersey Nets
    d. Memphis Grizzlies

207. This ESPN football analyst played eight seasons at running back for the Steelers and Bears, before retiring after the 1994 season.
    a. Brock Huard
    b. Tom Jackson
    c. Stuart Scott
    d. Merril Hoge

208. The "Harlem Globetrotters" weren't always the *Harlem* Globetrotters. Before that moniker, they were called the... what?
    a. Jersey Jivers
    b. Savoy Big Five
    c. Philly Phancy Phive
    d. Grand Central Globetrotters

209. Despite what most of us think about the NCAA, they've implemented the "death penalty" only a handful of times. Those include Kentucky basketball for its '52-53 season, SMU football for its '87 season, and the basketball program at this school for its '73–74 and '74–75 seasons.
    a. Western Kentucky
    b. Tulane
    c. Southwestern Louisiana
    d. San Francisco

210. In 1969, he/she became the first person to row solo across an ocean.
    a. Sylvia Cook
    b. George Harbo
    c. Frank Samuelsen
    d. John Fairfax

211. In rugby union, a "try" is worth how many points?
    a. 5
    b. 3
    c. 4
    d. 2

212. When this player went into the hall of fame, he chose to not have the logo of either team he played for (A's, Yankees) because he had good relations with both and didn't want to slight either.
    a. Catfish Hunter
    b. Rickey Henderson
    c. Billy Martin
    d. Reggie Jackson

213. Among the NFL Europe teams of the past, which of these team names belonged to Barcelona?
    a. Centurions
    b. Dragons
    c. Fire
    d. Sea Devils

214. Which of these sets of NHL teams have a "wing" (or "wings") in their logo?
    a. Montreal, Nashville, and Ottawa
    b. St. Louis, Philly, and Detroit
    c. Pittsburgh and San Jose
    d. New Jersey and Florida

215. Who's the only head coach to win league titles in the National Basketball Association, American Basketball Association, and the American Basketball League?
    a. Kevin Loughery
    b. Slick Leonard
    c. Alex Hannum
    d. Bill Sharman

216. In 2009, the Texas Legends made history by hiring this lady as their head coach, making her the first female to lead a NBA or NBA D-League team.
    a. Cheryl Miller
    b. Dawn Staley
    c. Nancy Lieberman
    d. Michelle Clark-Heard

217. Which Olympic sport has among its Gold medalists these fine folks: Natalya Sadova, Gerd Kanter, and Al Oerter?
    a. Javelin
    b. Shot Put
    c. Hammer
    d. Discus

218. He is the first basketball player in history to play on an NCAA championship team, an Olympics Gold medal basketball team, and a NBA championship squad.
    a. Clyde Lovellette
    b. Wilt Chamberlain
    c. George Mikan
    d. Paul Arizin

219. What do you call the two-wheeled, single-seat cart that is used in harness racing?
    a. Crawler
    b. Sulky
    c. Logger
    d. Trike

220. What college football coach reached 100 wins faster than any other in NCAA history?
    a. Gil Dobie
    b. Lance Leipold
    c. Bud Trickett
    d. Holand Wunn

221. Of these "Armstrongs" career included stops in Charlotte and Golden State?
    a. Darrell Armstrong
    b. Hilton Armstrong
    c. B.J. Armstrong
    d. Brandon Armstrong

222. Which of these "Washingtons" won four consecutive NCAA Women's Division III Basketball Championships?
    a. Washington & Lee
    b. George Washington University
    c. Washington & Jefferson
    d. Washington University in St. Louis

223. The melody of Oklahoma's fight song, "Boomer Sooner," is taken from this college's fight song.
    a. Yale
    b. Virginia Military Institute
    c. Tulane
    d. Dartmouth

224. What team began the trend of using poster-size graphics of singers, cartoon characters, logos, etc. to call signals for offenses and defenses?
   a. Jacksonville Jaguars
   b. Oklahoma State
   c. Northern Illinois
   d. Clemson

225. It's widely assumed that the Heisman Trophy refers to someone named "Heisman," right? But who was this Heisman fella?
   a. He was the head football coach at Auburn
   b. He played football at Brown University
   c. He originated the words "hike" or "hep" that a QB shouts to start every play
   d. He was the Athletics Director at New York City's Downtown Athletic Club

226. If a golfer makes a stroke at the wrong ball (Rule 19-2) or hits a fellow golfer's ball with a putt (Rule 19-5), the player incurs a penalty of how many strokes?
   a. 3
   b. 1
   c. 0
   d. 2

227. It's safe to assume that you know that the Univ. of Georgia and the Green Bay Packers share the same logo - a stylized oval "G" - albeit in different colors. What other college uses that logo, too?
   a. Grambling State (LA)
   b. Goddard College (VT)
   c. Gonzaga University (WA)
   d. Gettysburg College (PA)

228. Who took over as head coach of the University of Texas' football program when the legendary Darrell Royal retired?
    a. Ed Price
    b. David McWilliams
    c. Charlie Strong
    d. Fred Akers

229. It would probably never happen in this day and age, but the 1970 National Invitation Tournament (men's NIT) was unique because this coach, unhappy with his team's seeding, turned down a bid to the NCAA tourney and opted to play in the NIT instead.
    a. Dale Brown (LSU)
    b. Al McGuire (Marquette)
    c. Bobby Knight (Army)
    d. Pete Carrill (Princeton)

230. The only pro quarterback to play from start to finish and earn both a loss and a perfect passer rating is who?
    a. Chad Pennington
    b. Geno Smith
    c. Craig Morton
    d. Dave Krieg

231. Leading up to his gig as the head coach at Ohio State, Urban Meyer's previous four stops in order (including stints as assistant as well as head coach), were...
    a. Colorado State, Toledo, Iowa, Florida
    b. Illinois State, Utah, Notre Dame, Florida
    c. Ohio State, Bowling Green, Utah, Florida
    d. Notre Dame, Bowling Green, Utah, Florida

232. Ranging from high school to the pro level, what's the most popular team name in American sports with 1,603 teams?
   a. Warriors
   b. Panthers
   c. Tigers
   d. Eagles

233. Which of these things about professional (NBA) basketball is true?
   a. Hall of Famer Rick Barry and Walter Davis share the nickname "Bloodhound," which reflected their dogged style of play
   b. Shaquille O'Neal was the first player in NBA history to miss 5000 free throws
   c. Kareem Abdul-Jabbar was left unprotected by the Lakers for the Hornets' and Heat 1988 expansion draft
   d. If you trace their lines back to 1950, the Sacramento Kings were once the Tri-Cities Blackhawks

234. Which of the following sports figures has the nickname "The Glove"?
   a. Gary Payton
   b. Todd Helton
   c. Mike Tyson
   d. Wayne Gretsky

235. How many total balls in a game of snooker?
   a. 15
   b. 22
   c. 16
   d. 21

236. Which conference were Memphis State, Cincinnati, and Marquette all once a part of?
    a. Sun Belt
    b. The American
    c. Pac 12
    d. Conference USA

237. Not all "passers" in the NFL have been QBs. All of these "other position" players have passed for TDs. Which one had the most?
    a. Frank Gifford
    b. Marcus Allen
    c. LaDainian Tomlinson
    d. Walter Payton

238. Which of these sports balls' "official weight" is the lightest?
    a. Golf
    b. Tennis
    c. Squash
    d. Racquetball

239. Who was the first native-born American to win the British Open?
    a. Bobby Jones
    b. Tommy Armour
    c. Walter Hagen
    d. Gene Sarazen

240. Which one of Muhammad Ali's opponents was nicknamed "The Bayonne Bleeder"?
    a. Jean Pierre Coopman
    b. Henry Cooper
    c. Zora Folley
    d. Chuck Wepner

241. One of the following is the first and only woman to win NCAA Division I basketball titles as a player, as an assistant coach, and as a head coach. Who's that lady?
    a. Cheryl Ford
    b. Kim Mulkey
    c. Teresa Weatherspoon
    d. Betty Lennox

242. Basketballs were generally brown until this person introduced the orange basketball in the 1950s.
    a. Edgar Clayton
    b. Tony Hinkle
    c. Dr. James Naismith
    d. Amos Alonzo Stagg

243. Who was the first African-American head coach in the National Football League?
    a. Elyce Roberts
    b. Aloe Blannc
    c. Ray Camp
    d. Fritz Pollard

244. Where was the first Super Bowl played?
    a. Orange Bowl in Miami
    b. Sugar Bowl in New Orleans
    c. Tulane Stadium in New Orleans
    d. Memorial Coliseum in Los Angeles

245. Which of these golf greats was one of the pioneers of "croquet-style" putting?
    a. Sam Snead
    b. Gary Player
    c. Julius Boros
    d. Al Geiberger

246. At the 2010 Wimbledon Championships, what two pros played history's longest pro tennis match? One that lasted 11 hours, 5 minutes of play over the course of three days...
    a. John Isner and Nicolas Mahut
    b. Ivo Karlović and Radek Štěpánek
    c. Feliciano Lopez and Andre Agassi
    d. Radek Štěpánek and Joachim Johansson

247. By the time this QB's career ended, he had completed nearly 4,000 passes for 49,335 yards and 291 TDs – all that despite never being drafted by any NFL team.
    a. Len Dawson
    b. Bob Griese
    c. Sonny Jurgensen
    d. Warren Moon

248. This leftie won 363 games, more than any other left-handed pitcher in baseball history.
    a. Sandy Koufax
    b. Randy Johnson
    c. Lefty Grove
    d. Warren Spahn

249. Which of these foot races is the oldest annual running marathon (uh, for you math nerds, that would be 42.195 kilometers, or 26.21875 miles, or 461.45 football fields)?
    a. Marathon du Mont Blanc
    b. Bay to Breakers
    c. Boston Marathon
    d. Seoul International

250. Let's see how much you know about the men in the striped shirts. When an NFL referee has one arm above his head with an open hand, what does it mean?
   a. Dead ball, neutral zone established, or crowd noise
   b. Invalid fair catch signal
   c. Reset the play clock – 30 seconds
   d. Reset the play clock – 40 seconds

251. Why was Walt Frazier dubbed "Clyde"?
   a. It rhymed with "glide," a term he used to define his signature move.
   b. Because of the fedora he wore that was similar to that worn by Warren Beatty in the movie *Bonnie & Clyde*.
   c. Because teammate Phil Jackson said he looked like "Clyde" the orangutan from the movie *Every Which Way but Loose*.
   d. He was from Clyde Township, Illinois.

252. Which of these horses was a Triple Crown winner?
   a. Cannonade
   b. Jet Pilot
   c. Brokers Tip
   d. Gallant Fox

253. In terms of the length of the track, the Bristol Motor Speedway is considered a...
   a. Short track (less than 1 mile)
   b. Superspeedway (over 2 miles)
   c. Driveway (about 20 feet)
   d. Intermediate (1 to 2 miles)

254. In Joe Montana's first season with the 49ers, he spent most of the season as the backup on the depth chart behind whom?
    a. Marc Wilson
    b. Jim Plunkett
    c. Steve DeBerg
    d. Norm Snead

255. In the final verse of John Fogerty's "Centerfield," the song quotes this longtime broadcaster whose home run call was "Tell it goodbye!"
    a. Bob Fouts
    b. Gordy Soltau
    c. John Harrington
    d. Lon Simmons

256. This player was on three different NBA teams that won a championship in three different decades...
    a. John Salley
    b. Shaquille O'Neal
    c. Toni Kukoč
    d. Ray Allen

257. The New York Giants all-time leading scorer is...
    a. Pete Gogolak
    b. Lawrence Tynes
    c. Brad Daluiso
    d. Frank Gifford

258. Whose initials are painted in white on the manual scoreboard on Fenway Park's Green Monster?
    a. Ted Williams
    b. John I. Taylor
    c. Red Sox owners Tom & Jean Yawkey
    d. No one's, actually. Just testing you.

259. One of the following "factoids" is true and the other three completely false. Which one's for real?
     a. In '74, Chris Evert was one of the top three money winners in two different sports.
     b. NY Yankees first baseman Wally Pipp asked for a day off with a minor injury, which started Lou Gehrig's streak of 2,130 consecutive games played.
     c. Sports commentator Skip Bayless was an All-American baseball player at Vanderbilt.
     d. Ben Roethlisberger began his college career at N.C. State at the same time as Philip Rivers, but transferred to Miami U. (of Ohio) after the first year so he could get more playing time.

260. The only NCAA Division 1 basketball player to score 100 points in a single game is who?
     a. Frank Selvy (@ Furman)
     b. Elgin Baylor (@ College of Idaho)
     c. Jack Taylor (@ Grinnell)
     d. Larry Costello (@ Niagara)

261. Which of these ain't a real college football bowl?
     a. Quick Lane Bowl
     b. Cure Bowl
     c. Boca Raton Bowl
     d. Margarita Bowl

262. What golf course is certified by the Guinness Records folks as the oldest course in the world?
     a. Royal & Ancient Golf Club at St. Andrews
     b. Old Links of Musselburgh
     c. Leith Links
     d. De Baen (Holland)

263. Despite never arrested or indicted as part of a
rumored point-shaving scandal, this player was
expelled from the University of Iowa and pretty
much blackballed from the college ranks and
NBA. Still, he fought on by becoming the ABA
MVP and his team winning the ABA crown, then
successfully suing the NBA for reinstatement.
    a. David Thompson
    b. Connie Hawkins
    c. Walter Davis
    d. Larry Spivey

264. Since we're in Point Shavin' Land, gangsters
Henry Hill and Jimmy Burke perpetrated a point-
shaving scandal with this college's basketball
team in 1978-79.
    a. Providence College
    b. Arizona State
    c. Boston College
    d. Rhode Island

265. What university's football teams were coached by
the #1 and #2 coaches with the highest winning
percentage in NCAA Div 1 history?
    a. Notre Dame
    b. Alabama
    c. USC
    d. Ohio State

266. Which of these "cover stories" actually made it to
the cover of Sports Illustrated (Dec. 4, 1967)?
    a. Oakland A's: The Crass Menagerie
    b. The Aging Ali: No Float, No Fly
    c. Minnesota's Midget Masters
    d. The Case for the 12-foot Basket

267. Similar in concept to bowling and horseshoes, the aim of this game is to knock out groups of skittles arranged in patterns by throwing a bat at them.
    a. Mölkky
    b. Gorodki
    c. Pesäpallo
    d. Kimble

268. Golfer Ángel Cabrera (2007 U.S. Open, 2009 Masters winner) is affectionately known as...
    a. "El Molcajete"
    b. "El Pato"
    c. "El Maestro"
    d. "El Valiente"

269. This Heavyweight boxer was totally undefeated...
    a. Rocky Marciano
    b. Joe Louis
    c. Roland LaStarza
    d. Jersey Joe Walcott

270. In what sport would you find a technique called the "Fosbury Flop"?
    a. Sculling
    b. Weight-lifting
    c. Greco-Roman Wrestling
    d. High Jumping

271. Other than Princeton's appearance in the '65 Final Four, the only other Ivy League team to make the Final Four since was...
    a. Penn
    b. Harvard
    c. Cornell
    d. Dartmouth

272. What golfer notched 11 straight PGA Tour victories – a feat no one else has matched?
   a. Gene Sarazen
   b. Byron Nelson
   c. Dow Finsterwald
   d. Al Geiberger

273. Who was the first person in history to hit a home run (MLB) and score a touchdown (NFL) in the same week?
   a. George Halas
   b. Jim Thorpe
   c. Deion Sanders
   d. Brian Jordan

274. Which of these colleges is in Div II in the NCAA?
   a. Northwestern State (Louisiana)
   b. Western Michigan
   c. Western Carolina
   d. Western Oregon

275. Professional baseball began in St. Louis in 1875 with this team in the National Association.
   a. Centennials
   b. Brown Stockings
   c. Westerns
   d. Dark Blues

276. When Wayne Gretzky finally hung up this skates, he had scored 2,857 points, 54% more than the second-best scorer in NHL history, which was...
   a. Gordie Howe
   b. Ray Bourque
   c. Mario Lemieux
   d. Sid Smith

277. This pitcher pitched back-to-back no-hitters, a feat that's never been matched.
     a. Johnny Vander Meer
     b. Vern Law
     c. Ron Hansen
     d. Jim Bunning

278. The first U.S. college game/match in this sport was played between NYU and Manhattan on November 22, 1877.
     a. Volleyball
     b. Lacrosse
     c. Baseball
     d. Rowing

279. The first athlete to earn a million $ a year was...
     a. Catfish Hunter
     b. Bobby Hull
     c. Orel Hershiser
     d. Gail Goodrich

280. The only two cities that have met in the championship of all 4 major American sports are...
     a. Boston and Philadelphia
     b. Los Angeles and New York
     c. Philadelphia and Chicago
     d. St. Louis and Boston

281. In the game of "9 ball," where is the 9-ball placed in the rack?
     a. Front
     b. Rear
     c. Far right
     d. Center

282. On the morning of May 6, 1954, this med school student got up at the butt crack of dawn, went and made his hospital rounds in London, then moseyed over to Paddington Station and caught a train out to Oxford where he put on his track shoes, walked out onto the cinders for the first time that year, then ran a mile in 3:59.4, breaking the barrier of the four-minute mile. Who was it?
    a. Roger Bannister
    b. John Landy
    c. Eugene Landy
    d. Chris Brasher

283. As of 2016, five different coaches have won NCAA Men's Basketball national championships at this school.
    a. Kansas
    b. UCLA
    c. Kentucky
    d. North Carolina

284. This father/son tandem both played for the San Antonio Spurs but at different times, of course.
    a. Darren & Austin Daye
    b. Collis & Garrett Temple
    c. David Vaughn, Jr. & David Vaughn III
    d. James & Xavier Silas

285. Boxer Ken Norton played the character "Mede" in the movie about slavery in the antebellum South.
    a. Glory
    b. Mandingo
    c. Slaves
    d. Tamango

286. Which of these factoids is *not* something that happened to Doug Flutie?
    a. He made the only successful drop kick in the NFL since the 1940s
    b. Played briefly with his brother Darren on the Toronto Argonauts
    c. He was a candidate for a Rhodes Scholarship while at Boston College
    d. Flutie was selected in the 11th round of the NFL draft by the Rams

287. Bill Raftery, part of CBS Sports' college basketball coverage for 30+ years, also did an 11-year stint as head coach of …
    a. Seton Hall
    b. Rutgers
    c. La Salle
    d. Marist

288. The origin of a ram as this school's mascot dates back to the 1920s when star fullback Jack Merritt was given the nickname "the battering ram" for his performance on the field, as well as an initiation ritual he created for male freshman students.
    a. Colorado State
    b. Virginia Commonwealth
    c. Fordham
    d. UNC - Chapel Hill

289. The first female golfer to make the cut at a *men's* PGA Tour event was this lady…
    a. Babe Zaharias
    b. Nancy Lopez
    c. Annika Sorenstam
    d. Mickey Wright

290. From earliest to latest, which of these is the correct order of Heisman winners?
    a. Danny Wuerffel, Charles Woodson, Ricky Williams, Ron Dayne
    b. Charles Woodson, Ricky Williams, Danny Wuerffel, Ron Dayne
    c. Charles Woodson, Ricky Williams, Ron Dayne, Danny Wuerffel
    d. Ricky Williams, Charles Woodson, Ron Dayne, Danny Wuerffel

291. According to the Dickson Baseball Dictionary, the term "Grand Slam" originated in this card game.
    a. Contract Bridge
    b. Briscola
    c. Whist
    d. Pinochle

292. Which of these factoids about sports championship playoffs is true?
    a. The WNBA's first two playoffs were "best of 5," but now are "best of 7".
    b. The first "modern" World Series (1903) was a best-of-9 playoff.
    c. The Shaughnessy playoff system is the format used in Australian Rules Football.
    d. The NBA uses "2-1-1-1-2" for its playoffs.

293. This NBA team's first round draft picks have included Sidney Wicks, Geoff Petrie, Wally Walker, Rich Laurel, and Jeff Lamp.
    a. Portland Trailblazers
    b. Boston Celtics
    c. Milwaukee Bucks
    d. Phoenix Suns

294. Before they were the "Washington Redskins," they were this city's "Redskins"...
    a. Chicago
    b. Cleveland
    c. Boston
    d. Portsmouth (Ohio)

295. Who was the first African-American to play in the Masters Tournament? Happened in 1975, btw...
    a. Lee Elder
    b. Charlie Sifford
    c. Waco Turner
    d. Ted Rhodes

296. This pitcher's .397 lifetime batting average (31 hits in 78 @ bats) is the highest for any major leaguer in MLB history (w/ either 50 @ bats or with at least 15 years of major league experience).
    a. Terry Forster
    b. Silvio Martinez
    c. Paul Richards
    d. Richie Zisk

297. Didja know that use of instant replay in the NBA was instituted after an incident in the 2002 Western Conference Finals? It came at the end of the 2nd quarter of Game 4 when a Laker made a 3-point goal from half court. Although the shot counted, television replays showed the player had released the ball *after* the buzzer went off. Who was that player?
    a. Samaki Walker
    b. Robert Horry
    c. Brian Shaw
    d. Kobe Bryant

298. All but one person was killed when this college's basketball team plane crashed on its way to Nashville International Airport, taking the team to play Middle Tennessee.
    a. St. Louis University
    b. Evansville
    c. East Tennessee
    d. Marshall

299. After Evert and Navratilova, who became the third woman to win grand slam titles on grass, clay, and hard courts?
    a. Hana Mandlíková
    b. Serena Williams
    c. Monica Seles
    d. Zina Garrison

300. In the 4th quarter of Super Bowl XXXVIII, Tom Brady threw a 1-yard TD pass to this player, making said player the first defensive guy to make a Super Bowl TD on offense since Refrigerator Perry did it for da Bears in Super Bowl XX.
    a. Bruce Armstrong
    b. Tedy Bruschi
    c. Jim Nance
    d. Mike Vrabel

301. Johnny Weissmuller – better known to most of us as "Tarzan" in the movies – won five Olympic Gold medals for swimming and one Bronze medal in what other Olympic sport?
    a. Sailing
    b. Water polo
    c. Trampoline
    d. Diving

302. Can you pick out the flawed factoid below?
   a. Basketball legend Julius "Dr. J" Erving never fouled out of a game
   b. Eddie Shore's 978 career stitches are the most in NHL history
   c. Newspaper reporter Phil Klusman of the *Bakersfield Californian* was killed by a wayward hammer throw while covering the 1986 Division II track championships
   d. The Red Sox' Bill Buckner had more career hits than Red Sox' icon Ted Williams.

303. Who was the very first #1 overall draft pick in NBA history (1950)?
   a. Cazzie Russell
   b. George Yardley
   c. Chuck Share
   d. Frankie Bryan

304. The only NFL team to win championships in three different cities is...
   a. The Colts
   b. The Patriots
   c. The Raiders
   d. The Rams

305. One of the few differences between professional baseball in Japan and the MLB, is this one...
   a. There's a limit of 12 innings in a regular season game in Japan.
   b. The bat can't weigh more than 30 ounces in Japan.
   c. Home plate is 1.5" narrower in Japan.
   d. If a batter fouls a ball four times in Japan, he's called "out".

306. The "John Mackey Award" is awarded to college football's most outstanding tight end. Where did Mackey play his college ball?
    a. Ohio State
    b. Pittsburgh
    c. UCLA
    d. Syracuse

307. This college has gone through several nicknames since its athletic program began in 1893, including "Indians" and "Orange & White."
    a. James Madison
    b. Northeastern
    c. Towson State
    d. William & Mary

308. Here's a scenario from the NCAA football rulebook. Can you figure out the correct ruling? *Ball carrier A1, advancing in the field of play, becomes airborne at the 2-yard line. His first contact with the ground is out of bounds three yards beyond the goal line. The ball, in possession of the ball carrier, passed over the pylon. The ruling would be...*
    a. Ball is declared out of bounds @ 2-yd line.
    b. Whether or not a touchdown is scored depends on whether the player's body was inside or outside the sideline when the ball passed over the pylon.
    c. Not a touchdown. The goal-line plane is not extended because the player did not touch either the pylon or the ground in the end zone.
    d. Touchdown.

309. Believe it or not, there's different colors of "clay" tennis courts. The French Open, for example, is played on this color clay...
    a. Green
    b. Maroon
    c. Yellow
    d. Red

310. The first African-American coach in the National Basketball Association was...
    a. Nat Clifton
    b. Bill Russell
    c. Hank DeZonie
    d. Earl Monroe

311. Which of these collegiate athletic conferences is "Division III" in the NCAA?
    a. Lone Star
    b. South Atlantic
    c. Skyline
    d. America East

312. Which of these former NFL placekickers ditched their shoes and socks and kicked barefoot?
    a. Sebastian Janikowski
    b. Dirk Borgognone
    c. Rick Danmeier
    d. Tony Franklin

313. What Major League Baseball team wore "pill box" caps from 1976-1986?
    a. Pittsburgh Pirates
    b. Cincy Reds
    c. Houston Astros
    d. Detroit Tigers

314. In its early days, the AFL (American Football League) was thought to be pass-happy, and this little factoid may have made a wee bit of difference...
    a. The AFL's official football was slightly longer and narrower.
    b. The time between plays (play clock) was 5 seconds shorter than the NFL's.
    c. The AFL allowed two more "wide receivers" than the NFL.
    d. None of these are true.

315. What team entered the National League along with the New York Mets in 1962?
    a. San Diego Padres
    b. Houston Colt .45s
    c. Montreal Expos
    d. Seattle Mariners

316. Former Chicago Bulls forward Bob Love shares what nickname with boxer/wrestler/MMA fighter Eric Esch?
    a. Love Bug
    b. Yard Dog
    c. Pounder
    d. Butterbean

317. Steve Cauthen is the youngest jockey to win the Triple Crown (aboard Affirmed, '78). Who's the *oldest* jockey to win the Triple Crown?
    a. Victor Espinoza
    b. Gary Stevens
    c. Jerry Bailey
    d. Joel Rosario

318. After Gerry Faust left Notre Dame, his next stop as a college head coach was...
   a. Akron
   b. Bowling Green
   c. Toledo
   d. Youngstown State

319. Besides football, what other sport did Seahawks' QB Russell Wilson play in college?
   a. Basketball
   b. Track & Field
   c. Soccer
   d. Baseball

320. Which of these teams made the mistake of picking Jonny Flynn one spot ahead of Stephen Curry?
   a. New Orleans Hornets
   b. Houston Rockets
   c. Detroit Pistons
   d. Minnesota Timberwolves

321. Which of these athlete-becomes-Hollywood'er factoids is a FALSE one?
   a. Ed O'Neill, the future Al Bundy, played college football at Ohio U. and Youngstown St., and signed by the Steelers.
   b. *Duck Dynasty's* Phil Robertson was the QB ahead of Terry Bradshaw on the depth chart at Louisiana Tech.
   c. Before he was Superman, Dean Cain was a basketball star at Dartmouth where he led the team in assists (6.7apg) in 1987.
   d. Before Matthew Fox starred in shows like *Party of Five* and *Lost*, he was a wide receiver on Columbia U's football team.

322. Fact or fiction? One of these claims about football is false, but which one?
    a. An incomplete forward pass in football used to earn teams a 15-yard penalty.
    b. The Philadelphia Eagles and the Pittsburgh Steelers once combined to form the Steagles.
    c. The Seattle Seahawks paid Texas A&M $5k a year to use A&M's trademarked phrase "12th Man."
    d. NFL refs also receive Super Bowl rings.

323. What professional league allows the most (active) players on a roster at one time?
    a. Major League Soccer
    b. Major League Baseball
    c. National Basketball Association
    d. National Hockey League

324. While Disney/ABC and Hearst own ESPN nowadays, what was the first major corporation to hold a majority interest when the original owners sold 85% of the network in 1979?
    a. Getty Oil
    b. Atlantic Richfield
    c. General Motors
    d. Con Edison

325. Members of this coach's "coaching tree" include Jim Tressell, Nick Saban, Pete Carroll...
    a. Lou Holtz
    b. Earle Bruce
    c. Bob Davie
    d. Steve Spurrier

326. Which of these NBA teams did Shaquille O'Neal *not* play for?
    a. Cavaliers
    b. Celtics
    c. Jazz
    d. Suns

327. Which of these is an indoor variation of soccer?
    a. Füotron
    b. Board Ball
    c. Bacramma
    d. Futsal

328. In what sport would you find Ewa "The Striking Viking" Mataya Laurance?
    a. Wrestling
    b. Boxing
    c. Cricket
    d. Billiards

329. This gent became the first African-American ever to play in an NBA game.
    a. Chuck Cooper
    b. Nat "Sweetwater" Clifton
    c. Earl Lloyd
    d. Paul Henry Handley

330. Let's go back a few years, to like 17,000+ years ago, when cave paintings suggest that these two sports were played in the Upper Paleolithic.
    a. Sprinting and wrestling
    b. Swimming and javelin
    c. Boxing and fencing
    d. Marshmallow-toasting

331. In thoroughbred racing, how old does a female horse have to be to be considered a "mare"?
    a. At least 5
    b. At least 2
    c. At least 3
    d. At least 4

332. What athletic brand has a licensing deal with the NBA's Steph Curry?
    a. Nike
    b. Under Armour
    c. Adidas
    d. Reebok

333. Before golf tees, how did golfers set up their ball to hit their "tee shot" for each hole?
    a. Carry around buckets of sand and build a pile of sand before each shot
    b. Break off twigs and use them as a "tee"
    c. Would ask a fellow golfer to lay down and hold the ball on their lips
    d. None of these. They just set the ball flat on the ground and hit from there.

334. Drafted after LeBron James and before players like Carmelo Anthony, Chris Bosh, and Dwayne Wade, the Detroit Pistons wasted a lot of time, effort, and moola (close to $12 million) by choosing this 17-year-old kid with the overall #2 pick in the 2003 draft.
    a. Darko Milicic
    b. Greg Oden
    c. Michael Olowokandi
    d. Nikoloz Tskitishvili

335. Which of these sportscasters is connected to the catchphrase "Whoa, Nellie"?
    a. Keith Jackson
    b. Dick Enberg
    c. Dick Vitale
    d. Verne Lundquist

336. A "golden ferret" is...
    a. Holing out from a bunker in golf.
    b. When an outfielder catches a ball that bounced off the foul pole into fair territory.
    c. The gold-leaf statue Texas Tech football players touch when they're coming out of the locker room and on to the field.
    d. A type of smash played over the backhand side in tennis.

337. As of 2016, Joe DiMaggio holds the MLB hitting streak record with a streak of 56 consecutive games – a feat he achieved in 1941 – and a record he snatched from this guy.
    a. Pete Rose
    b. Bill Dahlen
    c. George Sisler
    d. Wee Willie Keeler

338. This NBA player was in the top 10 in free throw percentage five years in a row and finished his career at over 80% from the line. The interesting thing is that he shot "jumpers" from the free throw line instead of the usual method.
    a. Billy Cunningham
    b. Chet Walker
    c. Ed Conlin
    d. Hal Greer

339. The Golf Champion Trophy (presented to the
     British Open winner) is commonly known as the...
     a. Tooting Bec Cup
     b. Claret Jug
     c. St. Clifford Cup
     d. Royal Greens Cup

340. In 1997, MLB Commissioner Bud Selig number
     directed that this jersey number be "retired" by
     every single major league baseball club...
     a. 21
     b. 14
     c. 7
     d. 42

341. Which of the "Triple Crown of Motorsport" events
     is the oldest?
     a. Indianapolis 500
     b. Monaco Grand Prix
     c. 24 Hours of Le Mans
     d. European Grand Prix

342. Before the Hawks were in Atlanta, they were in St.
     Louis, and before that, they were in this city.
     a. Milwaukee
     b. Minneapolis
     c. Flint
     d. Ft. Wayne

343. In what sport did the phrase "hands down" (like
     winning hands down) originate?
     a. Boxing
     b. Horse Racing
     c. Hockey
     d. Speed Skating

344. At age 17 years, 137 days, this man became (and remains) the youngest American male track athlete to ever qualify for the Olympics. Drum roll, please, for...
   a. Jerry Milner
   b. Bob Seagren
   c. Jim Ryun
   d. Bob Beamon

345. The NCAA is dead set against it and Native American organizations rarely allow colleges to use "Native American (Indian)" names as athletic monikers. One of those is this college whose teams are called the Chippewas...
   a. Louisiana Monroe
   b. St. John's
   c. Southeast Missouri State
   d. Central Michigan University

346. Of the five major professional team sports, which one has the least actual action (like when a ball's in play) in terms of time?
   a. Football
   b. Basketball
   c. Hockey
   d. Soccer
   e. Baseball

347. Despite being born without a right hand, this man became a successful major-league pitcher and even threw a no-hitter.
   a. Jim Pollard
   b. Tim Abbott
   c. Tim Pollard
   d. Jim Abbott

348. This movement was part of the sport of Weightlifting in the Olympics until 1972, when it was removed due to difficulties in judging proper technique.
    a. Clean and press
    b. The snatch
    c. Clean and jerk
    d. Presto-chango

349. Who was the pitcher who gave up Babe Ruth's record-setting 60th home run in 1927? Hint: He also has the MLB record for most pitching wins without a loss in one season.
    a. Tom Zachary
    b. Ted Lyons
    c. Red Faber
    d. Pud Galvin

350. Who, pray tell, is Craig McTavish?
    a. The last helmetless player in the National Hockey League
    b. The golfer who won a PGA Championship with the longest putter (54 in.) ever used
    c. The boxer who scored the quickest TKO in boxing history
    d. The highest-drafter kicker drafted in NFL history

351. With a minimum of one game played per franchise, which of these NBA players has played for the most franchises?
    a. Caron Butler
    b. Chauncey Billups
    c. Juwan Howard
    d. Chucky Brown

352. This country did not win a medal at the Olympics (Winter or Summer) until 1984.
   a. China
   b. Paraguay
   c. Philippines
   d. Hungary

353. Which of these former NFL coaches has the best playoff winning percentage?
   a. Barry Switzer
   b. Joe Gibbs
   c. Mike Holmgren
   d. Chuck Noll

354. On January 19, '74, what college basketball team scored the last 12 points to defeat #1 UCLA, ending the Bruins' record 88-game win streak?
   a. Michigan
   b. Notre Dame
   c. Houston
   d. LSU

355. Muhammad Ali's first professional loss came in 1971 when he lost to who?
   a. Buster Mathis
   b. Ken Norton
   c. Sonny Liston
   d. Joe Frazier

356. Which of these "tournaments," "championships," or "playoffs" was established first?
   a. NFL playoff game
   b. Masters (Golf) Tournament
   c. NIT Men's Basketball Tournament
   d. NCAA Men's Basketball Tournament

357. 1976 is the last time the NCAA men's basketball tourney had two unbeaten teams in the tournament. One was Indiana. The other?
    a. Penn
    b. St. Bonaventure
    c. Rutgers
    d. Houston

358. On January 1, 1951, this team got a win over Oklahoma in the Sugar Bowl to snap the Sooners' 31-game winning streak.
    a. Ohio State
    b. Kentucky
    c. Florida
    d. LSU

359. The 1972-73 version of this team was undefeated, however they didn't play in the NCAA tournament because of sanctions.
    a. Marquette
    b. St. Johns
    c. NC State
    d. UNLV

360. Back when Joe Namath was drafted, there were actually two drafts – one for the NFL and one for the AFL. The NY Jets drafted Joe with the first pick in the AFL draft, but what NFL team drafted him 12th in the NFL draft?
    a. Green Bay Packers
    b. Dallas Cowboys
    c. Washington Redskins
    d. St. Louis Cardinals

361. The historical golf club was wooden-shafted and used primarily before the 20th Century. It would be most closely associated with today's 7-irons.
   a. Mashie niblick
   b. Cleek
   c. Mashie iron
   d. Jigger

362. What was Joan Whitney Payson's claim to fame?
   a. She was Billie Jean King's mixed doubles partner when the pair won nine Wimbledon championships.
   b. The inventor of the nylon net used on basketball goals.
   c. The first woman to found a major league baseball team.
   d. First woman to call play-by-play in the NFL.

363. After his football career (one that included the Heisman), this guy took on professional MMA and was also a member on the Olympic bobsled team.
   a. Mike Rozier
   b. Herschel Walker
   c. Billy Sims
   d. Earl Campbell

364. Back before both of us were probably born, ESPN college football analyst Lee Corso played on the gridiron at this school and with this famous dude...
   a. Florida State with actor Burt Reynolds
   b. Auburn with evangelist Jimmy Swaggart
   c. Texas Tech with Country singer Mel Tillis
   d. Ole Miss with writer William Faulkner

365. Who, what, when, or where inspired Nike's "Just Do It" slogan?
    a. Coach Vince Lombardi's terse message to his Packers in the famous "Ice Bowl"
    b. Mass murderer Gary Gilmore
    c. Harold Abrahams' (*Chariots of Fire*) dad encouraging him to run to overcome prejudice
    d. A line from the movie *The Natural*

366. POTUSes (that's Presidents of the United States) have been throwing out ceremonial first pitches at Opening Day baseball games for... well, let's just say a while. Who was the first Prez to toss one?
    a. William Howard Taft
    b. Grover Cleveland
    c. Dwight Eisenhower
    d. Harry Truman

367. After spending six years in the Toronto Blue Jays farm system, this player gave up baseball, enrolled at college where he became the oldest Heisman winner ever, at age 28.
    a. Jim Plunkett
    b. Andre Ware
    c. Chris Weinke
    d. Gino Toretta

368. Which of these sports figures coined the term "three-peat"?
    a. Lakers coach Pat Riley
    b. Yankees pitcher Lefty Gomez
    c. Steelers owner Art Rooney
    d. None of the above

369. What dapper pianist submitted (under an assumed name) his idea for a theme song for *The NBA on NBC*, a tune that NBC licensed and played more than 12,000 times from 1990 until 2002?
   a. Elton John
   b. Billy Joel
   c. John Tesh
   d. Barry Manilow

370. This college changed its nickname from the "Eagles" to the "Mean Green" in honor of its famous alum, Mean Joe Greene.
   a. Southern Illinois
   b. Western Carolina
   c. Eastern Michigan
   d. North Texas

371. Which of these "underwater" sports isn't for real?
   a. Underwater football
   b. Underwater baseball
   c. Underwater hockey
   d. Underwater rugby

372. The origin of the term "southpaw" for left-handed pitchers goes back to...
   a. Philadelphia A's lefty Eddie Plank who hailed from Greenville, Mississippi
   b. Jesse Petty, who was part-Pawnee Indian, and hailed from South Boston
   c. Back in the day, they built stadiums so the diamond part of home plate faces west which meant a left-handed pitcher's left arm was on the "south" side of his body
   d. Fact of the matter is no one really knows!

373. Which of these University of Michigan Wolverine QBs was selected the highest in the NFL draft?
    a. Chad Henne
    b. Tom Brady
    c. Elvis Grbac
    d. Brian Griese

374. Yelena Isinbayeva was named #3 in *Sports Illustrated's* "Top 20 Female Athletes of the Decade". What was Yelena's sport?
    a. Downhill Skiing
    b. Javelin
    c. Pole Vault
    d. 50-yard Dash

375. What NBA franchise retired the jersey number "613" in honor of their longtime coach's winning record with the team?
    a. Suns
    b. Celtics
    c. Lakers
    d. Knicks

376. In a meeting at the White House, President Nixon told this gymnast that their Olympics performance did more for reducing the political tension during the Cold War between the U.S. and Soviet Union than the embassies were able to do. Which one of these gymnasts was it?
    a. Olga Korbut
    b. Mary Lou Retton
    c. Nadia Comăneci
    d. Cathy Rigby

377. Doesn't take a rocket scientist to figure out that "football" has relationship to, duh, a foot and a ball, but where did the word "soccer" come from?
   a. A bunch of British school kids pulled it out of the phrase "association football" and, then, funked it up from there.
   b. The first "football" team at Oxford was captained by a chap named Bredford LeSocca who decided to try a version of the game using only the head and feet.
   c. Rugby players didn't wear socks, but football players did.
   d. It came from how one strikes the ball, e.g. "You just sock'er it with your foot."

378. "100 Miles of Hate" is the name of this annual college football rivalry that began in 1914.
   a. Alabama vs. Auburn
   b. Western Kentucky vs. Middle Tennessee
   c. Virginia vs. Virginia Tech
   d. Arizona vs. Arizona State

379. All of this U.S. city's major sports teams use the same two primary team colors.
   a. Pittsburgh
   b. Phoenix
   c. Atlanta
   d. Tampa

380. Which of these non-major sports was created before the rest of this bunch?
   a. Disc golf
   b. Racquetball
   c. Skeet shooting
   d. Grand Prix motorcycle racing

381.   Besides Boise State, which of these colleges has colored turf on its football field?
   a.   Northern Iowa
   b.   Eastern Washington
   c.   Central Florida
   d.   South Carolina

382.   This question is one of those "what am I" kind. It's long, too, so get a blanket... (This sport) is a "mini-baseball" game featuring a 1.6-ounce ball and a bat that measures 1.5 inches in diameter. Originally played on the streets of St. Louis, today the game has leagues formed around the country as a result of St. Louis servicemen introducing the game to their buddies during World War II and the Korean War. The game has many of baseball's trademark features, but can be played in a very small area because there is no base-running. What is it?
   a.   Pickleball
   b.   Town Ball
   c.   Corkball
   d.   Hoover Ball

383.   In the college ranks, there's a fair number of "human" or "live" mascots – like Georgia's "UGA," the Mountaineer dude at West Virginia, Southern Cal with the Trojan guy, Texas' "Bevo," etc. But, best as I can tell, there's only one "human" mascot in any of the four professional USA sports. Which of these teams has one?
   a.   Minnesota Vikings
   b.   Detroit Tigers
   c.   Anaheim Ducks
   d.   Tampa Bay Buccaneers

384. In American football, a 4-3 defense is a defensive alignment consisting of this configuration...
   a. Four linebackers and three rushers
   b. Four linemen and three guards
   c. Four tackles and three linebackers
   d. Four down linemen and three linebackers

385. What was the first major league-type sport that gave out rings to the champion team?
   a. Football
   b. Hockey
   c. Baseball
   d. Basketball

386. He was born in Mentor, Ohio and attended Baldwin-Wallace College, where he played football as quarterback under his father. He was hired by the Ohio State University prior to the start of the 2001 season to replace John Cooper. Who is he?
   a. Bo Pelini
   b. Ron Stoops, Jr.
   c. Luke Fickell
   d. Jim Tressel

387. When you get past the single-season records of Bonds, McGwire, Sosa, Ruth, and Maris, this trio of hitters are next in line with the most home runs in a single season (58).
   a. Hank Greenberg, Ryan Howard, and Jimmy Foxx
   b. Hack Wilson, Louis Gonzalez, and Alex Rodriguez
   c. Jose Bautista, Ken Griffey, Mickey Mantle
   d. David Ortiz, Ralph Kiner, Jim Thome

388. The moniker "Mr. Irrelevant" is the title bestowed each year upon the last pick of this annual pro league draft.
    a. NBA
    b. NHL
    c. NFL
    d. MLB

389. This golfer is one of three to win the Masters in his first appearance in the event. He also won the '84 U.S. Open and the namesake of a brand of vodka.
    a. Bernhard Langer
    b. Nick Faldo
    c. Fuzzy Zoeller
    d. José María Olazábal

390. Who was the first African-American athlete to play in an athletic contest of any kind in the Southeast Conference (SEC)?
    a. Stephen Martin
    b. Tom Payne
    c. Nate Northington
    d. Tom Jackson

391. Which of these distances is the longest in length?
    a. Home plate to pitcher's box
    b. Distance between soccer goal posts
    c. Three-point field goal line from the center of the basket in the National Basketball Association
    d. Overall length of a bowling lane (measuring from foul line to pit – not including tail plank)

392. In between Fran Tarkenton's two stints with the Vikings, he played for...
    a. NY Jets
    b. NY Giants
    c. Chicago Bears
    d. Atlanta Falcons

393. Which of these "firsts" would you not find on Ronda Rousey's curriculum vitae?
    a. First female fighter to step into the octagon
    b. First U.S. woman to win an Olympic medal in Judo
    c. First female UFC champ
    d. First female to win a UFC fight

394. During his junior year, Bob Pettit led this college to their first NCAA Final Four.
    a. Villanova
    b. Louisiana State University
    c. St. Louis Univ.
    d. Princeton

395. Karate was developed on these islands.
    a. Mitsukejima
    b. Wakasu
    c. Toshima
    d. Ryukyu

396. Which of these college football stadiums is the oldest (as in when it was built)?
    a. Autzen Stadium (Oregon)
    b. Gerald J. Ford Stadium (SMU)
    c. Mountaineer Field at Milan Puskar Stadium (West Virginia)
    d. Carrier Dome (Syracuse)

397. This baseball pitcher is the only player to have his number retired by three separate teams... the all-time leader in no-hitters with seven... one of only about 30 players in baseball history to have appeared in Major League baseball games in four decades... and the only pitcher to have struck out seven pairs of fathers and sons, among other superlatives (which we'll reveal in the answer!)
    a. Greg Maddux
    b. Randy Johnson
    c. Don Sutton
    d. Nolan Ryan

398. When the legendary Tom Landry retired as the Cowboys head coach, who did Jerry Jones hire as his replacement?
    a. Jimmy Johnson
    b. Barry Switzer
    c. Chan Gailey
    d. Dave Campo

399. Which of these factoids is true?
    a. Michael Jordan was cut from his high school basketball team at Laney High School in Wilmington, N.C.
    b. Future Cuban revolutionary leader Fidel Castro was once given a tryout by the Washington Senators.
    c. Golf courses have 18 holes because a bottle of Scotch contains 18 shots.
    d. The Kentucky Derby was the brainchild of Meriwether Lewis Clark Jr., grandson of William Clark (of Lewis and Clark fame).

400. The ABA (American Basketball Association) dissolved when four of its six teams were absorbed into the NBA. Who were the two teams left out in the cold at the end?
    a. Kentucky and St. Louis
    b. Dallas and Virginia
    c. New Jersey and Miami
    d. Houston and New Orleans

401. This collegiate star's uniform number (18) is used as the official speed limit on campus. Name the athlete and the school.
    a. Joe Namath/Alabama
    b. Archie Manning/Ole Miss
    c. Bart Starr/Alabama
    d. Herschel Walker/Georgia

402. In the NFL's numbering system, what number range is typically assigned to tight ends?
    a. 1-9
    b. 20-39
    c. 40-49
    d. 80-89

403. Since 1954 at this school, three football players who wore #44 earned All-American honors. To reflect the importance of #44, the university's zip code changed to 13244 and phone prefixes to 442 and 443.
    a. Syracuse
    b. Boston College
    c. Penn State
    d. Cornell

404. Who was the first woman to have a Nike shoe named after her?
   a. Sheryl Swoopes
   b. Lisa Leslie
   c. Krista Kirkland
   d. Maya Moore

405. Since his father, Dell, played for this college team and is in their Hall of Fame, Stephen Curry wanted to play for them, too, but they didn't think he had much of a game and only offered Steph a chance to walk-on.
   a. North Carolina
   b. Virginia Tech
   c. Virginia
   d. North Carolina State

406. The fastest pitch recognized by MLB was on September 25, 2010, at Petco Park in San Diego by this Cincinnati Reds left-handed relief pitcher.
   a. Pedro Villarreal
   b. Mike Leake
   c. Aroldis Chapman
   d. Brad Boxberger

407. You basketball fans probably complain about the refs as much as every other sport's fan, so let's pose this question and see how observant you are: This typical men's basketball referee signal – one hand tapping the top of the ref's head – indicates what?
   a. Player control foul
   b. Shot clock violation
   c. Charged timeout
   d. Crease violation

408. This Philadelphia Phillies' owner was banned for life for publicly asserting that umpires favored the NY Giants and making unfair calls against his team.
   a. Red Corriden
   b. Benny Kauff
   c. Jack O'Connor
   d. Horace Fogel

409. This Olympic hero has a town named after him...
   a. Jim Thorpe
   b. John Joe Nevin
   c. Jesse Owens
   d. Carl Lewis

410. Along with Chicago's Bears, this club is one of two NFL charter member franchises still in operation since the league's founding.
   a. Packers
   b. Cardinals
   c. Giants
   d. Bears

411. Best known as a basketball player, this Ohio State alum was also drafted by the Cleveland Browns.
   a. John Havlicek
   b. Jerry Lucas
   c. Bobby Knight
   d. Nate Archibald

412. All of these college teams are named after dogs except one – which?
   a. Butler
   b. Drake University
   c. University of Indianapolis
   d. University of Houston

413. This Yankee legend got a shout-out in episodes of
Seinfeld; posed nude for *Foxy Lady* magazine; won
three Gold Gloves; played first base...
   a. Marv Throneberry
   b. Chris Chambliss
   c. Joe Pepitone
   d. Moose Skowron

414. Besides Wilt Chamberlain, this guy's the only other
player to grab 50+ rebounds in an NBA game.
   a. Manute Bol
   b. Bill Russell
   c. Wes Unseld
   d. Tree Rollins

415. The term "Dream Shake" was this former NBA
star's name for his signature move.
   a. Hakeem Olajuwon
   b. Shaquille O'Neal
   c. George Gervin
   d. Dennis Rodman

416. At one point in history, paintings (or works of art)
were given to the winners in this historic event.
   a. The Olympics
   b. New York City Marathon
   c. U.S. Open (golf)
   d. French Grand Prix (auto racing)

417. The movie *Rudy* was based on the life of this
Notre Dame football player.
   a. Rutland Valdiserri
   b. Rudolph Baccaglio
   c. Vance Rudland
   d. Daniel Ruettiger

418. This ABA championship squad's roster included players named Moe, Bradds, Eakins, Jabali, Barry, Brown, Logan, Peterson, Clawson, Harge, Anderson, and Critchfield. Who was the team?
    a. Denver Nuggets
    b. Oakland Oaks
    c. Indiana Pacers
    d. Kentucky Colonels

419. According to Wikipedia, the first recorded use of this sports/game-oriented phrase appeared in the *Dallas Morning News* in March of 1976, attributed to a "Ralph Carpenter."
    a. "The opera ain't over until the fat lady sings"
    b. "It ain't over till it's over"
    c. "Nothing is carved in stone"
    d. "Don't count your chickens before they hatch"

420. Over the years, sports figures, implements (like Robert Redford's character named his bat "Wonder Boy" in *The Natural*), or events have been given certain names. For example, the name "Sceptre" would be related to which of these sports people, place, or thing?
    a. It was the name that Alex Rodriguez gave his baseball bat
    b. It was the first name submitted to the Jockey Club for the horse Secretariat
    c. It was the nickname golf great Tom Watson gave his putter
    d. It was the name of a defensive set built around Baltimore Raven Ray Lewis, setting him up for a possible interception.

421. Other than Babe Ruth, only one player in Major League Baseball, NCAA Softball, or NCAA Baseball has hit at least 70 homers <u>and</u> notched at least 70 wins as a pitcher. Who would that be?
   a. Sam Newby
   b. Lauren Haeger
   c. Eileen Canney
   d. Josh Hamilton

422. After admitting to doping, this athlete lost their Olympic medals, was banned from the sport, and spent six months in the hoosegow.
   a. Marion Jones
   b. Usain Bolt
   c. Brian Oldfield
   d. Pharaoh Hamilton

423. Prior to the school joining the A-Sun, it had been the only (last remaining) NCAA Division I basketball independent.
   a. Wagner
   b. UIPUI
   c. Radford
   d. New Jersey Institute of Technology

424. Coach Mike Krzyzewski's résumé includes the head coaching position at Duke and Army, plus an assistant's job at this school where the team won the NCAA Men's Basketball championship.
   a. Marquette
   b. Indiana
   c. Arkansas
   d. UCLA

425. Which of these "elements" is considered illegal in Olympic-eligible Pair Skating?
    a. A "Cincy Toast"
    b. A "Lebanese Lift"
    c. A "Goblet"
    d. A "Detroiter"

426. Of these ex-NFL coaches, who spent the most years as a pro football coach?
    a. Chuck Noll
    b. Curly Lambeau
    c. George Halas
    d. Tom Landry

427. He was captain of the '61 Notre Dame team, then appeared in three Super Bowls, and named the MVP of three Dolphins squads. Post-football, he was a host of Inside the NFL.
    a. Cris Collinsworth
    b. Nick Buoniconti
    c. Jimmy Johnson
    d. Chuck Bednarik

428. Which of these well-known sportscasters did *not* play a team sport in college?
    a. Brent Musburger
    b. Billy Packer
    c. Jim Nantz
    d. Curt Gowdy

429. In which country did Taekwondo originate?
    a. Korea
    b. China
    c. Japan
    d. Thailand

430. Prior to the 1970s there had only been two baseball players who had facial hair during the regular season. Who was the first player to break the modern day moustache barrier in 1972?
   a. Bert Blyleven
   b. Tony Kubek
   c. Sparky Lyle
   d. Reggie Jackson

431. This coach and school began the Midnight Madness tradition at 12:03 a.m. on October 15, 1971 by inviting the public to a 1.5-mile team run.
   a. Northeastern's head coach Jim Calhoun
   b. Maryland Terrapins' Lefty Driesell
   c. St. John's and Lou Carneseca
   d. UNLV and Jerry Tarkanian

432. This former Major League Baseball star's nickname was "Baby Bull."
   a. Roberto Clemente
   b. Jose Cardenas
   c. Juan Marichal
   d. Orlando Cepeda

433. Baseball'er Johnny Vander Meer is most well known for being what?
   a. The player who played for the greatest number of teams (13)
   b. The player with the record for errors committed as a third-baseman
   c. The only pitcher in Major League Baseball history to throw two consecutive no-hitters.
   d. Being the pitcher who pitched the most consecutive innings without allowing a run (43)

434. By the time this pro basketball player retired after 19 seasons in the NBA, he was the last former ABA player still active.
   a. Moses Malone
   b. Dan Issel
   c. Julius Irving
   d. Billy Cunningham

435. The first NBA coach to win 1,000 games with a single franchise was who? Think out West...
   a. Pat Riley
   b. Jack Ramsay
   c. Jerry Sloan
   d. Alex Hannum

436. Where did soccer great Mia Hamm go to college?
   a. UCLA
   b. Virginia
   c. Southern Cal
   d. UNC - Chapel Hill

437. After his time in Green Bay, Paul Hornung was selected in the expansion draft by this new franchise.
   a. New Orleans Saints
   b. Minnesota Vikings
   c. Tampa Bay Buccaneers
   d. Atlanta Falcons

438. We know Pat Summitt coached UT's Lady Vols from 1974-2012, but where did she play her college ball?
   a. University of Tennessee-Martin
   b. Louisiana Tech
   c. East Tennessee
   d. Middle Tennessee

439. In 1963, this person became the first black player ever selected for the United States Davis Cup team.
    a. Carol Thatcher
    b. Gabrielle Andrews
    c. Arthur Ashe
    d. James Blake

440. This NBA championship coach and HOF'er replaced Bob Cousy as Boston College's coach in 1969.
    a. Chuck Daly
    b. Don Nelson
    c. Phil Jackson
    d. Lenny Wilkens

441. Which of these coaches had the longest tenure as the head Football coach at the University of Michigan?
    a. Bo Schembechler
    b. Lloyd Carr
    c. Gary Moeller
    d. Fielding Yost

442. In North America harness races are restricted to this breed of horse.
    a. Coldblood Trotters
    b. Thoroughbreds
    c. Standardbreds
    d. Shires

443. One of this famous U.S. swimmer's two nicknames is "Reezy." He was a Florida Gator and his specialties are backstroke, butterfly, freestyle, and medley.
    a. Peter Rocca
    b. Ryan Lochte
    c. Don Schollander
    d. Tom Jager

444. Which of these factoids about sports traditions is the true one?
   a. Winners of the LPGA "ANA Inspiration" tourney jump into the lake
   b. As players leave the locker room at Notre Dame, they slap a sign that quotes JFK
   c. Until 1962, the U. of Illinois and Indiana U. players would exchange jerseys at the end of their annual football match
   d. The "7th Inning Stretch" was begun when President Eisenhower got up to stretch at a Senators game.

445. Which of these pitchers has racked up the most "saves"?
   a. Dave Righetti
   b. Jeff Russell
   c. Mariano Rivera
   d. Dan Quisenberry

446. In Super Bowl XVI, starting Defensive players from each side included Byron Hicks, Dwight Hicks, Carlton Williamson, Bobby Kemp, Eric Wright, and Ken Riley. Who are the teams?
   a. Dolphins and 49ers
   b. 49ers and Bengals
   c. Steelers and Cowboys
   d. Broncos and Giants

447. What's the only school to leave the ACC and move to the SEC?
   a. South Carolina
   b. Georgia
   c. Florida
   d. Mississippi State

448. Wilt Chamberlain was once a pro basketball coach. Really. For ABA's...
   a. Utah Stars
   b. Anaheim Amigos
   c. Los Angeles Stars
   d. San Diego Conquistadors

449. Despite a state ban on playing integrated teams, this college's all-white team snuck out in the dead of night to play Loyola (Chicago) in the '63 NCAA tourney.
   a. Auburn
   b. 'Ole Miss
   c. Mississippi State
   d. LSU

450. Who are Robin Herman and Marcel St. Cyr?
   a. The first female reporters ever allowed to enter into a men's professional team locker room
   b. The first Women's Doubles champions at Wimbledon
   c. The first two women allowed to participate in the Olympics
   d. The first girls allowed to play Little League baseball

451. Which of these pitchers would be considered a "knuckleballer"? A hint? Sure – he was the oldest player in Major League Baseball for each of his final seven seasons.
   a. Hoyt Wilhelm
   b. Lew Burdette
   c. Babe Ruth
   d. Roy Halladay

452. To capture the worn-down look of the era, *The Natural* movie was filmed at...
    a. Shibe Park in Philadelphia
    b. Colt Stadium in Houston
    c. Tulane Stadium in New Orleans
    d. War Memorial Stadium in Buffalo

453. Which of these sports has "seven-meter throw" as one of the scoring options that a referee can award.
    a. Cricket
    b. Team handball
    c. Water polo
    d. Curling

454. What college football team leads the pack of most 100+ point victories with 8?
    a. Georgia Tech
    b. Oklahoma
    c. Arkansas
    d. Old Dominion

455. This actor has owned part of eight minor league baseball teams, and his son has been an ass't coach for the men's basketball teams at Xavier, et al.
    a. Bill Murray
    b. Dustin Hoffman
    c. Billy Bob Thornton
    d. Dan Ackroyd

456. The last MLB player to take on the role as "player-manager" is this guy.
    a. Don Kessinger
    b. Joe Torre
    c. Frank Robinson
    d. Pete Rose

457. In 1950, this school became the only school to win both the NCAA Men's Division I Basketball Championship and the National Invitation Tournament (NIT) in the same season.
    a. Seattle
    b. CCNY
    c. Kentucky
    d. LaSalle

458. It was 38 years between the time that Ohio State joined the Big Ten and when the next school joined. What was that school?
    a. Penn State
    b. Northwestern
    c. Michigan State
    d. Iowa

459. As of 2016, this QB held NFL records for most career pass completions, most career pass attempts, most career interceptions thrown, most consecutive starts by a player, most sacked, and most fumbles.
    a. Dan Marino
    b. Warren Moon
    c. Brett Favre
    d. Terry Bradshaw

460. Let's talk about attendance figures. The NFL is #1 in average game attendance by a long shot – 68,776. But, which of these other leagues would be *second*?
    a. Premier League (association soccer in England/Wales)
    b. Bundesliga (association soccer in Germany)
    c. Indian Premier League (cricket in India)
    d. Major League Baseball (USA)

461. What professional ball player has played for the most franchises/clubs?
   a. Chucky Brown (basketball)
   b. Octavio Dotel (baseball)
   c. Shayne Graham (football)
   d. Mike Sillinger (hockey)

462. At SMU, this coach saw his football program brought down by sanctions that led to the "death penalty."
   a. Bobby Collins
   b. Forrest Gregg
   c. Ron Meyer
   d. Steve Orsini

463. With 2:12 to go in the NCAA men's national basketball championship, this team had a 9-point lead over Kansas, but wound up losing the game 75-68 (OT).
   a. Memphis
   b. Kentucky
   c. Michigan
   d. Utah

464. Who's the baseball player that was known as the "black Babe Ruth"?
   a. Josh Gibson
   b. Herb Souell
   c. Hank Thompson
   d. Lenny Pearson

465. In what sport would you find a ball called a "jack"?
   a. Four square
   b. Flickerball
   c. Bocce
   d. Polo

466. This major league baseball manager once did a commercial for Glad refrigerator bags, which poked fun at his infamous temper ("Don't get mad! Get Glad!").
    a. Yogi Berra
    b. Tommy Lasorda
    c. Lou Pinella
    d. Whitey Herzog

467. Oliver Luck, who happens to be the dad of Colts quarterback Andrew Luck, was also a QB in the NFL, spending five years with this team.
    a. Houston Oilers
    b. Chicago Bears
    c. Los Angeles Rams
    d. Detroit Lions

468. This hockey player, nicknamed "Mr. Goalie," holds the NHL record for most consecutive games started by a goaltender with a total of 502.
    a. Don Edwards
    b. Tony Esposito
    c. Chuck Rayner
    d. Glenn Hall

469. Tennis time, folks! There are three men who have seven Wimbledon men's singles titles to their name. There's Pete Sampras, Roger Federer*, and also this fella...
    a. William Renshaw
    b. Bjorn Borg
    c. Tony Trabert
    d. Andy Roddick
    *Didja know you can type all the letters in "Federer" with your left hand? You don't care, correct?

470. This football'er spent 57+ consecutive seasons in the NFL as either a coach or a player, including starting a record 171 games at cornerback.
    a. Herm Edwards
    b. Craig Newsome
    c. Deion Sanders
    d. Dick LaBeau

471. What conference was the first to hold a post-season basketball tourney to decide a conference champion?
    a. Southern
    b. SEC
    c. Patriot
    d. Big East

472. At what college did the term "redshirt" supposedly begin?
    a. Memphis State
    b. University of Nebraska
    c. St. John's
    d. University of Connecticut

473. What comic strip popularized the hockey re-surfacing machine, the Zamboni?
    a. Garfield
    b. Peanuts
    c. Doonesbury
    d. Beetle Bailey

474. Which of these Olympic gymnastics events do only Men participate in?
    a. Pommel horse
    b. Uneven bars
    c. Balance beam
    d. Rhythmic gymnastics

475. Which one of these is a real difference between racquetball and squash?
    a. There's no net to hit the ball over in racquetball, but there is in squash
    b. In squash, there's an area called the "tin" and if you hit it, your ball is "out"
    c. A racquetball can be any color, but squash balls are all green
    d. Racquetball rackets can be longer than squash rackets

476. Which of these sports is the oldest?
    a. Snowboarding
    b. Table tennis (ping-pong)
    c. Midget car racing
    d. Miniature golf

477. This MLB Hall of Famer ended his career as the baseball coach at Duke, but years earlier injured Jackie Robinson during a game by inflicting a 7-inch gash from his shoe spikes on Robinson's leg.
    a. Jim Bottomly
    b. Chick Hafey
    c. Enos Slaughter
    d. Johnny Mize

478. All but one of these four father & son duos each won an NCAA basketball championship. Who's the odd pair out?
    a. Derek and Nolan Smith
    b. Bill and Luke Walton
    c. Marques and Kris Johnson
    d. Scott and Sean May

479. Let's talk tennis shoes, ok? Specifically, the term "sneaker". How did we wind up with them being called "sneakers," anyway? Was it...
    a. Because the shoes were quieter than leather-soled shoes and one could "sneak up" on someone?
    b. Because they were first manufactured in the U.K. by the Jos. Sneaks & Son Rubber Co.?
    c. Because the first ones made had some sort of allergen in the formula that made people sneeze?
    d. Because the Greeks wore them for extra traction when it snowed and some wisecracker combined "snow" and "Greek" and called them "sneakers"?

480. Which of these famous golf players designed the Augusta National Golf Club, and co-founded the Masters Tournament?
    a. Bobby Jones
    b. Gene Sarazen
    c. Byron Nelson
    d. Henry Picard

481. There are four basic differences between candlepin and tenpin bowling. Which of the following ain't one? In candlepins...
    a. Players use three balls per frame
    b. The ball is smaller and has only two finger holes
    c. The pins are thinner
    d. "Downed" pins are not cleared away between balls during a player's turn

482.   This event was included only one time at the
       Olympics (1904) and the USA was the only nation to
       have athletes participate.
       a. Polo
       b. Alpinism
       c. Tug-of-War
       d. Roque

483.   Taro Tsujimoto is an imaginary player drafted by this
       NHL team in the 11th round of the 1974 NHL
       amateur draft.
       a. Washington Capitals
       b. Buffalo Sabres
       c. Minnesota North Stars
       d. Pittsburgh Penguins

484.   This NFL team failed to win a match for an entire
       season (or throw a TD pass in their first five games)
       and parlayed that into a 26 consecutive loss streak.
       Their first season's 0-14 record was finally broken
       when the Detroit Lions went 0-16 in 2008. What
       team is this?
       a. Tampa Bay Buccaneers
       b. New Orleans Saints
       c. Houston Oilers
       d. San Diego Chargers

485.   When Wichita State made it to the Final Four in
       2013, they were the first Missouri Valley Conference
       team to make it since this one...
       a. Loyola of Chicago
       b. Indiana State
       c. Butler
       d. Iowa State

486. Which of these sports has the *fewest* number of players on the field/court at the same time?
   a. Field hockey
   b. Ice hockey
   c. Polo
   d. Ultimate Frisbee

487. Which of these NCAA men's basketball tourney facts is actually false (as of 2015)?
   a. Texas has had more schools play in the tournament than any other state.
   b. The tradition of cutting down the nets began with coach Branch McCracken at Indiana, who stood on his players' shoulders to do it after the Hoosiers won the NCAA tournament.
   c. In 1975, Syracuse played the most overtime games in one tournament run.
   d. Kentucky vs. Marquette is the most frequent NCAA tournament matchup.

488. Legendary Kansas coach "Phog" Allen got the nickname "Phog" for the distinctive foghorn voice he had as a...
   a. Submarine captain
   b. Train brakeman
   c. Baseball umpire
   d. None of these are true

489. After Jerry Tarkanian got bounced from his job as UNLV's head b-ball coach, he landed a head coaching gig with this NBA team.
   a. Lakers
   b. Clippers
   c. Kings
   d. Spurs

490. The Society for American Baseball Research gives props to this N.Y. Knickerbockers player/exec for creating the concept of the shortstop position, and other historians pretty much give him the nod for baseball having nine players and nine innings.
    a. Alexander Cartwright
    b. Doc Adams
    c. Charles Schuyler De Bost
    d. Spike Harringay

491. Which of these sports factoids is false? Like not true, never happened, bogus, phony baloney!
    a. The reason why medalists at the Paralympics hold the medals up to their ear is so they can "hear" what medal they won.
    b. The overtime procedure in high school and college football, as well as the Canadian Football League is sometimes referred to as the "Ohio Plan".
    c. At one point in tennis star Andre Agassi's career, Nike outfitted him with stonewashed blue jean shorts – and he actually wore 'em in a match!
    d. Pitcher Rip Sewell is the only known 20-game winner who won all of his games throwing the "eephus," a "trick" pitch.

492. This MLB team held spring training on an island for 31 years... have had six ballparks they've called "home"... had pitchers nicknamed "Twiggy" and "Vulture"...
    a. Chicago Cubs
    b. New York / SF Giants
    c. Chicago White Sox
    d. Brooklyn / LA Dodgers

493. The only Heisman Trophy winner to have a stadium named after him is...
   a. Larry Kelley
   b. Nile Kinnick
   c. Clint Frank
   d. Davey O'Brien

494. Toward the end of his baseball career, this player did two Jazz LPs and got a Grammy nomination.
   a. Bernie Williams
   b. Rubén Sierra
   c. Raúl Mondesí
   d. Alfonso Soriano

495. This Olympic sprinter gave up running to become a Hall of Fame wide receiver in the NFL.
   a. Bob Hayes
   b. Calvin Johnson
   c. Don Hudson
   d. Jerry Rice

496. Who was the first QB to get to 100 wins?
   a. Bart Starr
   b. Johnny Unitas
   c. Brett Favre
   d. Joe Montana

497. After Nancy Kerrigan rebounded from Tonya Harding's whack job, she skated her tail off at the Lillehammer Olympics, but came in second. Who won the Gold in Ladies Singles that year?
   a. Oksana Baiul
   b. Michelle Kwan
   c. Vera Wang
   d. Tara Lipinski

498. Usually, MLB "home" uniforms feature the team's nickname, whereas "away" unis feature the name of the city the team is from (e.g. "Boston"). Interestingly enough, this major league team has never worn the full name of their hometown on any of their uniforms.
    a. Milwaukee
    b. Baltimore
    c. Kansas City
    d. Philadelphia

499. Let's talk "stadium naming rights," ok? Which <u>two</u> of these factoids would be true?
    a. Baseball commish Ford Frick wouldn't let the Anheuser-Busch company rename Sportsman's Park "Budweiser Stadium," so the Busch family asked if they could name it "Busch Stadium" after their company's founder. When Frick said "OK," Anheuser-Busch then released a new product called "Busch Beer" to capitalize on the name.
    b. What used to be the "Tangerine Bowl" is now the "Taxslayer Bowl".
    c. Before Wrigley Field became "Wrigley Field" it was called "Cubs Park".
    d. The Baltimore Ravens home field has had four different names – more than any other major league sports stadium in America.

500. Which of these names, places, events, etc. came into the sports world first?
    a. Baltimore's Camden Yards opened
    b. WWF's first WrestleMania was held
    c. The incubation of fantasy football
    d. Jim Nabors sang "Back Home Again in Indiana" for the first time at the Indy 500

501. Sometimes, athletes take things too far or they wind up being the central figure in a situation that calls for a rule change. With that in mind, which of these athletes had a "rule" named after them?
    a. Cedric "Cornbread" Maxwell (Boston Celtics)
    b. Jennifer Capriati (Women's Tennis Assoc.)
    c. Billy Sims (Detroit Lions)
    d. Rod Carew (Anaheim Angels)

502. Which of these famous inventors was inducted into International Swimming Hall of Fame?
    a. Ben Franklin
    b. Louis Pasteur
    c. Henry Ford
    d. Jonas Salk

— THE END —

Why 502 questions? 'Coz it's the area code for Louisville KY and the author is a bit of a home'r.

And, now, the answers

1. **D – Cleveland**, where they won the NFL championship in 1945, before moving to Los Angeles in 1946 to become the only NFL champion ever to play the following season in a different city.

2. **C – Bob McAdoo**, who was drafted second overall behind LaRue Martin (Dr. J was picked 12th). Martin was one of those "OMG" picks, probably because he kicked Bill Walton's butt in a game between Loyola and UCLA but he only lasted four years in the pros. Here's an interesting side note: McAdoo was twice a college All-American but with different teams. He played junior college ball at Vincennes where he won a national championship, then moved onto UNC where he led them to the Final Four.

3. **D – Oscar Robertson***. The "Big O" played 1,040 games over 14 seasons in the pros – 10 with Cincy and 4 with the Milwaukee Bucks where he won a championship with teammate Lew (pre-Kareem) Alcindor. He also became the only player in NBA history to average a triple-double for an entire season, with 30.8 points, 12.5 rebounds, and 11.4 assists. Oscar's most important contribution, however, may have been *Robertson v. National Basketball Association*, an antitrust suit that resulted in free agency for the players. *By the way, depending on how you do the math, Kenyon Martin may have played longer in the NBA than Oscar, but Martin's tenure included a year in China and a slew of little 10-day contracts.

Still, he played in only 757 NBA games, 28% fewer than Robertson.

4. **A – Bud Grant**. After his days as a Minnesota Gopher, Grant got drafted by the NFL (Eagles) and the NBA (Lakers). He only averaged 2.6 PPG in pro hoops, but he was on the 1950 Lakers championship team. As a pro football'er, Grant played defensive end for the Eagles and led the team in sacks, then moved to offense as a wide receiver for his second season where he was second in the NFL in receiving yardage. He then moved on to coaching, first as the head coach for the Winnipeg Blue Bombers – the youngest head coach in CFL history. In '67, he became the Vikings coach and the first coach to lead a team to four Super Bowls. He retired as the eighth most successful coach in NFL history.

5. **A – Jets**, who also retired Joe Namath's jersey and Weeb Ewbank's jacket. You probably remember Weeb from coaching the Jets to victory in Super Bowl III, but he also led the Baltimore Colts to NFL championships in 1958 and 1959, making him the only coach to win a championship in both the NFL and American Football League AFL. Weeb died, fittingly, on the 30th anniversary of the "Heidi Game," a match where his Jets were playing the Raiders. Thanks to lots of penalties and injuries, the game was running longer than expected. NBC had scheduled a broadcast of *Heidi* for 7pm, but as network execs watched the football game turning into a battle royale, they decided to postpone *Heidi's* start and let the Jets/Raiders play on. However, because viewers

were jamming the phone lines to make sure the golden-braided Swiss chick movie would start on-time, the execs couldn't get through the switchboard, so the network engineers flipped the switch right at 7pm with 1:01 remaining in the game – a point where the Jets were winning but right when Oakland was mounting a furious comeback and would go on to win the game. Football fans were teed-off beyond repair and NBC had some serious genuflecting to do. So much, in fact, that when NBC was set to air a special presentation of *Pinocchio* three weeks after the Heidi Game, the network promised football fans they'd be hands-off this time. They even ran a promotional ad for the broadcast where Pinocchio himself assured fans they would view the entire game before the film started and that he would sooner cut off his nose than "have them cut off" the action.

6. **B – Washington Senators**. Billy actually played for seven teams – Yanks, Tigers, A's, Indians, Braves, Reds, and Twins – and managed five different squads (two stints with the Yanks). One of Martin's more interesting detours was when he found Ron LeFlore at Jackson State penitentiary, got him out on parole for a day and a try-out with the Tigers. LeFlore went on to lead the majors in both runs scored and stolen bases. Doin' time on the lime!

7. **A – Dan Issel**, who played for the Kentucky Colonels and the Denver Nuggets, later become the Nuggets coach. His tenure ended on a rather sour note in 2001 when, after a close loss to the

Charlotte Hornets, Issel heard a fan taunting him as he walked off the court and taunted back, "Go drink another beer, you Mexican piece of s**t." Issel was suspended four games by the team. He publicly apologized the next day however, several members of Denver's Hispanic community thought the suspension was insufficient punishment and called for him to be fired. Issel decided to resign a few days later.

8. **D – Art Davie** who, by the way, was Donald Trump's roomie at the New York Military Academy (high school). The germination of UFC goes back to when Davie bought the U.S. rights to Japan's K-1 kickboxing franchise, then had the bright idea of letting martial artists of different disciplines (e.g. karate and boxing) go at each other. The first UFC event was held on November 12, 1993, at the McNichols Sports Arena in Denver. Ninety thousand households whipped out their wallet to watch it on pay-per-view, and Davie's dream soared from there. In the first UFC match, Dutch karate champion Gerard Gordeau went after Sumo wrestler Teila Tuli in a fight that lasted only 26 seconds and was stopped after Gordeau knocked out three of Tuli's teeth with a kick. The kick was so powerful that two of Tuli's teeth were lodged in Gordeau's foot but the docs didn't want to remove them because Gordeau had two more fights on that night's card and thought fighting with an open wound wasn't a smart thing to do. I have to apologize for the other answer choices... they were the original singer of REO Speedwagon, the guitarist from Kansas, and the dude who co-wrote "I Love Rock 'n' Roll." Shame on me.

9. **A – Tunney Hunsaker & Trevor Berbick**. After 17 wins, 15 losses, and 1 tie, Hunsaker hung up the gloves to become the youngest police chief in West Virginia (Fayetteville), an office he held for 36 years. A hobby of his was to turn the traffic signals off during rush hour and after the high school football games to direct traffic. Cops gotta get their happiness somewhere, right? Berbick? He beat Ali in Ali's last fight (at age 39) and, along with Larry Holmes, he's one of only two men in professional boxing history to have fought both Muhammad Ali and Mike Tyson (btw, Tyson kicked his butt).

10. **C – Archery and tennis**. Did that answer make you... uh... quiver with love (get it?)? No? Then, maybe this useless p.o.k. (piece of knowledge) will: Winning the Gold medal in tennis at the Summer Olympic Games in addition to the four majors in a one calendar year is known as a "Golden Grand Slam" or more commonly the "Golden Slam". Only one person has ever completed the Golden Slam – Steffi Graf. She's also the only tennis player to have won each Grand Slam event at least 4 times.

11. **A – Joe and Vince Dundee** whose real names were Samuel and Vince Lazzara. They changed to Dundee after emigrating from Sicily to the United States. Vince was middleweight champion and Joe was welterweight champ of the world.

12. **B – Tennis**. In Clopton's version of the game, it was played on an hourglass-shaped court and the net was higher (4' 8"). Service had to be made from a diamond-shaped box at one end only and

the ball had to bounce beyond the service line instead of in front of it.

13. **D – Magic Johnson**. Magic's also the only player to win MVP as a rookie. Now, you notice the question was Laker-centric, so that begs the question of who (as in anyone) has won the most MVPs of the Finals? That would be Michael Jordan with six, then Magic, followed by Shaq and Tim Duncan (tied with three each). Shaq's also the only player other than Jordan to win the award three times in a row.

14. **D – 7**. Jai alai once held the world record for ball speed with a ball that traveled at 188 mph, performed by José Ramón Areitio at the Newport (RI) Jai Alai, until it was broken by Canadian 5-time long drive champion Jason Zuback with a golf ball speed of 204 mph.

15. **A – American Football League** (also known retrospectively as the AFL III to distinguish it from earlier organizations of that name). The league lasted only two seasons and came to a halt after the Pearl Harbor attack since many players went overseas and that left several AFL and NFL teams with barely enough players to field viable teams. The teams in the league were the Columbus Bullies, New York Americans, Milwaukee Chiefs, Buffalo Tigers, and Cincinnati Bengals.

16. **B – The Preakness**. Why the name "The Run for the Black-Eyed Susans"? Because a blanket of yellow flowers arranged to resemble Maryland's state flower is placed around the winner's neck.

Why the name "Preakness"? Former Maryland governor Oden Bowie named the race in honor of the colt Preakness from Milton Holbrook Sanford's Preakness Stables in Preakness, Wayne Township, New Jersey, who won the Dinner Party Stakes on the day Pimlico opened (October 25, 1870).

17. **A – #9**. However, in some leagues, such as Europe's Super League, players can wear jersey numbers that do not have to conform to this system. The hookers I know had much longer numbers... and orange jumpsuits.

18. **C – Pigeon racing**. Yep, there's doping in pigeon racing to produce the same kind of results doping in other athletic contests does, 'cept that in pigeon racing, corticosteroids can be used to delay moulting, allowing a bird to race late into a season. Can't really see some NFL player worrying about moulting, can you?

19. **A – Graham Hill**. He is also the only driver ever to win the Triple Crown of Motorsport — the 24 Hours of Le Mans, Indy 500, and Monaco Grand Prix.

20. **A – Tony Conigliaro, Boston Red Sox**. He's the youngest *American League* player to reach 100 HR (in '67), but second-youngest to Mel Ott who hit that milestone for the NL Giants in '31 (Ott was also the first National League player to surpass 500 career HRs). Unfortunately, Tony was hit by a pitch toward the end of his record-setting season and, because he was wearing a helmet without an ear flap, the hit caused severe damage to his left retina.

He did make a comeback in '69 (Comeback Player of the Year), but eventually had to hang up the cleats because of his eyesight issues.

21. **D – University of Chicago**. Even though the school had some major success, e.g. the Sweet 16 in the NCAA basketball tourney and producing the very first Heisman winner (Jay Berwanger), the university chose to withdraw from the conference in 1946 after the school's president de-emphasized varsity athletics and dropped football.

22. **B – Alabama**. Stabler finished his career at Alabama with a 28-3-2 record as a starter. An interesting character, he had his own soft drink called "Snake Venom" and was featured on a SNL skit as the spokesman for a fictional product called the "Lung Brush."

23. **B – Baseball and cricket**, however innings can be either singular ("a good innings") or plural ("he batted well in both innings") in cricket.

24. **D – A.J. Foyt** or "Super Tex" to his amigos. He holds the USAC career wins record with 159 victories and the American championship racing (aka Indy car racing) career wins record with 67. And the Indy connection goes a little deeper than the raceway, too. The Foyts are also, via marriage, part of the ownership group of the Indianapolis Colts. A. J. Foyt IV is married to the daughter of Colts owner Jim Irsay.

25. **A – Elroy "Crazy Legs" Hirsch**. He gained his fame with the L.A. Rams where coach Clark

Shaughnessy made him the first full-time "flanker" in NFL history, splitting the talented receiver outside from his previous halfback position. Elroy was also one of the first to sport the molded plastic helmet that is the industry standard today. After his playing days were over, Hirsch served as the Athletic Director at the University of Wisconsin–Madison from 1969-1987. Within four years, he raised home attendance at football games from 43,000 to 70,000 and, during his tenure, the number of sports offered by the UW athletics department doubled and the Badgers won national titles in ice hockey, men's and women's crew, and men's and women's cross country.

26. **D – Two**. I won't bore you with a lot of useless cricket trivia, but it's a very complicated sport. For example, an "over" is a set of six balls bowled from one end of a cricket pitch (a 10x22' area). In a normal over, a single bowler delivers six balls in succession, from one end of the pitch, to the batsman at the other end. After six deliveries, the umpire calls 'over'; the fielding team switches ends, and a different bowler is selected to bowl an over from the opposite end of the pitch, while the batsmen do not change ends. The captain of the fielding team decides which bowler will bowl any given over, and no bowler may bowl two overs in succession. See? Told 'ya it was complicated.

27. **A – Grindstone and Thunder Gulch**. D. Wayne also trained Derby winners Charismatic and Winning Colors. But Mr. Lukas wasn't always a horse guy. He actually has a Master's Degree in Education from the University of Wisconsin-

Madison where he was an assistant coach on the Badger basketball team, then taught high school and coached basketball for nine years.

28. **C – Washington Senators**. The Senators' first go-round in D.C. lasted 59 years – a tenure that produced one World Series title (1924) and a Broadway play about the team ("Damn Yankees"). They moved to Minneapolis in 1960 and became the Twins, a move whose motivation may have had an ugly underbelly. Seems as though Senators owner Calvin Griffith reportedly told a Lions Club in Minneapolis-St. Paul in 1978 that he'd chosen Minnesota "when we found out that you only had 15,000 blacks here" as he and his father were well-known racists and segregationists. Their second stint in D.C. lasted only 10 seasons before they moved to Texas and became the Rangers. Wait! One more tidbit: What famous ballplayer was their manager from '69-72? Ted Williams!

29. **D – Long Beach State**. George's resumé goes like this: head coach for the Rams, then same gig for the Redskins, a little retirement, then a stint as the head guy for the USFL's Chicago Blitz and Arizona Wranglers. When Allen was with the 'Skins, he let President Tricky Dicky Nixon design a play which Allen ran against the San Francisco 49ers in the 1971 NFC Divisional playoff game. The result? A 13-yard loss on the play, and a game the Redskins ended up losing.

30. **A – Marquette**. Btw, do you know the first number officially retired by a team in a professional sport? It was hockey player Ace

Bailey, whose number 6 was retired by the Toronto Maple Leafs in 1934.

31. **A – Demons**. The team played at Pacific Bell Park in San Fran and, despite having the smallest stadium in the league, they had the highest average attendance (34,954). How do those numbers compare to an NFL team? Well, the Cowboys have the highest average attendance with about 90k and the Vikes the lowest with about 52k. The Demons' skipper was Jim Skipper who, as the Carolina Panthers running backs coach, helped make NFL history as two of his running backs, DeAngelo Williams and Jonathan Stewart, became the first set of teammates to rush for over 1,100 yards in the same season.

32. **B – Handball**. In Canada, the game was origi- nally called "Borden Ball" because a simplified version was introduced during WWII by European POWs detained at Camp Borden, Ontario.

33. **D – Fly pattern**. The famed "Hail Mary" play generally involves between three and five receivers all running fly routes in order to have the most chance of one of them catching the ball and scoring or gaining significant yardage. And while I'm educatin' you, do you know where the term "Hail Mary" came from? It goes back to a 1975 NFL playoff game between the Cowboys and Vikes, when Dallas' QB Roger Staubach (a good Catholic boy) commented that in his game-winning touchdown pass to wide receiver Drew Pearson, "I closed my eyes and said a Hail Mary."

34. **A – Hambone**. And to take the jargon a little further down the lane, six strikes and nine strikes in a row can also be referred to "Wild Turkeys" and "Golden Turkeys" respectively. A "perfect game" or 12 strikes in a row is also rarely referred to as the "Thanksgiving Turkey". Gobble gobble.

35. **B – Graceland University**. No, silly, Graceland's team name wasn't the Flying Elvises – and other than Jenner, their most famous alum was the guy who played the blue *Power Ranger*. Oops, almost forgot – here's another Jenner fact you can stump someone with: Despite not playing college basketball, Bruce was drafted 139th by the Kansas City Kings after he won the Men's Decathlon at the Olympics.

36. **A – Indiana–Michigan State**. The Old Brass Spittoon got its start in 1950 and more often than not goes home to East Lansing since the Spartans have won something like 75% of the matches. Actually, Michigan State spends like half its football season fighting for rivalry trophies. It's got the Land Grant Trophy with Penn State, the Paul Bunyan Trophy with Michigan, and the Megaphone Trophy with Notre Dame. Of course, nothing tops the geniuses at Illinois and Iowa – the Illini fight Ohio State for a trophy of a turtle (The Illibuck) and Iowa squares off against Minnesota for a trophy of a pig (Floyd of Rosedale).

37. **C – Buffalo Braves**. How the Braves got to California is kind of interesting. Because of the team's mediocre play in its final two years (30–52 in 1976-77 and 27–55 in 1977-78), along with rumors of the franchise relocating because of low season ticket

sales, John Y. Brown met with Irv Levin, who then owned the Celtics, and negotiated a deal in which the owners would swap franchises, with Brown taking control of the Celtics and Levin getting the Braves. Levin was a California businessman, and wanted to own an NBA team in his native state. However, he knew the NBA would not even consider letting him move the Celtics. He was therefore very receptive to Brown's offer. The deal was brokered by NBA general counsel (and future commish) David Stern in 1984. Following what would be the Braves' final season in Buffalo, the NBA owners voted 21–1 to let the team relocate. As Levin wanted, he became owner of a team in San Diego after the 1977–78 season, which became the San Diego (now Los Angeles) Clippers. As part of the transaction, the teams traded most of the players on their rosters. It could therefore be argued that the successor to the Braves franchise are the Boston Celtics. Got that? Then, go confound your Sports know-it-all buddies...

38. **D – Indiana University**. The bubbas VanArsdale were split apart upon graduating from IU (pre-Bobby Knight) with Dick going to the Phoenix Suns as their very first pick in the expansion draft and scored the Suns' very first basket when they made their NBA debut in '68. Tom, on the other hand – well, his claims to fame are the NBA record for most career games played (929) without a playoff appearance and the highest scoring player (14,232 career points) in NBA history without a playoff appearance.

39. **B – Spalding**. When Dr. Naismith invented the game of basketball in 1891, there wasn't a "real"

basketball, so players used a soccer ball. Naismith asked A.G. Spalding to develop the very first basketball, and in the first official rules of the game read, Naismith wrote, "The ball made by A.G. Spalding & Bros. shall be the official ball." And, ahem, what league has the bigger balls? The NCAA men's basketballs are a maximum circumference of 30 inches and NBA balls are 29.5 inches in circumference. WNBA balls are another half-inch smaller.

40. **D – Wrigley Field**. But you're sayin' "Wrigley Field... wtf," right? Well, it *is* Wrigley Field, but the one in Los Angeles, not Chicago. It's the ballpark the L.A. Angels used when they were in the Pacific Coast League and their residence the first year they were in the Majors. Back to the TV show, *Home Run Derby*, now – There were 19 players who participated in the series. Hank Aaron won the most duels with a 6-1 win-loss record. Mickey Mantle was second with a 4-1 record.

41. **D – 800 meters**. This event/race is a little like horse racing since all the runners converge on lane one where positioning on the cut-in is critical to the outcome of the race. The heptathlon didn't make its way into the Olympics until 1984 when it replaced the pentathlon by adding in the 800m and the javelin throw. Btw, there's a bit of sexism between the men's and women's version of the heptathlon. The men's is held inside; the women's outside.

42. **C – Ancient Polynesians**. And that "hang loose" hand gesture surfers make? The one where the thumb and smallest finger are extended while

holding the three middle fingers curled, and gesturing in salutation? That's called "the shaka."

43. **A – Mary Rand**, who is also the only Great Britain female athlete to win three medals in a single Olympics.

44. **B – Lisa Leslie**, who's also one of a handful of players who've scored 100+ points in a game. It was in high school, but still! Leslie scored 101 points in the first half alone – 49 in the first quarter and 52 in the second quarter. The opponent forfeited the game at halftime.

45. **D – Maryland**. Maryland was Bear's first gig as a head coach. He only lasted a year. Went 6-2-1, had a run-in with the school's president who reinstated a player who had been suspended by Bryant for a violation of team rules, then split for the University of Kentucky. Maybe a better trivia question would be "*What actors portrayed Bear Bryant in movies?*" and that answer would be Bryant was portrayed by Gary Busey in the movie *The Bear*, by Sonny Shroyer in *Forrest Gump*, Tom Berenger in *The Junction Boys*, and Jon Voight in 2015's *Woodlawn*. Or, better yet, I could ask you about Bryant's defamation suit against the *Saturday Evening Post*, a legal battle that went all the way to the Supreme Court. I'll leave you to research that one on your own...

46. **C – Mike Piazza**. Yep, this Miami-Dade Community College kid got selected in the 62nd round of the 1988 Major League Baseball Amateur Draft as the 1,390th player picked overall thanks to

his dad asking Tommy Lasorda for a favor. Lasorda asked Piazza to give up his preference as a first baseman and try out catching. Mike went on to become one of only 10 players to have over 400 home runs with over a .300 lifetime average while never striking out more than 100 times in a season *and* holds the career record for home runs hit by a catcher, with a total of 427. He also married a Playboy Playmate and is a Heavy Metal music nut, even getting a guest slot on Black Label Society's (Zakk Wylde) *Stronger Than Death* album.

47. **B – Terry Hanratty**. Hanratty was a 3x Heisman candidate (finished 8th, 10th, and 3rd) and led the Ara Parseghian-coached Irish to the national championship in '66 with a nation-leading 8.5 passing yards per attempt. In the pros, he was a second stringer to Terry Bradshaw* with the Steelers, but he did get two Super Bowl rings for carrying that clipboard. *Bradshaw was also a second stringer, behind *Duck Dynasty's* Phil Robertson on the depth chart at Louisiana Tech.

48. **B – Yellow**. The rider who has worn the yellow jersey the longest is the Belgian Eddy Merckx, who wore it for 96 days. And Lance Armstrong? Even if he'd played nice and didn't get all his records annulled, he was still ranked second in this list, leading the Tour for 83 stages from 1999 to 2005.

49. **A – Wichita** and it's been Omaha ever since (and will be until at least 2035). There are a lot of trivia questions that could be crafted out of College World Series stats, like *what team has appeared the most* (Texas – 35 appearances as of 2015, followed by

Miami with 24); *what conference has the most titles* (PAC-12 with 17); and *the coach who's won the most titles* (Rod Dedeaux @ Southern Cal with 11 including a record five straight. Btw, USC's first championship came against Yale, a team captained by George H.W. Bush).

50. **D – Plunge for distance**. It was an underwater diving event held at the 1904 Summer Olympics. Only five divers, all from the United States, competed. It was essentially a diving long jump. Competitors lined up in a standing position, then dove into the pool. Their attained distance was measured after either 60 seconds passed or their head broke the surface, whichever came first.

51. **A – from 0–100 points**. This must be the only sport where the animal gets points, 'coz the rider and the bull are both awarded points. There are usually two judges, with each scoring the bull from 0–50 points and the rider from 0–50 points. The combined point totals from both judges make up the final score for the ride. If you – and the bull – are good at your craft, you probably earn scores of 75 or more. Scores above 80 are considered excellent, and a score in the 90s exceptional. At that end of the spectrum would be this dude named Chris Shivers who holds the all-time mark for career 90-point rides. His total, which is close to a hundo, is double that of the second and third place riders combined. How much money can you make ridin' a bull? Well, Shivers' career total is $3,989,209.33 over 22 years or within a few dollars of what Darryl Strawberry made in a single year playing right field for the Dodgers.

52. **B – Washington University of St. Louis**, an institution that has a place in pop culture trivia given that Harold Ramis, one of the three writers of *Animal House*, pulled inspiration from his time as a member of Zeta Beta Tau to write the screenplay. Oh, and there was Tennessee Williams who dropped out of Wash U in protest of not winning the poetry prize. Wait – isn't this a sports trivia tome? Sorry.

53. **D – Swimming**. Dawn Fraser is one of only three swimmers to have won the same Olympic event three times – in her case the women's 100-meter freestyle. Ian Thorpe has won five Olympic Gold medals, the most won by any Australian.

54. **C – Ole Miss**. Hoddy Toddy! Casey helped coach the Rebels for a few months in 1914 before he headed off to spring training with the Dodgers. It was during that spring training that Casey would wax on and on about his experience in Oxford – so much that that's where he earned his nickname "The Old Perfessor."

55. **D – Idol of the Crowds**. In doing my homework for this, seems like John Wayne did quite a few sports-oriented movies: *Forward Pass* (football), *Salute* (football), *Brown of Harvard* (football), *The Drop Kick* (football), *Lady and Gent* (boxing), *That's My Boy* (football), *Maker of Men* (football), *College Coach* (football), and *The Drawback* (football).

56. **C – Twizzle**. What's the difference between a twizzle and a spin? As if you realllllly care, here's the diffs: 1) Twizzles travel and move down the ice.

THE GREATEST SPORTS TRIVIA THROWDOWN OF ALL-TIME

Spins stay in one place. 2) Twizzles can be done forward, backward, or any direction. 3) Twizzles can be done on both inside and outside edges.

57. **A – Henri Richard**. Henri won more Stanley Cups (11) than any other hockey player in NHL history. Oh, there's a dissenter among you? Probably one voting for Henri's former teammate and predecessor as team captain, Jean Béliveau, oui? Yes, Jean won 17 Stanley Cup titles, but only 10 as a player (the other seven as an executive).

58. **A – 2400 RPM**. And, while we're in physics mode, a pitcher's arm rotates around 8,500 degrees per second... the average MLB pitcher's stride is about 85% of their height... and faster pitchers rotate their hips earlier in the wind-up. How's it feel to be so Einstein-like?

59. **D – Indiana University**. You remember that when Spitz won the Olympics, he was sporting a mustache, right? Well, the Russian coach asked him why and Mark replied that the "mustache deflects water away from my mouth, allows my rear end to rise and make me bullet-shaped in the water, and that's what had allowed me to swim so great." The next year, *all* the Russian swimmers had mustaches.

60. **B – Mark Eaton**. So, you guessed Kareem, eh? Well, Kareem does have a larger *career* total of "total blocked shots," but he also played in nearly double the games Eaton did. According to Basketball-Reference.com, Eaton is currently the NBA's all-time leader in blocks per game, with a career average of 3.50 – ahead of Manute Bol

(3.34), Hakeem Olajuwon (3.09), and David Robinson (2.99). Kareem is ninth on the list with 2.57 blocks per game. And, of course, you Blink-182 fans do know Mr. Eaton from "Lemmings" off Blink's album *Dude Ranch*.

61. **A – Dara Torres** at the ripe (old?) age of 41 in the 2008 4x100m freestyle relay. However, getting to that point wasn't easy – or cheap! On Dara's payroll were a head coach, a sprint coach, two "stretchers," a chiropractor, a couple of masseuses, and a nanny. That set her back about $100k a year, but who else can claim they won 12 Olympic medals as a member of five different teams?

62. **D – Three strokes under par on a hole**. The odds of hitting an albatross are actually smaller than hitting a hole-in-one. The odds for an albatross are estimated at one in 1,000,000; the odds of a hole-in-one are around one in 3,700 to one in 12,500, depending on the hole and on skill. The first famous albatross was made by Gene Sarazen in 1935 on the 15th hole during the final round of the Masters Tournament. It vaulted him into a tie for first and forced a playoff, which he won the next day.

63. **D – Adam Vinatieri**, who was still playing in 2016 at the age of 44. The boy rules the Super Bowl stat histories with more Super Bowl appearances and rings than any other placekicker. He's also top-of-the-list for most postseason games played, most postseason points scored, and most overtime field goals made. He is the only player ever to score 1,000 points with two different teams.

AND – HE ONCE THREW FOR A TOUCHDOWN!
When he was playing for the Patriots in 2004, he
threw his first and only touchdown pass on a fake
to Troy Brown to help the Patriots score a "W". The
only other kicker I know to score a TD was the
"Polish Messiah," Chester Marcol, and his moment
came down like this: the Packers and Bears were in
an overtime game in 1980 and Green Bay opted
for a chip shot field goal for the win. Marcol's kick
was blocked, and it came right back to him. He ran
like a wascally wabbit around the left end to win
the game. As my ex-wife Kristey from Wausau used
to say, "After further review, the Bears... still...
suck."

64. **B – Joan Benoit**. In her very first Boston
Marathon ('79), she won the race in 2:35:15,
knocking eight minutes off the competition record.
She repeated that success with another victory in
'83, that took more than two minutes off the
world's best time, set by Grete Waitz in the London
Marathon just a day before. Then, in '84, she won
the first Olympic Women's Marathon in 2:24:52,
several hundred meters ahead of legends Grete
Waitz (the first woman in history to run the
marathon in under 2 ½ hours and also the winner
of nine New York City Marathons, more than any
other runner in history), Rosa Mota (the only
woman to be the reigning European, World, and
Olympic champion at the same time), and Ingrid
Kristiansen (the first athlete to win World titles on
the track, roads, and cross-country).

65. **D – Lorenzo Charles**. We've all seen that
moment a million times, haven't we? But, do we

remember where it was and what that moment capped off? The basket broke a 52–52 tie at The Pit in Albuquerque, New Mexico, as NC State scored the last eight points to defeat the top-ranked "Phi Slama Jama" Houston Cougars, led by Hakeem Olajuwon and Clyde Drexler. And, if I may, I'd like to add a little personal "God bless you, Jim Valvano." I don't think anyone could have captured an NCAA championship moment any better than he did when he was running around the floor, arms outstretched, and soaking in the unbelievable magic of what just happened.

66. A – Bret Boone, son of Bob (catcher and manager of the Reds and Royals), and grandson of Ray (infielder with a bunch 'o AL teams). The Boone family was also the first to send three generations of players to the All-Star Game, but they're not the only fam that am. Here's more generational jive: 1) Cecil and Prince Fielder are the only dad and son combo to both swat more than 50 home runs in a season. 2) Three families have had a father and son in a manager role: the Skinners (Bob & Joel), Macks (Connie & Earle), and da Sislers (George and Dick). 3) Finally, the Griffeys – Senior and Junior – were the first father-and-son combination to play in the majors at the same time. They started out on different teams but finally played together for the Mariners where, in one very OMG moment against the Angels, the Griffeys hit back-to-back home runs, becoming the first (and, so far, only) father-son duo to ever pull that off.

67. **A – booked**. It happens when a player gets a yellow card for "misconduct." At that point, a team

can substitute, but if a player gets a second yellow card, he's gone'ski and no one can come in to take their place. Basically, if you want a yellow card, all you have to do is bitch about something or act like a pouty little kid and hold up the game's or a player's progress. If you're lookin' for a red card, spit at someone or throw yourself on the floor like a two-year-old.

68. **C – Flip Saunders** with a .525 W-L percentage. Most peeps don't count Flip as a college coach, but he compiled a 92–13 record at Golden Valley Lutheran College, including a perfect 56–0 mark at home, in four seasons. Oh – and the others? Frank Layden who was at Niagara before he wound up as the Jazz' coach where he had a .485 W-L percentage; Rick Pitino (at Providence before the Knicks and Kentucky before the Celtics [.466]); and John Calipari (UMass before the Nets [.391]).

69. **D – Dayton 500**. If you're one of the naysayers who says it doesn't take a rocket scientist to drive a car, well you're wrong. Janet was originally an aerospace engineer and, after graduating from the University of Michigan, she worked with Republic Aviation. Her highest finish is sixth place at Bristol in 1977 and ranks as the best finish by a woman in a premier NASCAR event, (tied with Danica Patrick as of 2014).

70. **C – Horse racing and golf**. A "driver" is also a position in water polo, by the way.

71. **C – Gold medal in middleweight boxing**. When Floyd was 21, he became the youngest

boxer to win the world heavyweight title,* not to mention the first heavyweight to regain the title after losing it. An interesting side note: Patterson's manager, Cus D'Amato, adopted Mike Tyson after Tyson's mom died, trained him, and taught him the same "peek-a-boo" style that he had taught Patterson. *Although Mike Tyson later became the youngest boxer to win a world heavyweight title at the age of 20, Patterson remains the youngest *undisputed* heavyweight champion.

72. **A – Willie Mays** or for you nickname junkies, the "Say Hey Kid." Why "say hey"? One story is that sportswriter Jimmy Cannon crafted the nickname because Mays didn't know everybody's names when he first arrived in the minors. "You see a guy, you say, 'Hey, man. Say hey, man.'" Another angle was that Barney Kremenko, who wrote for the New York Journal, started calling Willie the "Say Hey Kid" after he overheard Mays say "'Say who,' 'Say what,' 'Say where,' 'Say hey.'" But, what we do know is that way before he became the "Say Hey Kid", he was called "Buck" back when he started his professional career with the Birmingham Black Barons.

73. **D – Midfielder**. Beckham is the first English player to win league titles in four countries: those being England (where he holds the appearance record for an outfield player), Spain, France, and the good 'ol U.S.A.

74. **C – Louis Meyer**. That victorious glass of milk – actually buttermilk at the time – got its debut in 1933, then when Meyer won the Indy in '36, he switched over to a milk bottle instead.

75. **D – Toronto Blue Jays.** Who else played more than one sport? We're probably gonna cover that in another Q&A, but a tangent on that are those who got *drafted* in other sports, like Pat Riley (mostly a Laker) was also drafted as a wide receiver by the Dallas Cowboys in the 11th round of the '67 NFL Draft, but never played... Troy Aikman, famed Dallas Cowboys QB, was drafted by the Mets but never suited up... and, besides the Padres where he wound up, baseball great Dave Winfield was also drafted by the Atlanta Hawks, the Utah Jazz, and the Minnesota Vikings.

76. **A – Cliff Hagan**. Hagan spent his entire 10-year playing career in a St. Louis Hawks uniform. After he retired, though, the Dallas Chaparrals were forming an ABA team and offered him the chance to be player/coach. Cliff laid 40 on the Anaheim Amigos in the Chaps' very first game, then went on to become the first player to appear in both an NBA and an ABA All-Star game. He was the first ex-University of Kentucky player inducted into the basketball HOF, too.

77. **D – Vasily Alekseyev**. You remember – the guy with the big sideburns that looked like comedian Marty Allen. Vas' (that's what I call him) was a smart man. The Russian government paid him bonus bucks every time he set a new world record, so he would simply increase his lifts by a pound each time he competed. That sly son-of-a-gun set 79 world records doin' things that way.

78. **C – Miami**. The Rrrrrrrock played defensive tackle for the 1991's undefeated 'Canes and on the same

national championship team as Warren Sapp and Gino Torretta, the one coached by Dennis Erickson. Dwayne didn't get drafted by any NFL team, so he went north and played for the Calgary Stampeders in the CFL, but was cut a couple of months into the season. That's when he said F-it and became a wrestler like his pop (Rocky Johnson) and grandpop (Peter Maivia). Maybe it's the swagger, but there's a number of TV & movie stars who spent time with a collegiate pigskin. Tommy Lee Jones was an All-Ivy offensive guard at Harvard; Mark Harmon QB'ed at UCLA in '72 & '73, going 17-5; and Nick Nolte went to Arizona State on a football scholarship, but flunked (or partied) out.

79. **A – Sacramento Gold Miners**. Not sure what our neighbors to the north were thinking, but they convinced seven U.S. cities – Baltimore (Stallions, who had an average attendance of 30k vs. the CFL average of 24k and the only U.S. team to win the Grey Cup), Sacramento, Memphis (Mad Dogs), San Antonio (Texans), Vegas (Posse), Shreveport (Pirates), and Birmingham (Barracudas) – to buy in. All but Baltimore lost money – collectively about $21 mil.

80. **D – Russia**. So, if I asked you who made more money on the court – Sharapova or Serena Williams – you'd probably say Serena and you'd be right because Serena's total winnings trumps Maria's. But, when it comes to overall earnings, *Forbes'* 2015 list of the world's highest-paid athletes shows that Maria is depositing more into the ATM than Serena. Why, you say? 'Coz Maria's *non-tennis-related* income – meaning endorsements

– is $23mil vs. Serena's $13mil. So, all told, Maria did $29.7mil in '15 and Serena did $24.6mil. Just for a reference point, the top three endorsement rainmakers overall are Roger Federer with $58mil; Tiger $50mil; and Phil Mickelson $48mil.

81. **C – Kansas City A's.** The year was 1967 and the Athletics were still in Kansas City. Good 'ol creative genius Charlie Finley saw Joe Namath wearing white shoes and got a wild hair to have his team do the same, something that no team had ever tried. The A's have stayed the white-cleated course and picked up the Astros, Giants, Padres, Angels, and Phillies along the way as white-shoe'd teams, but not all of 'em had the same long-term commitment as the A's. Another Finley wild hair while I've still got some ink left – he also tried using orange baseballs in 1973. The league office gave him enough rope to pull himself up or hang himself and, well, the noose prevailed. The experiment lasted two games and that was it. Hitters complained that they couldn't see the red laces on the ball and had difficulty telling what kind of pitch was on its way.

82. **D – Mickey Mantle.** Rather than me go off on a tangent, why don't I let the guy who scouted him – Tom Greenwade – tell you? This is from a letter Greenwade wrote to the publisher of *The Sporting News* in 1952. Here goes...
To the best of my knowledge and memory, the first person to talk to me about Mantle was his man-ager, Barney Barnett, in the Ban Johnson League. All the Midwestern scouts know Barney and drop by to see him. This must have been in the early

part of the 1948 season for I went to Alba, Mo.,
about August 1948 to see Mantle and other players that I had heard of on both clubs. Mantle, who
at that time was referred to as "Little Mickey Mantle," was small and played shortstop. He pitched a
couple of innings in this game. I wasn't overly impressed, but bear in mind he was only 16.

The following spring an umpire in the B.J. League,
Kenny Magness, told me about a game the night
before in which Mantle played, and he was very
high on him. I caught the Baxter club at Parsons to
see Mantle again. This was early in May, 1949.
Mantle looked better and must have put on 20
pounds since the past August, and I became interested in a hurry for that was when I discovered he
could really run, but wasn't hitting too much. So I
inquired from other sources, probably Barney,
when Mickey would graduate. It was to be the last
Thursday in May, 1949, from the Commerce,
Okla. H.S.

On Friday I drove to Commerce, and this is the first
time the Mantles ever knew there was such a person as Tom Greenwade. I found out the gradua-
tion exercises had been postponed till that night
for some reason. Since I had no desire to violate
the H.S. tampering rule, I was careful not to mention contract or pro ball either, but had under-
stood Mickey was to play in Coffeyville that night
and I wanted to see him play and I didn't mention
that I had seen him play before. Well, they talked
things over with the coach and superintendent and
decided to pass on the exercises since Mickey al-

ready had his diploma and go to Coffeyville instead.

Of course, I was there. Mickey looked better at bat, hitting left-handed. I still don't know he switches since the only pitching I have seen him against is right-handed. After the game Mr. Mantle tells me Mickey will play Sunday in Baxter Springs. I told him I would be at his house Sunday morning and go to the game with them. I was there about 11 A.M. I was scared to death for fear some scout had been there Saturday. I asked Mr. Mantle if anyone had been there. He said "no." I was relieved.

We all went to Baxter Springs, and for the first time I see Mickey hit right-handed. Mickey racked the pitcher for four "clothes lines," and I started looking all around for scouts, but none were there.

When the last out was made, Mr. Mantle, Mickey and I got in my car behind the grandstand and in 15 minutes the contract was signed. We agreed on $1,500 for the remainder of the season and the contract (Independence of the K.O.M.) was drawn calling for a salary of $140 per month. Mickey reported to Harry Craft at Independence. He was slow to get started and as late as July 10th was hitting only .225, but finished the season over .300. The following year at Joplin he hit .383, I believe. You know the rest.

The players Greenwade signed are an impressive list: Bill Virdon, Pee Wee Reese, Gil Hodges, Hank Bauer, Elston Howard, Ralph Terry, Bobby Murcer, *and* Jackie Robinson. Plus, he's credited with suggesting to the Yanks that they trade Marv Throneberry, Norm Siebern, Hank Bauer, and Don Larsen for Roger Maris.

83. **D – Syracuse Nationals**, a concept created by Daniel Biasone, the Nats' owner. How did he arrive at 24 seconds? Well, kiddos, it's like this: He conjectured that a good game pace was achieved when each team took about 60 shots a game. Then, since professional basketball games lasted 48 minutes, he divided 2880 (the number of seconds in 48 minutes) by 120 (total number of shots taken per game when each team attempted 60 shots each) and arrived at a number he considered dang near perfect and that was one shot every 24 seconds.

84. **C – Paul Hornung** in Notre Dame's 1956 season when they went 2-6. Wanna know why he was worthy of the Heisman? In that season, he led the Irish offensively in passing, rushing, scoring, kickoff and punt returns, not to mention punting. He also played the other side of the ball and led the team in breaking up passes, was second in interceptions, and second in tackles.

85. **A – George Sisler**. "Gorgeous George" hit .420 in 1920, hitting safely in 41 straight games, plus he led the American League in stolen bases, triples, and hits. Even though most of us have never uttered his name until this moment, the baseball gurus have been singing his praises forever, with *The Sporting News* naming him as #33 of

baseball's 100 greatest players, ahead of Bonds, Banks, Berra, Robinson, Ryan, Ripken, et al.

86. **B – Wilson**, who also makes the official basketball for the NCAA and the official volleyball of the AVP (remember "Wilson" in the Tom Hanks movie *Cast Away*?). Next time you look at a Wilson football, take note of the hand-sewn ends and lock-stitch seams. That (and triple-lining) was an advancement they made in 1931 in a football they called "The Duke." Why that? It's in honor of the late NY Giants owner, Wellington Mara. Mara was named Wellington by his father, Tim Mara, after the Duke of Wellington, then given the nickname "The Duke" by Giants players.

87. **C – Hockey**. The Rockies hockey franchise came to Denver from Kansas City where they were the Scouts. They were in Denver from '76-'82, then moved to Jersey where they became the Devils. IMO, the coolest trivia about the Rockies is that they were the first sports team to play Gary Glitter's "Rock & Roll, pt. 2" at a sporting event.

88. **D – Stanford**, known as the Cardinal, although it wasn't always singular and not always Cardinal or Cardinals. Cardinal – the color – was the original primary color of Stanford's teams. In 1930, the school adopted "Indian" as the mascot, and then dropped it in '72 after Native American students raised objections. At that point, they became the "Cardinals" (plural) and that lasted until '81 when the school's president decided Stanford's teams would be represented by the color "cardinal" in singular form. Why do they have that "tree," you

ask? Well, it's not an official mascot but rather a member of the band. It's 'spose to represent El Palo Alto, a redwood tree in nearby Palo Alto that appears in the Stanford seal and athletics logo.

Editor's note: This is a spur of the very first sports trivia question I wrote, way back in 1982 – that being something like "Name (the) 11 NCAA (Division 1) football teams whose nicknames don't end in the letter "s"." Back then I think my go-to answers were: Illinois Fightin' Illini, Notre Dame Fighting Irish, North Carolina State Wolfpack, UMass Minutemen, Alabama Crimson Tide, Tulsa Golden Hurricane, Navy Midshipmen, Stanford Cardinal, St. John Redmen (now the Red Storm), Syracuse Orangemen, and Tulane Green Wave. If you want, you could always go for the whole magilla and stretch it out to include Division II/III schools and others that fly under the radar of pedestrian consciousness: Cornell Big Red, Dartmouth Big Green, Elon Phoenix, Howard Bison, Harvard Crimson, Hofstra Pride, Loyola Wolfpack, Lipscomb Bison, Marshall Thundering Herd, Nevada-Reno Wolfpack, North Dakota Fighting Sioux, North Texas Mean Green, St Francis (Pa) Red Flash, William & Mary Tribe, Wisconsin-Green Bay Phoenix, Rhode Island Anchormen, Bucknell Bison, North Dakota State Bison, Univ. of Maine-Augusta Moose, Northern Kentucky Norse, and the Millikin Big Blue. If you can remember all of these, it could come in handy at tournament time or when you're anglin' for a free drink at the bar.

89. **A – Ryne Sandberg** who won nine consecutive Gold Gloves and appeared in 10 consecutive All-Star games. His career fielding % of .989 is a major-league record for second basemen.

90. **B – Chicago White Sox**. Those mid-'70s unis weren't only designed to be worn untucked, but they had collars and, get this, an option to wear SHORTS which they did but only once. Guess no one wanted to slide into third wearin' shorts, eh?

91. **D – Upset**. It was in the Sanford Memorial @ Saratoga and Man o' War lost by a nose. Upset and Man o' War raced against each other six more times and da Man won 'em all.

92. **C – A free turn in a handicap ma**tch. You wanna shoot me for asking you a blankety-blank croquet question, don't you? Just be glad I didn't ask you what a "sextuple peel" or a "pioneer" means in croquet!

93. **A – Leading off**. In fast-pitch softball games (at least ones sanctioned by the ASA), base runners can leave the base before the ball reaches the plate, *but* they gotta stay on the base until the ball leaves the pitcher's hand.

94. **D – 4**. It's complicated, but in polo each numbered position has a different responsibility as to defense, offense, passing to who, etc. For example, #1 generally covers the other team's #4. And, btw, polo must be played right-handed.

95. **B – Bobby Shantz** who was strictly a baseball player (Cards, As, Pirates, Yankees, Colt .45s, Cubs, Phillies). Dave DeBusschere played basketball and pitched a couple of seasons for the White Sox. Cotton Nash, the ex-Kentucky great, played for the Warriors and Lakers on the basketball side and the Twins and the White Sox in baseball. And Chuck Connors (yes, "The Rifleman") won an NBA title with the Rochester Royals, followed by a stint with the Celtics. On the diamond, he did a one-game stint with the Dodgers, then 66 games as the Cubs' first baseman. Chuck was also drafted by the

Chicago Bears but never suited up, and his legend also includes being the first professional basketball player to break a backboard.

96. **A – Masters**, whose field ranges somewhere between 90-100. It's an invitation-only event, and those invites usually go the top 50 players in the Official World Golf Ranking, past Masters winners, and lots of niche invitations to folks like the current Asia-Pacific Amateur champion, the current U.S. Mid-Amateur champion, and the first four players, including ties, in the previous year's U.S. Open.

97. **A – Rosey Grier**. While Rosey was a complete beast on the field, his heroics as a bodyguard for Robert Kennedy during the 1968 presidential campaign are far more honorable. Rosey was guarding the senator's wife, Ethel Kennedy, the night of RFK's assassination. Although he was unable to prevent Bobby's death, he did take control of the gun and subdued Sirhan Sirhan, the shooter.

98. **A – Fletching or flight**. I could bore you to tears with everything related to fletching – cocks, flu-flu, and the like – but I'll just leave it at this: fletching is designed to simply stabilize the flight of the arrow.

99. **D – Division 3**. As of 2015, there were 88 NCAA Division I men's lacrosse teams, 46 Division II men's lacrosse teams, and 208 Division III men's lacrosse teams. Hobart College (alma mater of the lead singer of Blue Öyster Cult) in lacrosse is kinda like UCLA was in basketball in the 60s. They won 13 out of the first 14 national championships,

which started in 1980. Salisbury State came on strong in the 90s and won 10 titles.

100. **B – Murray State**, where all teams were originally called the "Thoroughbreds." The backstory is that Thoroughbreds was too long for lazy sports reporters and editors to write so they started shortening it to T-breds, 'Breds, Racers, etc. until they all sort of landed on Racers. Then, in '61, the school adopted Racers as the official name for all its teams except baseball who stuck with Thoroughbreds (or 'Breds). That differentiation lasted until 2014 and, then, baseball gave in and became the Racers, too. Are there other schools with identity issues? Yeah, there's Furman. At one time, their basketball team were the "Paladins," the baseball team was the "Hornets," and the football team's nickname was the "Hurricanes". Finally, the student body decided to put it to a vote and "Paladins" became the official nickname of all of the university's athletic teams.

101. **D – Madden NFL game**. The game's cover had Madden on it for the first several years but, in '99, began putting top players on the cover starting with Garrison Hearst and that's where the jinx began and churned some bad mojo ever since. For example... After Hearst's appearance, he broke his ankle and was out for two seasons. After Daunte Culpepper's cover shot, he threw 23 interceptions, recorded the most fumbles in a season, and blew out his knees. Michael Vick? Broke his fibula. Favre? Traded to the Jets, ankle injury, shoulder injury, and a sex scandal. Shaun Alexander? Foot

injury that caused him to miss six games and a major slide in his stats.

102. **A – Major League Lacrosse**, a league that was developed by Jake Steinberg, the guy behind "Body by Jake," and a couple of his chums. It's a semi-pro league and most players hang on to their day jobs since the pay scale for the league runs only $10k-25k.

103. **D – Victor**. There's Victor E. Bear (Central Arkansas, where Scottie Pippen and Charlie Strong matriculated), Victor E. Bluejay (Elmhurst), Victor E. Bull (Buffalo), Victor E. Huskie (Northern Illinois), Victor E. Tiger (Ft. Hays), Victor E. Lion (Molloy), Victor E. Viking (Northern Ky., Western Washington, and Portland St.), and Victor E. Hawk (Viterbo U.). What name would be the second most used? "Bucky" and its variations. And, who's on David Letterman's list of worst mascots? Well, there's Speedy the Geoduck (Evergreen State), Sammy the Banana Slug (U. Cal – Santa Cruz), WuShock (Wichita St.), YoUDee (Univ. of Delaware), and the Fighting Okra (Delta State).

104. **C – Atlanta Hawks**. The Buffalo Bisons only lasted 13 games in the '46-47 season before moving to the Tri-Cities where they became the Blackhawks, then to Milwaukee where they shortened the name to the Hawks, which stuck with them thru their moves to St. Louis and Atlanta.

105. **A – Alpine Skiing**. What country has won the most Olympic medals in Alpine Skiing? Austria, far and away – close to double the number that

France, Switzerland, and USA have won. Be nice if you're ever crossing the border into Germany. Maria is a chief constable in Germany's federal customs corps and at 5'11" she could probably keep your butt from coming into the country.

106. **D – Welterweight**, a title he defended 19 times. Born Henry Jackson, Jr., Armstrong is a member of the exclusive group of boxers who've won championships in three or more different divisions. Additionally, he has the distinction of being the only pugilist to hold three world championships at the same time, when he wore the belts in featherweight, lightweight, and welterweight in 1938. In 2007, *The Ring* named Armstrong the second-greatest fighter of the last 80 years – behind Sugar Ray Robinson and ahead of Ali.

107. **A – Ara Parseghian**. Ara resigned as coach due to health reasons at the end of Montana's freshman season. When Dan Devine took over for Parseghian, Montana's rise to fame came in fits and starts, mostly bailing out the Irish in comeback situations, then landing the starting job permanently after the first two QBs on the depth chart fizzled or got hurt. Joe's storybook game at Notre Dame was the "Chicken Soup Game" – the 1979 Cotton Bowl – played the day after Dallas' worst ice storm in 30 years. During the game, Montana's body temp dipped to 96 degrees and so close to hypothermia that the ND medical staff took him off the field and fed him chicken soup. Joe came back to the field with 7:37 remaining and the Irish trailing Houston 34-12. Montana pulled rabbit

after rabbit out of his hat right up to the last tick of the clock when the Irish won the game 35-34.

108. **D – Iowa State**. Hornacek was a walk-on, mind you, but what a ride he gave the Cyclones fans. He carried ISU on his shoulders to its first NCAA tournament victory since 1944, beating Miami University. Two days later, he lifted the Cyclones to the "Sweet Sixteen" via a 72–69 upset of second seed Michigan. And Fizer and Tinsley? Both first round NBA picks, but out of the league inside a couple of years. My question about ISU is why do the Bulls keep hiring their coaches? Tim Floyd had a 12-18 Cyclones record and he replaced Phil Jackson? At least Fred Hoiberg was riding the wave of four 23+ win seasons when the Bulls came calling. Just sayin'...

109. **A – Oakland Raiders**. What 'zactly is "Ghost to the Post"? Well... On Christmas Eve, 1977, the Raiders and the Colts (the Baltimore ones) were playing in an AFC divisional playoff. It was in Baltimore and colder than hell. The matchups included Bert Jones QB'ing the Colts vs. Ken Stabler for the Raiders, and Ted Marchibroda coaching Baltimore vs. John Madden for the Silver & Black. The "ghost"? Raiders tight end Dave Casper. With 2:55 left in the game and the score 24-21 in favor of the Colts, Oakland was on its own 44. In the Raiders' playbook was something called "91 in" where the two receivers ran "in" patterns, and on that the tight end would run a post, then go deep, cleaning out the middle, while the receivers would come back to the inside. Tom Flores, the assistant coach had been keeping an

eye on the Colts safety who kept sneaking up, so
he told his team, "On '91 in' take a peek at Ghost
to the Post." Hike! Stabler back... pump fakes...
let's it fly... Casper looks up, adjusts his pattern,
splits two defenders, and hauls in the pass on the
Colts' 14-yard line. The Raiders go on to tie the
game with a field goal, then win it in double OT,
37-31. You can find video of the play on YouTube
if you want to watch it.

110. **C – BYU**, who made the Big Dance 29 times, but
never to the Final Four. The closest they ever came
was in 2011 when Jimmer Fredette helped them to
a #3 seed, but lost in the regional semis to Florida.
Mizzou and Xavier have missed the Final Four
25x, and Western Kentucky 22x.

111. **A – Michael Jordon**, who graced SI's cover 50
times, eclipsing Muhammad Ali's 37. And, it wasn't
always sports figures on SI's covers – Big Bird was
on there (with Mark Fidrych)... Steve McQueen
was, too, riding a motorcycle... Brad Pitt,
promoting *Moneyball*... Bob Hope as an owner of
the Cleveland Indians... Burt Reynolds and Kris
Kristofferson promoting the flick *Semi-Tough*...
Shirley MacLaine (really?) promoting the film *John
Goldfarb, Please Come Home*... Chris Rock,
wearing a Dodgers hat... actor Gary Cooper as a
scuba diver... even Stephen Colbert alongside the
headline "Stephen Colbert and His Nation Save
the Olympics." Reagan was on the cover twice, as
well as fellow presidents Ford, Kennedy, and
Clinton. I think that's enough tangents for now...

112. **D – Los Angeles Dodgers**. When you add the
      affiliations up year-by-year, the Dodgers have had
      a boatload of minor league connections – 768 of
      'em (of course, there's some repeats) – starting in
      1932 with the Jersey City Skeeters and the
      Hartford Senators. What MLB squad has had the
      most? The Cardinals with 917, but they've also
      been in biz longer than the Dodgers, too. The
      Cards' first affiliate goes way back to 1919 and
      the Texas League's Houston Buffaloes.

113. **C – Baltimore Orioles**. Jeffrey, Jeffrey, Jeffrey.
      Look what you've done! Orioles fans around the
      world are blaming you for the Baltimore Orioles
      not making it to or winning a World Series since
      1983. Do you remember that night in 1996,
      Jeffrey? It was the first game of the In Game 1 of
      the ALCS. Yankee Derek Jeter hit a fly ball to right
      field and you, in all your youthful exuberance,
      reached over the fence to retrieve the ball. Then,
      umpire Rich Garcia ruled it a home run instead of
      ruling it as fan interference, and that allowed the
      Yankees to win the game, the AL pennant, and
      eventually, the World Series. Now, since Oriole
      fans can't seem to let it go, some are blaming you
      for a) Rafael Palmeiro and Sammy Sosa testifying
      to Congress on steroid use in baseball; b) the
      Orioles' collapse in 2005 season; c) the Yankees
      winning the 2012 ALDS against the Orioles three
      games to two. I hear you've worked hard to put all
      this past you, Jeff. You were an all-conference
      selection when you played college ball at
      Wesleyan and even had a shot in the minors, plus
      a stint as Peter Gammons' personal scout in the

Cape Cod league. Don't worry, son – this stuff of legend eventually fades away or so I hear.

114. **A – Miami Dolphins**. Are there more? Sure. Here's a random sample of current/former owners: Will Smith owns a slice of the Philadelphia 76ers... Justin Timberlake a little bite of the Memphis Grizzlies... comedian Bill Maher bought into the Mets back in 2012... David Letterman co-owns an IndyCar racing team... Usher's got a piece of the Cleveland Cavs... in 2006, actor Russell Crowe bought part of the South Sydney Rabbitohs rugby team... singer/pot farm wannabe Nick Lachey co-owner of the minor league baseball club, the Tacoma Rainiers... and actor Bill Murray owns a stake in the St. Paul Saints.

115. **A – Volleyball**. Uh, did you know that after his professional basketball career was over, Wilt Chamberlain played volleyball in the International Volleyball Association, was the organization's president, and is enshrined in the IVA Hall of Fame for his contributions? It's true. Promise.

116. **C – Marcus Camby**, who got drafted 2nd in the '96 draft (to Toronto), right behind Allen Iverson. You remember Camby led UMass to the Final Four the same year, right? Except that somewhere along the way, Marcus took (ok, accepted) $28,000, jewelry, rental cars, and prostitutes from two sports agents who were hoping that Camby would hire them to be his agent. The NCAA sort of frowns on that stuff and later nullified UMass' Final Four visit. As part of the penalty, UMass had to return $151,617 in revenue from the NCAA tournament.

Camby later reimbursed the school for the amount lost.

117. **A – Honus Wagner** (in 1905). Who are the Hillerich and Bradsby guys associated with the Louisville Slugger (originally called "Falls City Slugger")? Well, Bud Hillerich was the woodworker dude who came up with the idea of making the bats and Frank Bradsby was a company salesman. Bradsby was so good at selling bats that the company gave him gave a piece of the action and changed the company's name from "J.F. Hillerich & Son Co." to "Hillerich & Bradsby" (1916).

118. **A – University of Michigan**. Some people think the design on Michigan's helmets has some wolverine connection, but they're actually wings. When Crisler was at Princeton, he ordered stock helmets bearing leather wings straight out of the Spalding catalog, because he had this notion the design might make receivers easier to spot downfield. When Crisler got the gig at Michigan, he just added maize and blue colors to the stock design, debuted the helmets against Michigan State (1938), and they've been worn ever since. Interestingly enough, Michigan State began wearing a variation of the winged helmet before 1938, pre-dating the Wolverines. There's only one other college I know who uses that design and that's U. Delaware who's been using it since 1951. In pro football, the Bears, Giants, and the short-lived football versions of the Cincy Reds and Pittsburgh Pirates all used it at one time in the '30s & '40s.

119. **D – Basketball** at 94 ft. long. Why did I put "U.S. version" in the question? Because the FIBA (international) version of the basketball court is shorter, narrower, the distance from the foul stripe to the backboard is a smidge longer, the key is a wee bit wider, the 3-point line is a little closer to the basket – heck, everything overseas except the rim height is just a little bit different.

120. **A – 1-wood** (driver) with a loft of 8-11 degrees. Recently, researchers have found that modern golf balls fly further with a higher loft, and 12 degrees has become closer to the norm. The 1-wood is the longest, and more often than not, the lightest club, and meant to launch the ball the longest distance of any stick you've got in your bag.

121. **B – Patrick Ewing**. Actually Patrick went from the Knicks to the Sonics first, via a masssssssssive 4-team trade, then after a year as a Sonic, got waived and was picked up by the Magic where he retired. We all know about Patrick's contribution to the game as a big man, but how many of you know his contribution to the *rules* of roundball? The man was famous for his carries (palming the ball), which led to stricter monitoring league-wide. And there are other players whose play contributed to rule changes, too, like: George Mikan and the 3-second rule; Wilt Chamberlain and the rule preventing shooters from crossing the free throw line while during free throws (Wilt would throw it against the backboard for dunks). Another Wilt-related rule was that the ball cannot be in-bounded over the backboard (in-bounders standing under the basket would sometimes lob the ball over the

backboard for Wilt to dunk); Charles Barkley and Mark Jackson for the 5-second rule where players have only 5 seconds to make an offensive move; Reggie Miller and the eradication of the "leg kick" where players would kick out their legs on shot attempts in an effort to get fouled; and Rajon Rondo and the headband rule prohibiting players from wearing a headband with the NBA logo up-side down. Guess there are no "style points" in basketball, huh?

122. **D – 24**, but Jeff didn't want 24 when he started out on his 90+ victory career. He wanted #46. Why didn't he get what he wanted? You can blame Paramount Pictures because they put Tom Cruise into a #46 car for *Days of Thunder* and there evidently were some licensing issues that prevented Jeffy from getting his way.

123. **B – Professional wrestling** (yes, the kind some or all of you think is fake). There's lots more where those came from, too, including the Kiss My Foot match, Bra & Panties match, Casket match (to win the match, a wrestler has to throw the other guy in the casket and close the lid), Empty Arena match, Tables match (where a wrestler must put their opponent through a table with an offensive move in order to win), and my personal favorite, the Fans Bring the Weapons match. What's Luchas de Apuestas? It's a type of match popular in Mexico where both wrestlers put something on the line, usually their hair or their mask.

124. **C – Liz Heaston**. Lizzy played at Willamette, an NAIA school and, on 10/18/97, she successfully

kicked two extra points (PATs). My research proved there are lots of proud women who scored in the college ranks. First one to dress for a bowl game, first one to kick a field goal, first woman to play a non-kicking position in a professional football league made up predominately by men, etc. Kudos to Brittany Ryan from Lebanon Valley College who holds the record for the most points scored by a female college football player with 88 (as of 2015). I guess we should also mention kicker Lauren Silberman who was the first woman to try out at a NFL Regional Scouting Combine. She didn't make it any further.

125. **D – Ron Artest** (aka Metta World Peace*) who had to sit out 86 games to Sprewell's 68, Kermit's 60, and Gilbert Arenas' 50. Artest's pocketbook took a salary hit of nearly $5 million due to the suspension, a drop in the bucket compared to the $75 million he banked from his NBA start in 1999 up to 2015. *Metta is a Buddhist word meaning loving kindness and friendliness towards all, except when they pee in your Cheerios.

126. **B – The guy who coined the golf term "birdie."** Ol' Ab came up with that term in 1899, at the Atlantic City Country Club in Northfield, New Jersey. It seems that one day Ab, his brother, and their friend George Crump were playing together when Crump hit his second shot mere inches from the cup on a par-4 hole after his first shot had struck a bird in flight. Ouch. Well, the Smith brothers exclaimed that Crump's shot was "a bird." Crump's short putt left him 1-under-par for the hole, and from then on the three of 'em

referred to a 1-under-par score as a "birdie."
Being that there wasn't much going on in 1899 and
the guys at the clubhouse weren't too busy tweetin'
or textin' and in need of something to talk about,
they all started using the term. Since the country
club was also a resort, it had many out-of-town
visitors, and the expression spread like wildfire.
Two quick tangents on that: 1) the "perfect round"
(e.g., a score of 54 on a par-72 course) is
commonly referred to when you score a birdie on
all 18 holes, although I couldn't find records that
any player had ever recorded a perfect round in a
professional tournament. 2) During the 2009 RBC
Canadian Open, Mark Calcavecchia scored nine
consecutive birdies at the second round, breaking
the PGA Tour record.

127. **A – 4 horses**. Chariot races were run pretty much
like the thoroughbred horses of today – a race
card, starting boxes, a drawing for position,
different colors for the drivers, etc. The race was
made up of seven laps (8.4 kilometers or 5.22
miles) and typically lasted about 15 minutes.

128. **A – University of Idaho and the University
of Montana**. Back in '59, there was a little pay-
for-play scandal at USC, UCLA, Cal, and
Washington, and the Pacific Coast Conference
(PCC) broke apart and those four schools talked
Stanford into creating a new conference called the
Athletic Assoc. of Western Universities (AAWU),
and hired the AD at Pitt, retired admiral Tom
Hamilton, to be the commish. Hamilton then came
up with the idea of a "power conference" and
pretty much had talked Duke, Penn State, Notre

Dame, Georgia Tech, Penn, Army, Navy, Air Force, and his AAWU schools into becoming members of what would be the first "super conference," one called the "Airplane Conference." Well, the Pentagon put the kibosh on the service academies involvement and the idea died on the vine. The AAWU continued to evolve into the Pac-8, then Pac-10 and, little by little, brought all the original members of the PCC – sans Montana and Idaho – back into the fold.

129. **D – NHRA Top Fuel Funny Car champions**. Don Prudhomme was the first Funny Car driver to go faster than 250mph. He drove a yellow '70 Barracuda that became part of the legendary (and valuable – up to $500 for an original set) Hot Wheels' "Mongoose & Snake Drag Race Set." The "Mongoose"? Tom McEwen and his '70 red Duster.

130. **C – Don Budge**. And Don's six consecutive Grand Slams ain't the only thing he's cornered the market on: a) he achieved the "Triple Crown" winning singles, doubles, and mixed doubles titles at one Grand Slam event a total of three times – Wimbledon (1937-38) and the U.S. Championships (1938); b) he had a 34 match win streak; c) the highest career winning percentage (92.06% [58-5]); d) the highest career grass court winning percentage (91.22% [55-5]); e) 14 consecutive tournament wins; f) and he's tied with Jimmy Connors re: 100% (24-0) Single Season winning percentage. Beat that, will 'ya! And only a handful *might* – in a 2006 survey done of former greats and experts, *Tennis Week* assembled a draw for a

best-of-all-time fantasy tourney. Budge was picked sixth behind Federer, Laver, Sampras, Borg, and Tilden, and ahead of Kramer and McEnroe.

131. **A – Diving**. From what I can tell, the origin of the term "pike" goes back to Middle English or Old English terms pik, pyk, or piic which refer to a "pointed tip" of something so, when "pike" first appeared in 1928, it probably meant that the diver (or gymnast 'coz they pike, too) was in the position of tapering to a point.

132. **B – Rich Brooks**, an Oregon State grad who gave their in-state rivals, the U.O. Ducks, 18 good years of his life and amassed a 36-60-4 record in his first nine seasons and a not-much-better 53-48 in his last nine. Yet, you could never count Brooks among the quitters. When he played high school ball in Grass Valley, California, he was easily the best player on the team, and while his team was having their heads bashed in in the rain-soaked league championship game one year, Brooks kept fighting. The other team ripped his jersey off, so Brooks battled on in his T-shirt. Then, they ripped his t-shirt off. Then, all he had left by the second half was his pants and shoulder pads (no, folks, this isn't "strip football"). Brooks' school was so impoverished, there were no extra unis, so he had to play with what he had. Brooks getting hired by the Rams was a big "huh?" maker. It made so little sense that Dwight Jaynes of The (Portland) Oregonian penned – with tongue firmly in cheek – some of the reasons the Rams hired him. My favorite being "Gerry Faust turned them down." Ooh.

133. **D – Calvin Hill**. Hill was a highly touted QB in high school and went on to Yale with the goal of becoming the first black QB in Yale history. However, on the second day of practice, the coaching staff moved him to linebacker and gave the QB job to Brian Dowling whose claim to fame was having cartoonist Garry Trudeau as his roomie and winding up as the character "B.D." in the *Doonesbury* comic strip. But I digress. Calvin was moved to halfback a few days later and led Yale to an undefeated season in 1968. He was selected by Dallas as the 24th pick in the draft – the first player from an Ivy League school drafted in the first round. After four years of medical setbacks, Hill's career finally found its groove in 1972 when he finished with 1,045 yards, a 4.2-yard average, and 6 TDs. He followed that up in '73 by breaking his own record with 1,142 yards and six touchdowns. And, yes, he's Dukie Grant Hill's papa. Grant Hill's mama? She was Hillary Clinton's roomie at Wellesley.

134. **A – Cycling**. Señor Quintana is a Colombian racing cyclist who won the "Giro" in 2014. The Giro d'Italia is one of cycling's Grand Tour races and starts in a different foreign country each year and finishes in Italy. The idea to do the race came from a newspaper (*La Gazzetta dello Sport*) after seeing how well the Tour de France did. The newspaper is printed on pink paper, so the winner's jersey is pink, too. Quintana's other claims to fame? He has twice finished 2nd in the Tour de France, as well. That's about it.

135. **A – Indiana State's Memorial Stadium** had the first outdoor use of "AstroTurf" in the college or pro ranks, but "Chemgrass," Astroturf's original name, was first installed at the Moses Brown School in Providence, Rhode Island. And, yes, you pop culture know-it-alls, the backyard of the Brady Bunch house is covered with AstroTurf.

136. **D – Outfield**. Billy was a roamer for six years in the majors and minors, playing for the Mets, Twins, Tigers, and Athletics and all their farm teams. He came into the league with a lot of promise born from the Mets picking him as the 23rd pick in the 1980 draft. The Mets even thought Bill had more upside than his fellow Mets draft pick Darryl Strawberry and they sent Darryl to play a lower rung of the minors than Billy. Hmm. After his last go-round with Oakland and growing tired of being sent down to the Little Falls'es of the world, he went to Oakland's GM, hat in hand, and asked if he could become a scout instead of being reassigned to the minors. It turned out to be a good move, one where he learned Saberemetrics – the analysis of baseball statistics that measures in-game activity – and turned that knowledge into making the A's one of the most cost-effective teams in baseball. A prime example would be the 2006 season where Oakland had the fifth-best record but ranked 24th out of 30 teams in player salaries. That begat playoffs and division crowns and impressive side notes like the Athletics becoming the first team in the 100 plus years of American League baseball to win 20 consecutive games. Beane was so good at what he did that the Red Sox offered him $12.5 mil to be their GM, but he believed, just like my

grandpappy, that "you dance with who brung you" and he decided to keep his laces tied to Oakland. Oakland, in turn, showed its appreciation by giving Beane a piece of the team and a 7-year contract extension. After Beane's analysis model being copycatted to death by other MLB teams, he started concentrating on high school players and a draft strategy focused on defensive efficiency. And the shift worked like a charm – the A's led MLB in defense, allowing the fewest runs in the league and the highest percentage of balls put into play by opponents that resulted in outs. Once again, that leveraged more playoffs and division championships. I know I've probably spilled too much ink on Mr. Beane, but indulge me one last bit of trivia: When Billy Beane played on one of the Tigers minor league teams, he played in the same outfield as Billy Bean (sans the last "e"), the second Major League Baseball player to publicly come out as gay. Who was the first? Dodger Glenn Burke. Glenn was also (with teammate Dusty Baker) credited with inventing the "high five" (in ESPN's "30 for 30" film *The High Five*).

137. **C – Mike Eruzione**. Of the "Miracle on Ice's" 20 USA players, 13 eventually wound up in the NHL. Even though Eruzione scored the winning goal against the Soviet Union (btw, voted the greatest highlight of all time by ESPN viewers in March 2008), he was one of the ones left undrafted. Of the team's players who did make it to the pros, center Neal Broten probably had the most impressive NHL career with 1,099 pro games over 17 seasons. He was the first American player to record 100 points in a season and the first player

in hockey history to win a championship at the collegiate (Minnesota), professional (Devils), and Olympic levels.

138. **C – Jack McKinney**. You probably don't remember, but Jack's first head coaching job was with the Lakers in 1979 and he was off to a 14-5 start when he damn near died in a bicycle accident where he suffered a near-fatal head injury. That's when assistant Paul Westhead took over as interim coach. Jack never got a chance to get back to the sidelines as his recovery was longer than expected and the Lakers were well on their way to the NBA championship under Westhead. The Lakers fired McKinney shortly after the confetti hit the floor, so he headed off to the Pacers where he got his due. However, the ball started bouncing the wrong way in Indy and he was fired a few years later after the Pacers posted the league's worst record.

139. **B – Dave Meyers** who was part of one of the biggest trades in NBA history a mere 19 days after he started his NBA career. He played pro ball for four years (averaging 11.2 PPG) and, then, suddenly announced he was retiring to devote time to his family and his Jehovah Witnesses faith. You might remember his sister, Ann, who was the only woman to sign a free-agent contract with an NBA team (Indiana Pacers).

140. **A – Nolan Ryan**, who not only holds the record for walking the most batters in a career with 2,795 walks, but is also the only pitcher in MLB history to walk more than 2,000 batters. Steve Carlton comes in second with 1,833.

141. **A – Deion Sanders**, who played in a World
Series with the Braves and Super Bowl with the
Forty-Niners (and, later, with the Cowboys). In that
Super Bowl (XXIX), there were several firsts –
Sanders becoming the first to play in a World
Series and a Super Bowl; Ken Norton, Jr. who
became the first player to win three consecutive
Super Bowls (albeit as a member of two different
teams); Chargers QB Gale Gilbert who became the
first player to be a member of five straight Super
Bowl teams (and on the losing side of each); and,
the first Super Bowl to have two players each score
three touchdowns (Jerry Rice and Ricky Watters).

142. **D – Marshall**, home of the Thundering Herd – a
nickname a local sports reporter plucked from a
1925 Zane Grey novel and plopped on the team.
It was never an "official" name, though, and the
school played around with others like Boogercats,
Green Gobblers, and Judges (the school's name
came from John Marshall, a U.S. Supreme Court
chief justice). In 1965, the nickname was put to a
vote and Thundering Herd won out.

143. **A – Los Angeles Rams**, and you can thank Fred
Gehrke for the idea. Fred, halfback and half-artist,
had been playing around with painting helmets for
a while when the Rams coach Bob suggested he
paint a helmet with ram horns on it. Fred did...
Snyder showed it to the owner, Dan Reeves...
Reeves got okay from the NFL... then, paid Fred a
dollar a helmet to do 75 of 'em... and the helmet
got its debut in a pre-season matchup with the
Browns in 1948. Gehrke's creativity didn't stop
there, either. After he had his nose broken three

times in a single season, he came up with the idea for the facemask.

144. **B – Speed racing car**. Specifically, a modified Duesenberg Special driven by Ab Jenkins. The Ab man was instrumental in bringing attention to the Bonneville Salt Flats as a place to run cars hard and hang 'em up wet. In 1940, Ab's Mormon Meteor III did 3,868 miles in 24 hours at an average speed of 161 mph, a record no one dared challenge until 2005. In 1958, General Motors introduced the Pontiac "Bonneville" in honor of Ab's accomplishments making it the first, and perhaps the only car to warrant its name as opposed to being donned with a moniker by an automaker.

145. **C – Rose Bowl**, which, interestingly enough, hasn't always been in Pasadena, Cali. After Pearl Harbor, there were concerns about Japan looking for West Coast bombing targets and 90,000 folks at a football game seemed like a frightening option. It was recommended that the Rose Bowl (and Rose Parade) be canceled, but Duke University stepped up and offered to host the game and Oregon State as its opponent on Duke's home turf in Durham, N.C. Duke was unbeaten and ranked #2 in the country and Oregon State #16, but the Beavers pulled off the win, 20-16, their only Rose Bowl win to date (as of 2016).

146. **B – Seventies** or, more specifically, the year of 1970, one of the more trivia-filled years in baseball. Here's why: Curt Flood filed a lawsuit challenging MLB's reserve clause... Bud Selig

bought the bankrupt Seattle Pilots for $10.8mil and moved 'em to Milwaukee... Hoyt Wilhelm became the first pitcher to appear in 1,000 games... Hank Aaron bangs out his 3,000[th] hit, making him the first member of the 3,000/500 club... Pirate Dock Ellis pitched a no-hitter while on LSD...

147. **A – Gordie Howe** and his boys. That's it far as I can tell. I looked as far back as 1917 and could find: a) 47 pairs of brothers who played together on the same team; among them, 10 who won the Stanley Cup together. b) brothers who squared off against each other five times in the Stanley Cup finals; c) 26 sons who followed in their daddy's footsteps and played for the same team as their dad; d) But only once has a dad played with his sons (at the same time), and that was when Gordie Howe played with sons Mark & Marty for a single season with the Whalers.

148. **D – 24 Hours of LeMans**, which is one leg of the Triple Crown of Motorsport – the others being the Indy 500 and the Monaco Grand Prix – and one loooooooong son-of-a-gun. Over that 24-hour period, drivers can cover more than 3,000 miles (in 2010, 3,360 miles), which is like driving from New York City to Los Angeles. And if you win, you have USA's Dan Gurney to thank for the celebratory twist. Back in '67, Gurney – not wanting his moment to be pallid like an Indy car driver chugging a bottle of milk – started a trend of his own when he became the first winning driver to celebrate by spraying champagne on anyone nearby instead of drinking it.

149. **A – Ralph Sampson**. Despite the University of Virginia's #1 rankings in three of Ralph's four years as a Cavalier, you can thank a Jordan'less UNC squad in the '81 Final Four, a lucky UAB team in '82, and NC State on their way to the '81 NCAA crown for Ralph's lack of a championship ring. In pro ball, the Celtics kept Ralph's Rockets from winning the '86 championship and that's as close as Ralph got. I think before I bug out here, I should give a little-used shout-out to Rick Carlisle, one of Sampson's Virginia teammates (transferring in from Maine), who went on to NBA coaching good'ness. If we have to give a high five to Ralph, there's two choices: 1) it might be his buzzer-beating shot to dethrone the Los Angeles Lakers as Western Conference champions, screwing up L.A.'s hopes for back-to-back NBA titles and, with that, rocketing Houston to the second NBA Finals in their team's history; or, 2) it might be that, at 7' 4", he's the tallest player inducted into the Naismith Memorial Hall of Fame.

150. **B – Cincy's Riverfront Stadium**. Sliding pits were designed to save re-configuration time converting the playing field between baseball and football and, now, since most places have separate baseball and football stadiums, it's unnecessary.

151. **A – A marked ski run/path** down a mountain for snow skiing. How do you pronounce that little booger? The Brits use a long "e" (like "least") and the American skiers go for the short "I" (like "mist"). If you've ever gone skiing, you know that the pistes are graded by difficulty, going from green for easiest up to black double-diamond for "whoa, sister!"

North America's longest continuous black double-diamond run is at North Face, Alyeska, Alaska, while the shortest (about 150 meters) is Corbet's Couloir in Jackson Hole, Wyoming. Corbet's is a run that ski experts call the scariest in the world and #4 on the "Top 50 things for skiers to do before they die" (the top three are not really quantifiable – "ski ironically," "ski South America," and "ski your nemesis."). How scary is it? Well, this description from Forbes.com is a good, quick insight: "Few emerge from the first 25 feet still on their skis. You enter the chute's narrow, flinty mouth in free fall, dropping two stories onto a 55-degree slope. Fail to execute a hard right turn immediately, and you smash into a face of Precambrian rock. Survive, and you then smear speed by executing two nervy turns, exiting down a 45-degree slope as the chute fans out." Slightly more difficult than giving an after-dinner speech, eh?

152. **C – Arad McCutchan/Evansville University**. Why Arad over everyone else? Well, five national championships at Evansville is enough, don'cha think? And the name "Arad"? McCutchan said it was Hebrew for "wild ass".

153. **C – Football**. When the NY football Giants were playing at the old Yankee Stadium from '56-'63, chequered flags were posted at each corner of the end zones. Why? Basically, because chequered flags were symbolic with finishing or completion.

154. **D – Ken O'Brien**. While Kenneth's not on anyone's frequency of QB instant recall, his

numbers are staggering. Besides the ones in the question, dig these...

✓ 1st QB (of 2) to combine 400-yard game with a perfect rating (Nick Foles of the Eagles was the other).

✓ 1st QB (of 2) to maintain completion % on 30+ attempts (Kurt Warner was the other).

Ken's career faded hard and fast after 10 years with the Jets. At age 32, he was traded to the Packers for a fifth-round pick and was behind Brett Favre, Ty Detmer, and Mark Brunnel on Green Bay's depth chart. Rather than paying O'Brien the $1.8 mil due him to just carry a clipboard, they sent him home to mama.

155. **B – Ozzie Virgil, Sr.,** who also the 17th African-American to play major league béisbol. They don't make 'em like Ozzie, Sr. anymore. He was a true utility player and, over 13 years with six different teams, he played every single position 'cept pitcher and centerfield.

156. **D – Richard Lee ("The King") Petty**, winner of seven Daytonas, the NASCAR championship seven times, a record 27 races in 1967 alone (including 10 in a row), and 200 races in his career. Yep, the same guy who was cast as Strip "The King" Weathers in the movie *Cars*... the same guy who ran for Secretary of State in North Carolina and lost his arse ("If I had known I wasn't going to win, I wouldn't have run.")... and the same guy we've never seen without his sunglasses or wearing a Charlie 1 Horse cowboy hat.

157. **C – Bowling**, specifically "sport bowling." Think about the times you've gone bowling. Have you ever noticed a little slippery stuff on your ball when it came back? Well, pardner, that's oil. Not the cooking or car variety, but a formulation that breaks down dirt, does a little cleaning, conditions the wood, etc. Your mom & pop alleys typically use a pattern that's tapered from the outside to the center where most of the oil is applied. However, for competitions, the patterns get whacky. The names of these patterns attempt to describe the pattern and how to play it. For example, the "Shark": This pattern forces bowlers to play deep inside the center of the lanes, like sharks that troll the depths of the ocean.

158. **D – Larry Doby**. Doby's route to the bigs was a little zig-zag'y. He had a basketball scholarship to Long Island University, but joined the Navy instead and, after the war, played ball in the Negro League for the Newark Eagles. On the heels of Jackie Robinson's entrance into the league, Larry became the second Negro in MLB and the first in the AL, signing with Cleveland... *and* the first to go directly from the Negro League to the Major League (Jackie went from the Negro League to the minors, then the majors)... *and*, along with Satchel Paige, the first African-American players to win a World Series crown when the Indians won in '48.

159. **A – Sam Barry @ USC.** Yep, Tex Winter gets referenced the most in the modern era because of the success he had with the triangle with the Bulls and Lakers, but Tex picked it up playing for Barry in the Forties. The triangle-O set wasn't the only thing

Sam brought to the game. Most give him credit for eliminating the center jump after every basket, as well as spearheading the drive to create the center line and the 10-second rule, and along with Phog Allen, the chief proponent of the "stalling offense" that Kansas and UNC did so well with.

160. **D – Mintonette**. Why that name? Because the game is similar to bad<u>minton</u>! Morgan's idea was to create a game that was safe to play and gave athletes something to do indoors in the cold weather months. Morgan was like a sports "remixer" – borrowing pieces of handball, tennis, badminton, and baseball (originally badminton had "innings" and three serves per inning). Don't get any wise ideas, you creative types. Not sure that golfette or footette would fly. Oh, yeah, this – Did you know when Morgan first devised the sport, he tried to use a basketball? However, he found it too heavy for what he had in mind, so he played with the basketball's inflatable rubber inside instead.

161. **B – Charlie Weis**. Charlie did play football in high school, however when he got to Notre Dame as an undergrad, he never put on the cleats. We haven't heard much about Weis' pre-NFL career, but the short story is that he was an assistant at the high school level for five years in New Jersey, then went to U. of South Carolina as a graduate assistant, then back to Jersey where he won the state high school championship, then to the Giants, Patriots, etcetera, etcetera, etcetera. Oh, yeah – Lou Holtz played ball at Kent State, Jon Gruden at U. Dayton, and Joe Gibbs at San Diego State.

162. **A – Pesky's Pole**, rightly named after Johnny Pesky who played second, short, and third for the Red Sox. Folklore has it that former Red Sox lefthander Mel Parnell came up with the nickname when he called the games on radio in the 1960s. Mel loved to talk about how Pesky, a left-handed hitter with limited power, would sometimes profit from a rare fly ball that would hit the pole and go for a home run. The right-field fence at Fenway is the shortest in the majors – something that came about as a result of the bullpen area built in front of the right-center field bleachers in 1940. It was built there mostly for Ted Williams' benefit, so he and other left-handed batters could hit more home runs.

163. **D – Joe Torre replaced Bobby Cox**. Is there any connection, other than managing the Braves, between Torre and Cox? Well, Torre managed and Cox played for the Yankees and they both wore #6 uniforms.

164. **C – Lenny Wilkens,** the man who 1) was the first to have his jersey retired at Providence; 2) did one of the rare simultaneous player-coach stints when he was with the Seattle Sonics; 3) won an NBA crown as the Sonics coach; 4) 3x Naismith HOF inductee – as a player, a coach, and member of the 2010 Dream Team.

165. **D – Millionaires**, won the Stanley Cup in 1915, and then later became the Maroons (the color of the uni). The team played in Denham Arena, which at the time, was the largest indoor ice rink in the world. The Vancouver Canucks now own the rights

to the Millionaires and wear their throwback jerseys once or twice a year.

166. **C – "Down the Field."** I know, I know – ya'll were thinkin' "Rocky Top," weren't 'ya? "Down the Field" is the *official* fight song of UT, although "Rocky Top" is more popular or _unpopular_ if we're to believe *Bleacher Report's* "Top 10 College Football Traditions Fans Love to Hate". In that poll, "Rocky Top" came in at #2, ahead of Florida State's Indian Chief, and right behind Stanford's "tree" mascot.

167. **D – The American League champ**. Who's William Harridge? He was the president of the American League from 1931-59 and seems like a pretty okay guy. However, he did create headlines a few times. First, he allowed a crony of the Yankees' owners to buy the A's and move 'em from Philly to K.C. without giving local Philly businessmen a chance to buy the team and keep it there. Then, on July 4, 1932, in a game between the Yanks and the Senators, Harridge fined Yankee catcher Bill Dickey a thousand bucks and suspended him for 30 days for chasing down Senator Carl Reynolds and breaking his jaw after the two collided at home plate. The funniest thing came in 1951 when St. Louis' owner, Bill Veeck, signed a dwarf (little person) to play (and did!). Harridge thought Veeck was making a mockery of baseball and cancelled the dwarf's contract the next day. Yeah, the same Veeck who came up with the idea of the ill-fated "Disco Demolition Night" when he owned the White Sox.

168. **A – They're orange,** just like they were at Mets Stadium, the only team who doesn't have 'ol yeller poles. I'll throw another bit of useless knowledge your way if you like – neither the first hit, nor the first pitch, nor the first home run in Citi Field were hit by anyone on a major league team. All of those came from the first game played in the park, one that featured the Georgetown Hoyas and St. John's Red Storm two weeks before the Mets had their first regular-season game in the stadium.

169. **D – Ulnar Collateral Ligament Reconstruction**, a surgical graft procedure in which the ulnar collateral ligament in the elbow is replaced with a tendon from another part of the body. It's mostly done on pitchers, but there are some fielders who man'ed up and did the surgery, including Jose Canseco. Jose did it to himself, though. When he was with Cleveland, Canseco asked his manager to let him pitch the eighth inning of an out-of-control loss to the Red Sox. The dumb butt screwed up his arm, had to undergo Tommy John surgery, and was lost for the rest of the season.

170. **C – Belmont**. Chrome, if you remember, was the key figure in "Nasalgate," a dust-up caused after the New York Racing Commission balked on letting the horse wear nasal strips like he had in the Derby and the Preakness. They eventually relented, but it was for naught as Cali Chrome got stepped on in the gate by an adjacent horse, tore some heel tissue, and finished fourth.

171. **C – Tyson Chandler & Eddy Curry**. Matter of fact, none of the first four players selected that

year played college ball. You've got the first pick, Kwame Brown – the first number one draft pick to be selected straight out of high school – whose career lasted 12 years and hit $63 mil in salary; Tyson Chandler was the #2 pick and has a salary history that's hit $135 mil and still going as of 2016; then, Pau Gasol who's amassed $163 mil and still cashin' checks as of 2016; followed by Eddy Curry who raked in $70 mil in an 11-year career. Curry is the only one who came close to going to college. He signed a letter-of-intent to DePaul, but the temptation of the NBA was too strong and he declared himself eligible for the draft. No relation to Wardell Stephen "Steph" Curry II, btw.

172. **D – Albert Belle**. How did he acquire the tag "Mr. Freeze"? Seems like big Al liked to have the temp in the clubhouse nice and chilly (below 60°). And, as the story goes, one of his teammates was feelin' the chill and turned up the heat. So, Belle sauntered over, turned down the thermostat and – *WHACK!* – smashed it with his Louisville Slugger, thereby earning the nickname "Mr. Freeze." Even though Belle became the first player to hit 50 doubles and 50 home runs in a single season (1995), and was also the first player to break the $10 mil/yr. compensation contract in Major League Baseball, he was still a little twerp. When he was at LSU and playing in the College World Series, he went after some dude who was heckling him and labeling him with some uggggly racist insults. So, the NCAA kicked him out of the series. Then, a few years later, there was a fan up in the stands taunting Albert about his purported alcohol problem, so Albert threw a ball at him. Then, there was

a corked bat incident that included sending in a teammate to the umps' dressing room and replacing the corked one with a non-corked one. Let's not forget the time he knocked down Fernando Vina of the Brewers who was blocking Albert's base path. And, if that's not enough, he refused to speak to the media and when he did, he'd sometimes lose his wheels and go on a tirade. Of course, karma is a bitch and the first time he was eligible for the Hall of Fame, he only got 7.7% of the baseball writers' votes and missed election by a mile. The next time he was up for the HOF, he got even less. Oh, and the money thing? When he signed with the White Sox, his deal made him the highest-paid player and his White Sox contract had a rather odd clause that allowed Albert to demand he would remain one of the three highest-paid players in baseball. So, what did he do two years later? He invoked the clause, 'cept the White Sox declined to give him a raise, so he declared himself a free agent and went to the Orioles where he once again became the game's highest paid player. Two years into that deal, though, he got osteoarthritis and had to lay down his (corked) bat forever, but only after he homered in his very last at-bat.

173. **B – Mark Rypien**, who did pretty well for a sixth-round pick and the eighth QB overall, behind Jim Everett, Chuck Long, Jack Trudeau, Bubby Brister, Hugh Millen, Robbie Bosco, and Doug Gaynor. Here's two interesting side notes: 1) Rypien caught the same NASCAR bug that Redskins coach Joe Gibbs did and became the original owner of the #97 team driven by Kurt Busch that won the 2004 Nextel Cup

championship. 2) Rypien's daughter, Angela, was a star QB in the Lingerie Football League. Yes, there is such a thing. It's a full-contact, 7-women-to-a-side sport similar to indoor football. Their uniforms include shoulder, elbow, and kneepads, performance wear, and ice hockey-style helmets with clear plastic visors. Prior to the 2013 season, players wore garters, bras, and panties. No, they are not allowed to put on eyeliner while driving down the field. Lots of (lonely?) ex-NFL players have signed on to be LFL coaches – there's Jim McMahon, Eric Dickerson, Willie Gault, Lawrence Taylor, and the Packers' Gilbert Brown.

174. **D – Yale and the "Yale Bowl."** When it was constructed in 1913, it had 70,896 seats, but renovations have helped scale that back to 61,446. The real impact the stadium made is in the word "bowl." It was the first stadium to *look* like a bowl and the first one to use the *name* "bowl." And, oddly enough, there's not a locker room to be found, so players have to dress in another building 200 yards away.

175. **D – The President's Cup**. The format is pretty much the same as the Ryder Cup. And like the Ryder, there is no prize money awarded and the proceeds are distributed to charities nominated by the players and captains. The Presidents and Ryder Cups aren't the only USA vs. Europe or the World golf competitions, mind you. There's the Chrysler Cup (senior men), the Palmer Cup (collegiate-level), the Solheim Cup (women), and the Handa Cup (senior women). If you can leave your putter

for a sec, there's even a Mosconi Cup for 9-ball pool players and a Weber Cup for bowling.

176. **A – Minnesota**. "On, Wisconsin's" roots go back to 1909 and the campus of the University of Minnesota. William Purdy wrote the tune as "Minnesota, Minnesota" with the intent of entering it in a contest for the University of Minnesota's fight song. One of his buds – a Wisconsin grad – convinced him to pull out of the contest and change "Minnesota, Minnesota" to "On, Wisconsin" and the rest is history. Well, almost. Paul McCartney owns the worldwide rights to "On, Wisconsin" (it's in the public domain in the U.S.) as well as ''The Buckeye Battle Cry,'' ''Rambling Wreck from Georgia Tech,'' and the ''Notre Dame Victory March.'' The governor of Wisconsin asked Paul to gift the song's rights back to the state in honor of John Lennon, but Paul refused to utter the words "...and I'll send it along, with love from me to you."

177. **D – New Orleans Buccaneers**. When the ABA was founded, there were seven Bucs investors (including Morton Downey, Jr.) who got a heckuva bargain – a franchise fee of $1,000 where the rest of the ABA franchises were going for $30,000. The team was actually pretty good. It included future NBA coaches Doug Moe and Larry Brown on a squad coached by Babe McCarthy who had won four SEC championships at Mississippi State. The Bucs made it to the ABA finals the first year, the division semis the next, then broke even with a .500 record the third. It looked like things were starting to slide, so they rechristened the team the Louisiana Buccaneers with the intent of playing

their home games all over the Bayou State. That's where the new owner came in and moved 'em to Memphis where they became the Pros, then the Memphis Tams, and finally the Memphis Sounds. If you keep connecting the dots, you'll see the team's lineage dying in 1974 when some Maryland businessmen bought the team and moved 'em to Baltimore where they became the Hustlers, then the Claws, even bought the rights to Dan Issel from the Kentucky Colonels. They played three pre-season games while the ABA home office waited for a "performance bond," but the money never came and the commissioner had enough and terminated the franchise.

178. **B – A college basketball coach who's won more than 1,000 games.** Actually, Statham (coach at McKendree) is one of five as of the writing of this book. The others are: Pat Summitt (Tennessee), Danny Miles (Oregon Tech), Herb Magee (Philadelphia U.), and Mike Krzyzewski (Duke). Sticking with the "1,000" theme, Scotty Bowman is the (only) NHL coach who's won more than 1,000 regular season games. Joseph Franklin "Jumping Joe" Fulks (Murray State and the Phila Warriors) was the first NBA player to score 1,000 in a single season (he also set the single-game scoring record four different times).

179. **A – Cross-country skiing and rifle shooting.** Why do we have a biathlon, anyway? Well, we have the Norwegians to thank for that. Seems like it began as an exercise alternative for military training, then an actual military contest where soldiers would shoot at a mark while skiing at top

speed, race downhill among trees, and a long race on level ground while carrying a rifle and military pack. I guess this is why no country has ever even thought of trying to invade Norway. :-)

180. **C – Ray "Boom Boom" Mancini.** I'll keep this brief because it's sad. It was a 14-rounder between 21-year old Mancini and 27-year old Kim in Vegas in 1982. Kim suffered brain injuries that led to his death four days later. Everyone took it hard. Mancini fell into a serious state of depression and blamed himself for Kim's death. Kim's mother committed suicide a few months later, then the fight's ref killed himself soon after. There are a couple of good things that came out of this tragedy, one being the reduction of rounds from 15 to 12 in a title fight. Others include an extra ring rope to prevent fighters from falling through the ropes and out of the ring, plus EKGs, brain and lung tests before the fight. Before Kim's death, the only tests they performed were blood pressure and pulse.

181. **D – UCLA** and when I say "most," I'm talkin' 24 national championships. Pepperdine's second with only five. However, you've gotta take into consideration that there are only 39 schools that field a *men's* volleyball team and it takes a blend of Div. 1 and Div. 2 schools to cobble together that many. You won't find 'em in the same conferences as football and basketball, either. For example, Harvard and Princeton play in the EIVA instead of the Ivy League; Ohio State plays in the MIVA rather than the Big Ten; and Stanford, UCLA, and USC play in the Mountain Pacific, as there is no men's volleyball in the PAC-12. And the little guys

do pretty well, too. Heck, Lewis University (Romeoville, IL) has a national championship to its name. So does Hawaii. Loyola Chicago has a couple, and UC-Irvine has at least four.

182. **D – Stand by Me** (yessir, the Ben E. King hit). It was part of Muhammad Ali's only album *I Am the Greatest* – an album consisting of monologues and poems pretty much about Clay himself that Columbia Records put out as a prelude to Clay's first title match. After Clay turned Muslim and all that controversy arose, Columbia pulled the record from the shelves. It was another 13 years before Ali made another record, one where he teamed up with Frank Sinatra and Howard Cosell to record "Ali and His Gang vs. Mr. Tooth Decay" in 1976.

183. **A – Blake and Flynn.** You remember – Mudville was down two runs when the alleged weak hitters Blake and Flynn hit a single and double respectively. All they needed was for Casey to bring 'em home and either tie or win the game. But the backstory of the poem? Let me do some generous quoting from Baseball-Almanac.com...

It all started in 1885 when George Hearst decided to run for state senator in California. To self-promote his brand of politics, Hearst purchased the San Francisco Examiner. At the completion of the election, Hearst gave the newspaper to his son, William Randolph Hearst.

William, who had experience editing the Harvard Lampoon while at Harvard College, took three Lampoon staff members to California with him. One of those three was Ernest L. Thayer who signed his humorous Lampoon articles with the pen name Phin.

In the June 3, 1888, issue of The Examiner, Phin appeared as the author of the poem we all know as Casey at the Bat. The poem received very little attention and a few weeks later it was partially republished in the New York Sun, though the author was now known as Anon.

A New Yorker named Archibald Gunter clipped out the poem and saved it as a reference item for a future novel. Weeks later Gunter found another interesting article describing an upcoming performance at the Wallack Theatre by comedian De Wolf Hopper - who was also his personal friend. The August 1888 show had members from the New York and Chicago ball clubs in the audience and the clipping now had a clear and obvious use.

Gunter shared Casey at the Bat with Hopper and the performance was nothing short of legendary.

184. **C – The defender contacts the ball-handler/ dribbler with an arm-bar**. Dribbling's roots? (I know, you didn't realize that dribbling actually had roots.) If you look at Dr. Naismith's original rules, there was nothing in there about dribbling. It just said that passing the ball was the legal way of advancing it. Some creative player somewhere soon came up with the strategy of "passing to themselves," a move that Naismith both endorsed and admired for its cleverness, and that evolved into the dribble as we know it today. The first known team to dribble? Yale University in 1897. Boola!

185. **D – Tom Seaver**, who until Ken Griffey Jr. got 99.3%, was the highest-voted HOF inductee (98.84%). Other than the amazin' stats in the question, another wow'er or two was that he threw 27 3-hitters, 10 2-hitters, 5 1-hitters (all as a Met) and 1 no-hitter. More? He has the major league record for consecutive strikeouts in a game – 10. Tom's ascent to the majors was a little disjointed. He was pitching for USC when the Dodgers drafted him in the 10th round, but he wanted $70k to sign and the Dodgers said nope. A year later he got drafted and signed by the Braves, but the commissioner voided the deal because USC had played two exhibition games that year, so Tom decided to go back to college except the NCAA ruled him ineligible because he had signed a pro contract (even though it had been voided). Tom's dad stepped in and threatened to sue, so the MLB backed off a little and said any team that matched the Braves' offer could have him. The Phillies, Indians, and Mets all did, so there was a lottery and the Mets won. The Mets were a good place for Tom Terrific, especially at the teller's window. At age 27, Seaver became the youngest Major League player to hit the $100,000 salary level when he signed a $120,000 contract (1972).

186. **D – Linebacker**. The etymology of "linebacker?" Simple – a linebacker plays three to five yards behind the line of scrimmage and behind the defensive linemen, so they're "linebackers." What's their purpose, sayeth ye non-football fans? Simply add a little run or pass protection and, when needed, blitz and sack the dang quarterback. Another way to tell a linebacker from a defensive lineman is that

defensive linemen usually put one or two hands on the ground and linebackers stand upright.

187. **C – Mariano Rivera**. A "cutter" (aka "cut fastball" or "buzz saw") falls somewhere in between a slider and a fastball. It's usually faster than a slider, slower than a fastball, and has more stuff on it than a fastball. The cutter is a "four-seamer" and the pitcher can create more spin if they shift the grip by rotating the thumb inwards and the two top fingers to the outside. What happens is the pitch will shift in or out by a few inches and, then, break late, like a long skinny "S". When it's working its magic, it can be nasty. Case-in-point, the 1999 World Series and Ryan Klesko of the Braves is facing Mariano Rivera. Rivera's well into the zone and Klesko breaks three bats in a single at-bat, hence the nickname "buzz saw." Besides Rivera, other cutter pitchers are Andy Pettite, Al Leiter (who got a no-hitter out of his cutter), Brian Wilson, and Roy Halladay (who says the cutter messed up his arm).

188. **D – Minnesota Twins**, who had nuthin' but bad luck with Ortiz. Between the moment he debuted in a Twins uniform in 1997 and got to the Red Sox in 2003, he split time between the majors and minors, suffered wrist injuries, and had knee problems. Finally, the Twins threw in the towel and released Big Papi from his contract. Boston signed him as a free agent and, at first, didn't use him much – mostly as a DH or pinch hitter. But, a couple of months into the season, manager Grady Little benched Jeremy Giambi and put Ortiz in the lineup as the full-time DH. Ortiz started slammin' HRs like

crazy, the fans in Beantown fell in love with him, and his career took off from there.

189. **A – 6**. Because if a ref tried to hold up 6 fingers to show whom the foul was on, it would look like 51. The only numbers that are legal are numbers you can demonstrate with the digits on your hands, plus 0 or 00 (but not *both* 0 and 00).

190. **A – Gene Stallings**. Gene was one of Bear Bryant's "Junction Boys" and returned to A&M as head coach after assisting Bryant with two national championships at Alabama. At A&M he had the unmitigated gall to beat Bear in the '67 Cotton Bowl – the only winning season Stallings had out of seven as the Aggies coach. Years later, he went back to 'Bama where he led the Crimson Tide to their first national championship in 13 years and the last one until Nick Saban showed up in town.

191. **B – The Rutgers Queensmen & Princeton** (then called the College of New Jersey) **Tigers**, a game that Rutgers won 6-4. As a matter of fact, that first season (1869) had only two games and the second pitted the same schools, but with Princeton winning that one 8-0. There's a huge difference in how they played the game then and how it's played now – no running with the ball, 25 players to a side, and the ball was round. The rules Harvard played Tufts under in 1875 are closer to what we have today – 11 to a side, running with the ball, and a spherical ball – but every game has to have its roots somewhere and Rutgers and Princeton get the nod as the first colleges to play

football and the first intercollegiate football co-champions.

192. **B – Vin Scully**, who got his big break in the '53 World Series between the Yanks and Dodgers thanks to Red Barber's salary squabble with Gillette. Barber, by the way, had actually recruited Scully to do CBS' college football games. Scully isn't just a baseball guy, mind you. You might not remember this, but he did the NFL (w/ John Madden) as well as PGA tournaments (like The Masters). If you're a fan of *The Simpsons*, Harry Shearer does an impersonation of Scully as the "Gabbo" puppet character.

193. **D – Tampa Bay Lightning**, the team that turned a few heads in 1992 when they hired Manon Rheaume to become the first woman to play in an NHL game.

194. **C – Dodgers**. This was the Series where Reggie became "Mr. October" and it came down like this: Some reporter was interviewing Thurmon Munson and Munson proposed that Reggie might be a better interview target thanks to his past post-season performances. Munson said, "Go ask Mr. October," giving Jackson a nickname that would not only stick, but merited forewarning to the opposition. Jackson didn't fail Munson, either. He hit homers in Games Four and Five of the Series, then smacked three off three different pitchers in Game Six.

195. **D – Brad Daugherty**. Seven-foot Brad was a Tar Heel and the second UNC player taken as the first

pick in the NBA draft (James Worthy was the first). He played for the Cleveland Cavs his entire nine-year pro career where he wore #43, a tribute to his favorite sportsman, driver Richard Petty. After back problems cut short his NBA career, he bought into the NASCAR Camping World Truck Series, then leveraged that into a racing analyst for ESPN.

196. **A – The Palestra**. Often called the "Cathedral of College Basketball," this gym on the U. of Pennsylvania campus was built in 1927 and named after the Greek term "palæstra," which was the Greek wrestling school. Given all the college teams it's served (and still serves), it's figured that the Palestra has hosted more games, more visiting teams, and more NCAA tournaments than any other facility in college basketball. Btw, the "Big 5" is not really a conference, but all the teams play each other once a season (so four games per team).

197. **B – Elo**. No, no, not the '70s band. The Elo rating system – created by Marquette physics professor Arpad Elo – is a way to calculate the relative skill levels of players in competitor-versus-competitor games. Originally, it was created for chess and, then moved into soccer, American football (part of the BCS weighting for 15 years), baseball, and basketball. The basic principle is that the difference in the ratings between teams or players can predict who wins the match/game. Say you and I have equal ratings, we're each expected to score an equal number of wins, but if my rating is 100 points greater than yours, I'm expected to score 64%; if the difference is, say 200 points, then the expected score for me is 76%. Real world examples? Sure.

In basketball, the Top 5 Elo all-time ratings are Larry Bird, Tim Duncan, Hakeem Olajuwon, Oscar Robertson, and David Robinson. In football, the all-time Top 5 are Jim Brown, Y.A. Tittle, Gale Sayers, Anthony Munoz, and Otto Graham. If you want to test out this theory, go to Sports-Reference.com.

198. **D – Barry Bonds**. Bonds was *intentionally* walked 688 times to Pujols' 297 (as of 2015), Aaron's 293, and McGwire's 150. Oh, and by the way, Roger Maris was never intentionally walked the year he hit 61 HRs, maybe because Mickey Mantle was right behind him in the line-up. Not that there's a pro baseball etiquette guide, but it's considered a no-no if you actually *walk* to first base, which is how Pete Rose got his nickname "Charlie Hustle." He ran to first base when he was walked.

199. **B – John Paul Jones Arena at the University of Virginia**. Its capacity is 14,953 but when they played Arizona in 2006, they squeezed 15,219 in there. One of the special traits that the Virginia fans bring to the games is that they all stand and cheer for the Cavaliers defense when there's 10 seconds left on the opposing team's shot clock.

200. **A – Sisal fibers**, which are glued on their end. Sisal is a grass grown in Africa and China, and a little like hemp. The cheaper boards use cork or paper, but sisal is the real deal because it has a "self-healing effect." Meaning when a dart lands next to where the previous dart landed, the sisal is parted and closes the original hole. Genius.

201. **D – 7** (six field players and one goalie). As little as most of us know about water polo, it's loaded with trivial nuggets. The ultimate mash-up sport, water polo combines rules from basketball, hockey, soccer, wrestling, and, duh, swimming. There's a lot to remember, so here goes: a) Players can only use one hand to hold the ball, but the goalie can use two hands as long as they're within five meters of their own goal. b) Like soccer, the object of the game is to score in the opposite team's net. c) Players advance the ball by passing to teammates or swimming with the ball in front of them. d) There are personal fouls and shot clocks just like basketball. And one more trivia nugget you can leverage with your pals: (men's) water polo (for men) was the first Olympic *team* sport, dating back to 1900 (women's water polo wasn't included until 2000).

202. **A – 19.** It's rumored baseball players wore numbers on their unis before 1900 but the Baseball Hall of Fame displays a newspaper clipping that contradicts that. The clipping says, "In 1907, Alfred Lawson, manager of Pennsylvania's Reading Red Roses, decided to number his club's uniforms in an effort to aid fans' identification of players. With 14 men signed to his Atlantic League team, Lawson ordered numbers 1 through 12, 14 and 15, avoiding 13 in fear that no player would wear the unlucky figure. Though it is unclear if the club ever took the field with numbered duds, this marks the earliest known instance in which a team experimented with numbering its players." It was another nine years before a major league team took up the idea when the Cleveland Indians added numbers, albeit on the left sleeve and on

home uniforms only. Then, in 1929, both the Yankees and Indians popped numbers on the backs of their jerseys. And, to wrap up this uniform trotting, the Dodgers were the first to add numbers to the *front* of the uniforms.

203. **C – Frank Vogel**, who is actually a leaf on Rick Pitino's coaching tree* (as video coordinator for the Celtics), but this question is about Larry Brown so I should give him first crack at showing his limbs. Brown's tree has these folks on it: Bill Self, John Calipari, Alvin Gentry, Maurice Cheeks, Bob Hill (Pacers, Spurs, Sonics), Danny Manning, Mark Turgeon (Maryland), and Tad Boyle (Colorado). Where'd I come up with Gregg Popovich? He was a D-III coach at Pomona-Pitzer (home of the Sagehens!) and took a year off to go to Kansas and absorb all the Larry Brown one man can. Bleacher Report claims Dean Smith (UNC) is the "Zeus" of coaching trees since his offspring includes Larry Brown, which means all of the Caliparis and Popovichs are on his tree, too. And, if you take Dean Smith all the way back to Dr. Naismith, you get the most badass coaching tree in the universe. Phog Allen, the great Kansas coach, played for Naismith and Dean Smith played for Phog. *BleacherReport.com calls Pitino's coaching tree a "sequoia," given all these branches and sub-branches: Mick Cronin (Murray, Cincy), Billy Donovan (who begat Shaka Smart and Anthony Grant), Jim O'Brien (Celts, Pacers, Sixers), Herb Sendek (who mentored John Groce [Illini], Thad Matta, and Sean Miller), Tubby Smith, Reggie Theus, Jeff Van Gundy, and Ralph Willard (who had Tom Crean on staff (and who had Buzz Williams on his at Marquette). Capiche?

204. **A – New Hampshire**, the same school that produced NFL and college coaches Chip Kelly and
George O'Leary, baseball great Carlton Fisk, and
a kazillion NHL players. What I love most about
these Wildcats is their fish-tossin' tradition at
hockey games. After UNH scores its first goal,
alllllllll the fans drop what they're doing and turn
their heads toward the visiting team's net, then a
fish is thrown up and over the rink boards right
onto the ice. Take that, Mr. Visiting Team person!

205. **A – Balance Plus** created a broom that had
directional fabric, which made redirecting the stone
way too easy, and it slowed it down like it was
making love to some Barry White ballad.
Originally, curling brooms were made of corn
strands, kind of like your grandma's whiskbroom.
Then, there was hog's hair, and now directional
fabric. One pundit commented that it's akin to
hitting a golf ball 500 yards. After some teams got
their ice buckets whipped, there was a major
outcry from curling associations, especially the
Canadians who, and I quote, "... want a level
playing field and not an arms race with
technology." Guess it's back to grandma's
whiskbroom, eh?

206. **D – Memphis Grizzlies**. When that job
happened (in 2002), Hubie hadn't sat courtside
without a microphone in front of his face for 16
years and was pushin' 70 on his own biological
clock, but the boy took to Beale Street like a duck
to water and the Grizz' made the playoffs for the
first time in team history and he was named NBA
Coach of the Year. But a couple of years later, the

grind of pro ball and the attitude of the players wore him down and he hung up his polyester sport coat for good. And, just because this is what I do and this book is all about sports trivia, here's a Hubie Brown one: At Niagara University, Brown was a roommate/ teammate of Frank Layden, future Utah Jazz coach. Another? Ok – he was an assistant coach at Duke for four years. Still another? His first NBA gig was as an assistant with the Bucks when they had Kareem and Oscar Robertson and went down in the finals to the mighty Celtics.

207. **D – Merril Hoge**. You know, I've been seeing Hoge on ESPN for several years and kept scratching my head as to who he is and why he's there. It's certainly not for the fashion statement he makes with those short, fat ties. Hoge played college ball at Idaho State, so most of us never saw him on Saturday TV. Then, he was a Pittsburgh Steeler – picked in the 10th round and did a darn good job playing running back for seven seasons (34 TDs including 10 in one season) before moving on to the Bears for part of a year. The biggest thing that happened to Merril is a sad one. In the middle of a game between the Bears and the Chiefs, Hoge received a concussion and, then, only five days later, the Bears' doctor gave him the green light to resume playing in a freakin' phone call without examining him to see if he had actually recovered. Even though he still suffered post-concussion symptoms, the coach kept putting him in. He suffered a second concussion mere weeks later and stopped breathing. He spent two days in ICU and had to hang up the cleats because of the brain injury. He

had memory lapses, periods of confusion, and headaches galore – even had to learn how to read again. He sued the Bears' doctor and awarded a $1.5 mil judgment. He thought about trying to make a comeback, but his former doctor at the Steelers re-evaluated him, noted a "marked discrepancy," and told Hoge that he was risking permanent brain damage. That's all it took.

208. **B – Savoy Big Five**. Flashback to the Twenties when Abe Saperstein, age 24, organizes and coaches a new team called the "Savoy Big Five," named after famous Chicago's Savoy Ballroom. Saperstein then changed their name to the New York Harlem Globe Trotters. He picked Harlem as the team's home since many thought Harlem to be the center of African-American culture and he figured having an out-of-town team name might give the squad more of an aura. However, it took four decades before the Globetrotters actually played a game in their "hometown" of Harlem. Did you know that, in 2002 & 2003, the Globetrotters decided to put their silliness aside and play some college teams? Yeah, no buckets of confetti, no wild ball-handling, just straight-up basketball. They played (and lost) to Maryland, Vandy, and UTEP, but they did beat Michigan State (w/ guest player Magic Johnson), UMass, and defending national champ Syracuse.

209. **C – Southwestern Louisiana**. Yep, the year was 1973 and the Ragin' Cajuns became only the second school to receive the NCAA's "death penalty" thanks to racking up 120 violations ranging from cash, cars, and clothes to players; an assistant

THE GREATEST SPORTS TRIVIA THROWDOWN OF ALL-TIME

coach forging a principal's signature on a transcript; and surrogates taking ACT/SAT tests for recruits. The NCAA was so ticked off that they wanted to kick the school out of the NCAA for good, but the university was able to cut a deal by wiping out two whole seasons as their penance. The school blew it again in 2004 and 2005 because it allowed Florida transfer Orien Greene (Celtics, Pacers, Kings, Nets) to take correspondence courses from another institution – an NCAA no-no – which meant another two years of probation. As a spur of this question, what would be the answer if I asked for the school that's vacated and/or forfeited the most games over the years? Michigan, with 113 regular season and tournament wins and 4 tournament losses vacated covering six of eight seasons between 1992 and 1999. Syracuse next with 106, then Ohio State with 82.

210. **D – John Fairfax** was the first to cross any ocean – in this case, the Atlantic. Two years later, he became the first to cross the Pacific Ocean, albeit with Sylvia Cook alongside to help. Mister Fairfax wasn't shy about getting from point A to point Z. In 1959, he flew to the U.S. and drove from NYC to San Francisco (2,905 miles). Then, he ran out of money and figured he'd ask mommy for some. The only problem was that mom lived in Argentina. So, he found himself a bike and took off for South America. The bike got him as far as Guatemala, and from there, he hitchhiked to Panama where he hooked up with some pirates and ran guns, liquor, and cigs for a coupla years. He eventually got tired of that life and hopped on a horse and went on about his merry journey to Argentina.

It was there in Argentina that he read about fellow Brits Chay Blyth and John Ridgeway who, together, rowed across the North Atlantic in a 20 ft. open dory in a matter of 92 days. He figured that the cat was out of the bag about rowing across The Pond and it was only a matter of time before some fool would want to try it solo. So, he went back to England and worked on getting everything ready. It took him two years, but he made it. In the middle of winter, 1969, he set off from the Canary Islands and finally landed 180 days later on the Florida shore. Then, two years later, he and fellow rowboat'er Sylvia Cook took a year off their lives – literally – and rowed, rowed, rowed their boat from San Francisco to Australia in 363 days. That made them the first people to row across the Pacific, and Cook the first woman to row across an ocean. Years later, Tori Murden became the first *American* to row solo across the Atlantic (81 days). Tori's also the first woman and first American to ski to the geographic South Pole. My daddy told me he walked 10 miles to school – uphill in both directions. That counts for something, right?

211. **A – 5**. And a subsequent conversion kick scores 2 points. Maybe I'm a lazy American who likes his sports simple, but, IMO, rugby is too darn complicated. Proof? Ok, this: If a scrum is formed correctly there should be a space between the two teams and it is into this space that a scrum-half feeds the ball. The space is known as the "tunnel" and there is an opening on either side of the scrum. This allows the scrum-half to decide which side would be the most tactically advantageous. If the ball comes out of the other side of the tunnel, the

scrum has to start again. Sounds too much like childbirth to me. Wonder if they offer rugby players an epidural?

212. **A – Catfish Hunter** (or James Augustus Hunter to his family). It was baseball love at first sight for A's owner Charley Finley. Even though Hunter was hobbled by a hunting accident where he had lost a toe and still had shotgun pellets still in his foot, Finley signed the kid, sent him to the Mayo Clinic to get this foot fixed up, then had him stay at Finley's farm in Indiana so he could recuperate. When he was fully recovered, he skipped the minor leagues entirely and went straight to the majors and Kansas City where Finley gave Hunter a $3,000/yr. salary and the "Catfish" name because he thought the kid needed something flashy. Hunter made the All-Star team in his second and third season, and in his third season he became the first American League'r to pitch a perfect (regular season) game since 1922. He had four consecutive seasons with 20+ wins and four World Series without a loss. He died at age 53 from Lou Gehrig's disease.

213. **B – Dragons**. For the entire duration of the Dragons' history they had only one head coach, and that was Jack Bicknell. Jack had been the head coach at Boston College where he coached Doug Flutie in his Heisman Trophy year. Jon Kitna played for Barcelona. So did 1985 Outland Trophy winner Mike Ruth... the #4 overall pick in the '80 NFL Draft, Penn State defensive lineman Bruce Clark... former Notre Dame QB Tony Rice, who led the Fighting Irish to the 1998 national title... and former UConn linebacker Eric Naposki, who was

sentenced to life in prison for a murder-for-hire of a dude in California. It was a true "cold case," one that went unsolved for 15 years before they nabbed Naposki and a female accomplice. Disturbingly, Naposki continued to play for Barcelona for two years after doing the dirty deed.

214. **B – St. Louis Blues, Philadelphia Flyers, and Detroit Red Wings**. While the Red Wings had been in the NHL for, like, ever (previously as the Cougars and Falcons – just like Ford car models), the Blues and the Flyers were part of the NHL's largest expansion. It was 1967 when they came into the league with the Kings, Penguins, Minnesota North Stars (now in Dallas), and the California Seals (which merged with Minnesota in '78). The Blues entry into the NHL came fully equipped with drama. St. Louis was in a fight with Baltimore to land the last of the six expansion franchises and the only reason it got one is because there was an arena that was part and parcel of the franchise application. Even though Cardinals' great Stan Musial was part of a consortium applying for the franchise, the owners of the Blackhawks and Red Wings owned a white elephant of an arena in St. Louis they wanted to unload. They found a group of investors who didn't mind paying 3x what they had paid for the arena (and minus an adjoining 50 acres that were an original part of the real estate). So, with arena in hand and the Blackhawks and Red Wings owners with fatter wallets and Cheshire grins to match, that group was given the franchise over the more obvious, sports-centric group that included Musial.

THE GREATEST SPORTS TRIVIA THROWDOWN OF ALL-TIME

215. **D – Bill Sharman**. It's true that Alex Hannum did
with a championship with an ABA franchise (Oakland) and a couple of NBA titles (St. Louis and
Philly), but Sharman has a hat trick of titles – an ABA
one (Utah Stars), an NBA one (L.A. Lakers), and an
ABL one (Cleveland Pipers). Sharman, one of only
four people in the HOF as both a player (four rings
with the Celtics) and as a coach (Wooden, Wilkens,
and Heinsohn being the others), not to mention a
baseball player worthy of getting called up by the
Dodgers but never seeing any game action and,
also, holds the distinction of being the only player
ejected from a major league game without appearing in one. Howzat? Well, it came as a result of a
1951 game in which the entire Brooklyn bench was
ejected from the game for arguing with the umpire,
and Sharman just happened to be riding the bench.
Shifting to the ABL, now... What, pray tell, was the
ABL? It was the brainchild of Abe Saperstein, the
Globetrotters guru, as payback to the NBA for not
giving him a franchise after years of him having the
Globetrotters play warm-up games as precursors to
regular season NBA games. In the ABL, originally,
were teams in Chicago, Cleveland, Kansas City, Long
Beach, L.A., Oakland, Philadelphia, and Pittsburgh.
Saperstein brought some twists to the game that have
become commonplace – the 30-sec. shot clock, the 3-
point basket, and a wider free throw lane. Among
the cadre of ABL owners was one George Steinbrenner who had the Cleveland Pipers franchise. In a
sneaky move, Georgy boy signed All-American Jerry
Lucas to a contract worth $40,000 as part of a secret
deal with NBA commissioner Maurice Podoloff
whereby the Pipers would merge with the Kansas
City Steers and join the NBA. They even went as far

as printing up a schedule for the 1963-64 NBA season with the Pipers playing the NY Knicks in the first game. Steinbrenner and Podoloff's scheme worked, but the ABL sued to block the move, which left Steinbrenner with a team but no league. Instead of returning to the ABL on bended knee, Steinbrenner folded the team, took his $2 mil loss medicine like a big boy, put his ball in his backpack, and went home.

216. **C – Nancy Lieberman**. In November 2009, Nancy wan named the coach of the Texas Legends (the Mavs' affiliate) in the NBA's D-League. Later, she became the second female assistant coach in NBA history (after Becky Hammon of the Spurs) when she signed on with the Kings. One more superlative? Ok, she became the WNBA's oldest player in history when, at 39, she suited up for the Phoenix Mercury in their inaugural season.

217. **D – Discus**. Sadova was a serial enhancement drug'y and got busted three times and lost several titles... Kanter won discus Gold in the 2008 Olympics... Oerter was the first athlete to win a Gold medal in the same individual event in four consecutive Olympics.

218. **A. Clyde Lovellette** – the first (and one of only seven) to do that litany of excellent'ness in the question. At Kansas, he won a national title alongside teammate Dean Smith; at the Olympic level, he won Gold on a team coached by Warren Womble, the coach for the Peoria Caterpillars, a National Industrial Basketball League team based in Peoria, Illinois. (btw, Womble was 34-0 against international competition); and, at the pro level, he

won championships with the (Minneapolis) Lakers and the Celtics. Even though Clyde was selected in the first round of the NBA draft, he decided to play for the Phillips 66 Oilers, an AAU team that won 11 national championships of its own and, combined with Adolph Rupp's "Fabulous Five," formed the squad that won the 1948 Olympics.

219. **B – Sulky**. Why are they called "sulkies"? Because the driver would rather be alone... and sulk. Sigh.

220. **B – Lance Leipold**, coach of the Wisconsin-Whitewater Warhawks, who got to 100 wins in only 106 games. Yep, that's a record of 100-6, one that broke the previous mark of 108 games set by Gil Dobie in 1921. In that 8-year stretch, Sir Lance Winalot had five undefeated seasons and six Div. III titles with all of those victories being against Mount Union (the same school they also lost three titles to).

221. **C – B.J. Armstrong**, the little guy from Iowa that the Chicago Bulls selected as the 18th pick in the first round of the 1986 draft. Armstrong won three NBA title rings as a member of the Bulls but when he was picked numero uno by Toronto in the 1995 expansion draft, he refused to play for the Raptors and sat out the year. He eventually returned to Chicago to finish out his career and retire without pouting. He's now a sports agent and sits in his office counting the cash coming in as Derrick Rose's agent.

222. **D – Washington University in St. Louis** who snagged four titles in a row between 1998 and 2001, then another in 2010. Although some of you of never heard of Wash U, pay attention: besides the women's basketball titles, they've got 10 national titles in women's volleyball and two in men's basketball. They play in the UAA Conference, aka the "Egghead Eight," with NYU, University of Chicago, Emory, Case-Western, U. of Rochester, Carnegie Mellon, Brandeis (whose nickname is "The Judges"), all dem smart'y schools.

223. **A – Yale and "Boola Boola."** That's right, Okies – your school song's melody comes from one of them preppy schools out East! But, the Yale'ies version wasn't completely original, either. If you drill down further, "Boola Boola" was itself borrowed from an 1898 song called "La Hoola Boola" (by African-American singer-songwriters Bob Cole and Billy Johnson) whose lyrics talk about Boston girls who'll treat you nice if you have money and Philly girls who will call you "honey" irrespective of your net worth. So, if you're an OU fan, the lack of originality might sting a bit, but your own alum, Robert Alden, who's credited with crafting "Boomer Sooner," borrowed even more – he tagged on an ending taken from the University of North Carolina's "I'm a Tar Heel Born." What does that phrase "Boomer Sooner" mean anyway? It's about the Land Run of 1889, specifically the land around the modern university. A "boomer" was someone who campaigned for the lands to be opened to the general population before passage of the Indian Appropriations Act of 1889. And a "sooner" was a land thief who settled before the

lands were officially opened, which gave them an unjust benefit in finding, fencing, and claiming farm land.

224. **B – Oklahoma State**. Roll the video back to 2008 and a grad student @ OSU named Glen Elarbee who came up with the idea when coach Mike Gundy threw down the gauntlet to find a means of speeding up messaging between offensive coaches and players. What started out as PowerPoint printouts of different colors and random numbers and letters has blossomed into pictures of Jay-Z, Will Farrell, even Dr. Pepper and Pepsi logos at Cowboys games in an obvious way of pampering their sponsors. The trick, however, is deciphering which frames of the posters are "live" and which are "dead." Sometimes, they put up posters that are completely void of meaning, just to throw off the fool teams that are videotaping them.

225. **Any/all of the answers are correct** (sorry for the trickery). John Heisman was all that and several bags of chips – head football coach @ Oberlin, Auburn, Buchtel (now U. of Akron), Clemson (where he was also baseball coach), Georgia Tech (also basketball and baseball coach), Penn, Washington & Jefferson, and Rice; and player at both Brown and Penn. The longest he ever stayed at one place was 15 years at Georgia Tech where he amassed a football record of 102-29-7 and one national championship. Here's some odds-and-ends: Heisman's got streets named after him on both Clemson's and Auburn's campuses... he was one of the innovators of the "jump shift" and the QB hollerin' out "hike" to signal the center

to toss him the ball... the Downtown Athletic Club was near the World Trade Center and closed down after 9-11 It never reopened, and eventually went belly-up.

226. **D – 2-stroke penalty**. Didja know that (in stroke play) if the flagstick is in the hole, unattended, and your putt strikes it, that's a 2-stroke penalty? Or if you have too many clubs in your bag (more than 14), you get penalized 2 strokes for each hole on which the breach occurred, up to a max of 4 strokes? And, grounding your club in a bunker or water is a serious no-no as Dustin Johnson found out in the 2010 PGA Tourney. He grounded* his club in what was deemed to be a bunker which led to a 2-stroke penalty on the 18th hole and cost him a spot in the playoffs. *Grounding is allowing the golf club to touch the ball or the ground while the golfer is addressing the ball.

227. **A – Grambling State.** The origin of that infamous "G" dates back to 1961 when the Packers' Vince Lombardi asked his equipment folks to create a logo and they whipped up a "G" inside of football shape. Three years later, Vince Dooley, Georgia's coach, copied the idea, tweaked it a smidge, and got permission from Green Bay to use it. In '65, Grambling decided to join in the fun and also got Green Bay's okay to use it, but with a gnat hair's tweak of their own.

228. **D – Fred Akers**. The University of Texas isn't easy on their coaches, but Fred stuck around for nine years, thanks to incubating Earl Campbell to Heisman status, and going undefeated in two sea-

sons (only to lose their bowl games in those seasons). But, just like any Texas pigskin coach, if you a) don't beat Oklahoma and A&M; b) produce the school's worst W-L record in 30 years; and, c) lose four bowl games in a row, you are a goner!

229. **B – Al McGuire** (Marquette). The Marquette Warriors were 26-3 and ranked 8th in the U.S., but they spurned the NCAA for disrespecting them by putting them in the Ft. Worth regional rather than the Dayton one where they felt they belonged. They were, then, invited to the NIT, which they won. A year after the insult, the NCAA instituted a rule which forbid NCAA Division 1 men's basketball teams from rejecting an NCAA bid in favor of an NIT bid. The NIT filed an antitrust case over the issue, and the NCAA backed down and settled out of court. McGuire's move was pride-driven, but maybe going to the NIT was smart since the '70 NCAA tourney was anything cakewalk. You had Wooden and UCLA with Wicks, Rowe, and Bibby; Jacksonville with Artis Gilmore; Bob Lanier at St. Bonaventure; Villanova with Chris Ford; and Notre Dame with Austin Carr who set an NCAA record with a 61-point game against Ohio U. and averaged 52.7 points in the tournament. Nonetheless, McGuire's Marquette team got to cut down the nets in '77 when they beat UNC's Tar Heels. You need something further back on McGuire? Maybe this'll suffice: McGuire played ball for St. John's, the Bullets, and the Knicks (as did both his dad and uncle) where he once legendarily pleaded with his coach for playing time by making this guarantee: "I can stop Cousy." So,

the coach put him in and McGuire proceeded to foul Cousy on his next six trips down the floor.

230. **A – Chad Pennington** and, yes, others have pegged perfection in a loss, but none who played from start to finish. Perfect passer ratings (PPR) were created in 1971 (for little to no reason that we can find) and are dang complicated. A perfect rating is the odd number of 158.3 and based on the % of completions per attempt, the average yards gained per attempt, the % of touchdown passes per attempt and the % of interceptions per attempt. To qualify, a quarterback has to attempt a minimum of 10 passes, have zero interceptions, and have minimums of a 77.5% completion percentage, 11.875% touchdown passes percentage, and 12.5 yards per attempt. There's several QBs who scored perfect <u>and</u> zero ratings in their careers, like Johnny Unitas, Joe Namath, Terry Bradshaw, Len Dawson, Bob Griese, James Harris, Bob Lee, Craig Morton, Dan Fouts, Eli Manning, and Peyton Manning. If you go back far enough – to 1948 – you'll find that the Chicago Cardinals' Ray Malouf was the first quarterback in NFL history to achieve a perfect passer rating in a game. More firsts? Drew Bledsoe was the first rookie to get a PPR... Ben Roethlisberger was the first QB with multiple perfect ratings in a single regular season (2007)... and Peyton Manning was the first to gain four PPRs.

231. **D – Notre Dame, Bowling Green, Utah, Florida**. I don't think I have to wax poetically about Urban's coaching career, but I can spin a few trivial bits about his career. Here goes... Urban

Frank Miller III (born July 10, 1964) whose first love was baseball and was actually selected at age 17 by the Braves in the 13th round of the 1982 MLB draft where he played two seasons of summer league ball. Had he not thrown his arm out, he might have never thrown the dice as a walk-on at the University of Cincinnati where he mostly held the ball for FGs and extra points. Later, as a college football coach, he paid his dues – 15 years as an assistant (including six @ Colorado State, five under Lou Holtz and Bob Davie @ Notre Dame, and two under Earle Bruce @ Ohio State) and he also gave a lot of assistants a chances to grow into head coaches including Charlie Strong @ Louisville and Texas, Steve Addazio @ Boston College, Tim Beckman @ Illinois, Dan Mullen @ Mississippi State, Tom Herman @ Houston, et al.

232.   **D – Eagles**, followed by (in order of popularity) Tigers, Bulldogs, Panthers, Wildcats, Warriors, and the Lions. Not sure who was the first team to have the Eagles as their team name, but the Philadelphia Eagles' origin goes back to 1933 when Bert Bell and Lud Wray purchased the bankrupt Frankford Yellow Jackets. The new owners renamed the team the Eagles in honor of the symbol of the National Recovery Act, which was part of President Franklin D. Roosevelt's "New Deal." More? Okay... Broadcast exec George Richards bought the Portsmouth Spartans in 1934 and moved their helmets and pads to Detroit and renamed them the Lions, a nickname most likely derived from Detroit's baseball team, the Tigers, who won 101 games and the AL pennant that year. As George explained it, "The lion is the monarch of the jungle,

and we hope to be the monarch of the league."
And one last piece of useless trivia for you *Star
Wars* fans: there *is* a school that has the
"Millennium Falcons" as their nickname. It's
Millennium High School in Piedmont, California.

233. **C – Kareem left unprotected in the draft**.
GM Jerry West was pretty crafty with the dangling
o that carrot and defensively traded a draft pick to
both the Heat and Hornets with the assurance that
neither would select Kareem, who was entering his
20th and final season.

234. **A – Gary Payton**, who got the moniker when his
cuz called him up during the 1993 Western Conference Finals series against the Suns and told him,
"You're holding Kevin Johnson like a baseball in a
glove." Payton was a true badass, raking in the
third-most technical fouls of all time (behind Jerry
Sloan and Rasheed Wallace) and, alongside Michael Jordan, the only guard to have won the NBA
Defensive Player of the Year award (since 1988).

235. **B –22** (15 unmarked red, six colored balls, and a
white cue ball). I would imagine most of us are
unwashed when it comes to the differences are
between billiards, snooker, and pool and they're
far more that I had imagined so I'll save a tree and
just give you two: 1) a billiard cue is shorter than a
snooker or pool cue; 2) billiard balls are a bit
larger than both American-style pool balls and
snooker balls – 2 11/16" vs. 2 1/4" vs. 2 1/15".

236. **D – Conference USA**. The central idea behind C-
USA's creation in 1995 was to create a conference

that featured football by merging the basketball-centric Metro and Great Midwest conferences. Short of Southern Miss and UAB, the current C-USA has little resemblance to the original one with 14+ defections. The most interesting twist as to who's in C-USA comes in men's soccer where Kentucky, South Carolina, and New Mexico are in as "affiliate members." Uh, are they afraid of playing their regular SEC or Mountain West peers?

237. **A – Frank Gifford** with 14 TDs thrown, then Walter Payton with 8, Tomlinson with 7, Marcus Allen (and a bunch of others) with 6. Back in the day, there were lots of both-sides-of-the-ball guys and Giff played defensive back, running back, and flanker (what we call a wide receiver, now). Why did Frank throw so many touchdowns? Because he was a master of the option pass from his halfback slot. There, he completed 29 of the 63 passes he threw for 823 yards and 14 TDs. In his first couple of years with the Giants, most of Gifford's action was on the defensive side of the ball and, despite his prowess making him a Pro Bowl'er, he wasn't real thrilled with the position. His big offensive break came in year three when the Giants hired a young offensive assistant named Vince Lombardi who made Gifford the starting halfback, where he racked up 5.6 yards per carry, and became the first player to move from defense to offense in the Pro Bowl in consecutive years. In 1960, in a game against the Philadelphia Eagles, he was knocked out by Chuck Bednarik on a passing play, and suffered a head injury so severe it led him to retire from football for 18 months. Upon his death, that blow to the head increased the focus on

concussions when an autopsy revealed that Frank had Chronic Traumatic Encephalopathy (CTE), a disease closely related to repeated head trauma.

238. **C – Squash balls**, weighing 23 to 25 grams. Racquetballs weigh 40 grams; tennis balls weight 56 to 59.4 grams; and golf balls weigh 45.93 grams. The *lightest* ball is a table tennis ball, weighing 2.7 grams. The *heaviest* ball? A bowling ball, weighing 7.26 kg. If you want to argue that a shot put is a "ball," you can, but it weighs the same as a bowling ball, so there!

239. **C – Walter Hagen**, who won the British Open four times, the PGA Championship a record-tying five times, and an overall 11 major championships, putting him third behind Jack Nicklaus (18) and Tiger Woods (14). Hagen also impacted the game of golf in the respect the game's professionals were due. Odd as it may seem, amateurs had the upper hand over pros in golf in the early 1900s. For example, pros weren't allowed to go into a clubhouse through the front door or even use the clubhouse facilities. So, Hagen decided to get in their face a bit. On one occasion at the British Open, he rented an expensive Pierce-Arrow car to be his personal dressing room. He hired a chauffeur, parked the car in the clubhouse's driveway, and changed clothes there.

240. **D – Chuck Wepner**. Chuck went toe-to-toe with Ali in '75, a bout where he floored Ali in the 9th, but wound up losing a TKO in the 15th. The fight later precipitated a lawsuit against Sylvester Stallone because Wepner heard that Stallone wrote the

script for *Rocky* after seeing the fight, using Wepner as the inspiration. Like most all lawsuits, they settled on the courthouse steps. I reckon Wepner thought he could get away with just about anything, because in 2002, he was nabbed by the FBI for his part in a counterfeit scheme that included him forging Muhammad Ali autographs on a variety of Ali merchandise.

241. **B – Kim Mulkey**, who won an NCAA crown as a player and as an assistant at Louisiana Tech, then as a head coach at Baylor. On the male side of the balance sheet, there are three who have won an NCAA title as a player and coach (Joe B. Hall, Dean Smith, and Bobby Knight), but no men who have the same hat trick that Kim has. In 2012, Mulkey made NCAA history by leading Baylor's Lady Bears to the most wins in the annals of college basketball, men or women with a perfect 40-0 season, one capped by the national championship.

242. **B – Tony Hinkle**. Let me tell 'ya, Tony was a coach for all seasons. Over the course of his tenure at Butler, he was head football coach, head basketball coach, and head baseball coach. He was a stud of a player, too – twice All-Big Ten and twice All-American on a University of Chicago team that was the runner-up to Penn in the 1920 national championship. And, yes, Tony's the "Hinkle" in Hinkle Fieldhouse where they filmed *Hoosiers*. The fieldhouse was the largest basketball arena in the USA (9,100 seats) when it was built in 1927 and retained that distinction until 1950 when Williams Arena at the University of Minnesota opened its doors to 14,625 seats. Hinkle is the fifth-oldest

college basketball arena still in use behind Rose
Hill Gym @ Fordham, The Palestra, Hec
Edmundson Pavilion at the Univ. of Washington,
and Williams Arena @ Minnesota.

243. **D – Fritz Pollard**. As a collegiate, Pollard played
ball at Brown. He was on their Rose Bowl team in
1916 and also the first black running back to be
named an All-American. After Brown, he (along
with Bobby Marshall) became one of the first two
African-American players in the NFL when he
joined the Akron Pros, a team he would lead to the
1920 NFL championship. The next year, he was
named co-head coach of the Pros but they wouldn't
let him hang up his cleats so he pulled double-duty.
After a stint with the Hammond Pros, Pollard re-
joined the Akron team, but they cut him because he
"failed to play up to the form expected of him."
Historians think that was probably a lie. Their rea-
soning? Well, Red Grange's wannabe AFL had
folded after a single season which made available
a glut of white players eager to sign on with the
NFL, making black players expendable. The NFL
went from five black players in 1926 to just one in
1927. By 1934, no black players were signed to
NFL contracts. All that didn't bother Fritz much –
he created and coached a black-only football team
that played all-white teams around the country.
Much like the showboating the Harlem Globetrotters would employ later, Fritz' players would dance
and sing spirituals during games.

244. **D – Los Angeles Memorial Coliseum** was the
site for the Packers vs. Chiefs championship game.
And it was fitting that the Chiefs were in the match

since it was their owner, Lamar Hunt, who first used the term "Super Bowl." In a July '66 letter to NFL commissioner Rozelle, Hunt wrote, "I have kiddingly called it the 'Super Bowl,' which obviously can be improved upon." Hunt's co-owners agreed and decided to use "AFL-NFL Championship Game," but the media liked Hunt's "Super Bowl" name from the get-go and beginning with the third annual game, that became the official moniker.

245. **A – Sam Snead**. But, like they say, no good idea goes unpunished, so the USGA banned Sam's technique. Being the creative guy that he was, Sam then went to putting "side-saddle," where he would crouch and angle his feet towards the hole. Must've worked – he won three PGA Senior Championships using that method.

246. **A – John Isner & Nicolas Mahut**. Naturally, because of the time it took, both players broke several Wimbledon and tennis records, including each serving more than 100 aces. Heck, the final set alone was longer than the previous longest match recorded. I don't know if there's tennis "Viagra," but Isner can go for hours on end (without calling his doctor). He also played the then 10th longest singles match, a 5-hour 41-minute battle in the second round of the 2012 French Open.

247. **D – Warren Moon**. Moon was born to QB, but the sports world wasn't going to make it easy for him. Despite being All-City in L.A. as a high school quarterback, many of the colleges recruiting him wanted him to switch positions because black play-callers just weren't part of the norm in those days.

So, he headed off to West L.A. College and rocked the record books in his first year. After seeing what he could do, a few major schools came knockin' and he picked the U. of Washington thanks to their guarantee that they wouldn't switch him to another position. He went 11-11 his soph and junior year, but led the Huskies to a Rose Bowl victory-and-MVP season as a senior. Still, despite his success, not a single team called his name in the NFL draft, so he went north to Edmonton where he led the team to five straight Gray Cups and became the first pro QB to pass for 5,000 yards in a season. After showing Canada what he could do, he thought he'd try the NFL one more time and picked the Oilers where he marched them to their first winning season in seven years. Before the '89 season kicked off, Moon scored a five-year, $10-million contract extension, making him the highest-paid player in the league. After a division-winning season in '93, Warren was traded to the Vikings where he passed for over 4,200 yards. But, as it is with most football players, the body starts to slow down, the halo's glow starts to fade, and there's always a young buck climbing the ladder right behind you. And that went down in Minnesota for Moon when they asked him to take a $3.8 mil pay-cut and carry the clipboard for Brad Johnson. Warren refused, got released from the team, moved over to Seattle as a first-stringer, then the Chiefs as a backup. Moon's NFL numbers are unrivaled: 3,988 completions for 49,325 yards, 291 touchdown passes, 1,736 yards rushing, and 22 rushing touchdown – and if you add in his CFL stats, the numbers go up another 50%. Add to that individual NFL lifetime records for most fumbles recovered (56) and (at the time of his retirement) Top 5 all-time for passing yards, passing TDs, pass attempts, and pass completions. His only smear was most fumbles made (161), but that was only temporary because Brett Favre decided to play beyond his usefulness and he's now the all-time fumbler (166).

248. **D – Warren Spahn**. Most people don't know how Spahn's career started, but he was called up by the Boston Braves in 1942 at the age of 20. He clashed with Braves manager Casey Stengel, who sent him back to the minors after Spahn refused to throw a brush-back pitch at Dodger batter Pee Wee Reese in an exhibition game. But he eventually made it back up to the majors and that's when the real fireworks started. Spahn won 363 games, more than any other left-handed pitcher in history, and more than any other pitcher who played his entire career in the post-1920 live-ball era. He's the 6th most winning pitcher in history, trailing only Cy Young (511), Walter Johnson (417), Grover Cleveland Alexander (373), Christy Mathewson (373), and Pud Galvin (364). You want more? He threw two no-hitters... won four ERA titles... he holds the NL's record for home runs by a pitcher (35), hitting a round-tripper in 17 consecutive seasons... and he appeared in 14 All-Star games, the most of any pitcher in the 20th century. And if you're an oldster, this should make you feel good: Warren led or shared the lead in the NL in wins from age 36-40 and he even had a 23-7 record at age 42.

249. **C – Boston Marathon**, which dates back to 1897 where 18 runners ran the race, and is one of

only two major sports events that were held during both WW1 & WW2 (the Kentucky Derby being the other). The 1996/centennial race set a record as the world's largest marathon with 38,708 entrants.

250. **A – Dead ball, neutral zone established, or crowd noise.** Really. Guess you have to go over to ~~Mr.~~ Zebra and ask ~~him~~ which one ~~he~~ meant. By the way, if ~~he~~ does the same gesture but with a closed fist, it means "fourth down." 'Ya know, I shouldn't have referred to refs as a "he" since Sarah Thomas ref'ed college football starting in 2007, then became the NFL's first full-time female official in 2015 (line judge – #53). You go, Sarah!

251. B – Because he wore a fedora that looked like the one Warren Beatty wore in *Bonnie & Clyde*. Puma honored Walt's passion for fashion by making him the first NBA player to have a shoe named after him – the "Clyde." The first version of the shoe was outfitted in blue suede (to match Clyde's Knicks uni), and the kicks got a nice little cultural kiss thanks to the Beastie Boys and other hip-hop'ers wearing 'em and giving them shout-outs in their songs. By the way, Puma and Adidas were born out of a rift over Nazi loyalties between two brothers, Rudolf and Adolf Dassler. Puma was originally called "Ruda" (after Rudolf) and Adidas got its name from "Adi" (Adolf's nickname) and "das" (the first part of "Dassler").

252. **D – Gallant Fox**, the second winner of the Triple Crown and the first to bestowed with the moniker "Triple Crown." When Sir Barton won all three races in 1919 (Kentucky Derby, Preakness, and

Belmont), those three races were just, well, three races! But starting around 1923, journalists would sometimes refer to the triad as "Triple Crown." It wasn't until Gallant Fox did the deed in 1930 that the phrase found its way into popular use when Charles Hatton of the *Daily Racing Form* started using it with regularity.

253. **A – short track**. In 2016, the speedway was host to college football's largest ever crowd thanks to what was dubbed as "The Battle at Bristol" between Virginia Tech and Tennessee (UT won 45-24). All told, an official count of 156,990 were on-hand, surpassing the NCAA record for highest single-game attendance of 115,109 that happened in 1913 in a game between Michigan and Notre Dame. Why Bristol? Well, one, the track does have the room and, two, it's on the Virginia/Tennessee state line, which places the game about 125 miles from the Virginia Tech campus in Blacksburg and about 110 miles from the UT campus in Knoxville.

254. **C – Steve DeBerg**, who was never in the right place at the right time. He was with the Niners when Montana got drafted, then he was with the Broncos when John Elway was drafted, and with the Tampa Bay Buccaneers when both Steve Young and Vinny Testaverde were drafted. Despite those ouchies, he can still say he a) led the NFL in completions (1979); b) set the NFL single-season record for lowest interception percentage (1990); c) played on an NFC champion (1998 with the Falcons); d) became the oldest QB to ever start an NFL game (when he led the Falcons against the Jets); and, e) became the oldest player ever

included on a Super Bowl roster (at age 45 years, 12 days, when the Falcons appeared in Super Bowl XXXIII, though he did not play in the game).

255. **D – Lon Simmons**. Fogerty grew up on the West Coast at a time there were no major league teams, so he drew his inspiration from center field at Yankee Stadium since the Yankees were the closest thing the Bay Area had thanks to San Francisco native Joe DiMaggio. Once the A's and Giants made it west, Simmons' sportscasting gave Fogerty all the inspiration he needed as Simmons did either Giants or A's games for 35+ years, not to mention 25+ seasons with the football 49ers (with Bob Fouts, Dan Fouts' dad, as his co-anchor).

256. **A – John Salley**. Robert Horry is the only other player (as of 2016) who's won a championship with three different squads, and Tim Duncan is the only other player who's won a championship in three different decades. We can drill down a little further if you like: Frank Saul (Rochester Royals & Minneapolis Lakers) and Steve Kerr (Bulls & Spurs) are the only players to win two championships with two different teams in consecutive seasons.

257. **A – Pete Gogolak**, whose contribution to football wasn't only pioneering the soccer-style kick, but he was a key participant in the merger of the AFL and the NFL. Say what? Yep, it happened when he was with the Bills. He was making about $10k/yr. and, rather than sign a new contract for more, he opted to take a little less and play out his options (a la what's become to be known as "unrestricted free agency"), which meant that the

Bills had to meet any other team's offer. That's when things got screwy. At the time, the NFL owners had a gentleman's agreement that they wouldn't poach players from another league, basically to keep salaries down and prevent any inter-league squabbling over good players. However, the NY Giants said to heck with that agreement and plucked Pete from Buffalo and plopped him down in the Bronx. Shortly thereafter, Al Davis of the AFL Raiders started working his poaching magic and the competition for good players became expensive and started to get out of control, which greatly contributed to the two leagues' owners agreeing to merge. Gogolak wasn't only the Giants leading scorer with 646 points, but has the team's franchise records for most points after touchdowns attempted (277) and made (268). League-wide, he has the records for the most PATs in a game (eight vs. Philadelphia on 11/26/72), most consecutive PATs (133), and most field goals attempted (219) and made (126).

258. **C – Former Red Sox owners Tom & Jean Yawkey**, and their initials are written in Morse Code, just to make the recognition a little more difficult to interpret. Tom Yawkey (at the time of his death) was the sole owner of the Red Sox (for 44 seasons, longer than anyone else in baseball history), and how he got there is a neat story. His dad had a deal in place to buy the Detroit Tigers in 1903 but died before they got to the closing table, so Tom's uncle stepped in and bought the team, held it for a few years, sold it, and left his estate to Tom. Unfortunately, little Tom was only four at the time and the will stipulated that Tom couldn't touch

the money until he was 30. Four days after his 30th birthday, Yawkey got a poke from his buddy Eddie Collins (A's and White Sox) about the Red Sox being up for grabs. He wasted no time in buying the team for $1.2 million and holding onto it until the day he died where it went on to his wife, Jean, until she died. At that point, their estate sold the team for $700 mil. Nice return on investment, eh? Oh – and Eddie Collins? Tom thanked him for tipping him off about the team being for sale by making him GM of the Red Sox.

259. **A – Chris Evert** was one of the top three money winners in two different sports. Am I serious? Yes, Chris Evert, the female tennis player, and Chris Evert, the horse! Chris the horse was owned by Carl Rosen, a guy who made sportswear for the budding tennis superstar Chris Evert. The horse did well – 10 Wins, two Places, and two Shows out of 15 starts, plus the filly Triple Crown in1974, a year where she beat out Secretariat and Foolish Pleasure as the top money winner in thoroughbred racing. She and Secretariat got it on later in life, too, when the two got all lovey and produced a filly named "Six Crowns" (what you get when you put two Triple Crown winners in the same sugar sack). Six Crowns, in turn, was bred to Danzig to produce Chief's Crown, who won $2 million and the 2-year-old title in 1984. Chris, the tennis player's, love life? Three-time loser.

260. **A – Frank Selvy**, who notched 100 points in a game against Newberry College, February 13, 1954. In a way, it was sort of a gimme 'coz the school was having "Frank Selvy Night" to

celebrate Frank leading the nation in scoring and being named an All-American, so the coach told the team to get him the ball as often as they could. And, boy, did they! He drilled 41 of 66 field goals – his last two points coming on a desperate heave near midcourt at the buzzer – and 18 of 22 free throws. Selvy went to become the #1 pick in the NBA draft by the Baltimore Bullets, but spent his better years as a Laker alongside Jerry West and Elgin Baylor. Btw, this question has a couple of catches to it: 1) There was one other Division 1 player who scored more than 100 points in a game. That was Paul Arizin (Villanova) but he scored those points against a junior college so the NCAA doesn't count them. 2) There's also Div II and Div III players who went over the century mark. Bevo Francis of Rio Grande went for 116 against Ashland Jr. College (the NCAA discredited those, too); then, there's Grinnell's Jack Taylor who lit up the scoreboard for 138 in a Div III game.

261. **D – Margarita Bowl**. Quick Lane's played at Ford Field in Detroit, the Cure Bowl in Orlando, and the Boca Raton Bowl in, duh... Who's been to more bowl games than anyone else? Alabama, which has 63 to their credit (as of 2016), followed by Texas, Nebraska, and USC who are all 10 or 11 bowl bids behind, so I think the Crimson Tide's record is safe for a good long while.

262. **B – Old Links of Musselburgh would** be the oldest golf course in the world, not to mention the oldest on which play has been continuous all the way back to 1672. It could even go back another hundred years if someone could prove the rumor

true that Mary Queen of Scots played there in 1567. The course started out with only seven holes but, by its 200th anniversary, had gotten up to nine. Outside of its historical value, the course's lone legacy is to golf's rules. The 4.25" diameter of a golf hole was the same width of the implement used to cut the holes at Musselburgh.

263. **B – Connie Hawkins**, the recipient of some bad mojo. He grows up in Bed-Stuy, averages 25+ PPG in high school, and takes Iowa up on their scholarship offer. While a Hawkeye freshman, there was a point-shaving scandal that broke out in NYC, and while he wasn't officially implicated, he had borrowed (and his bro repaid) $200 from the central figure in the scandal. As a result of the investigation, Iowa sent Connie packing and no one – not even an NAIA school – would touch him and the teams in the NBA draft ran as far away from him as they could. Enter the ABL (American Basketball League). He did a year there, made the league's MVP, then went Harlem Globe'trotting. While he was spinning balls on his fingertips, he decided to file a $6 mil lawsuit against the NBA for unfairly banning him without substantial evidence. While he was waiting for a gavel in his favor, he went to the ABA and the Pitt Pipers where he, once again, won the league's MVP title. After that, the NBA decided he might have a real gripe, paid him $1.3 mil, and assigned his rights to the Suns. In Phoenix, he averaged 24.6 PPG in year one, then 21 PPG, then 16 PPG, then off to Atlanta. Still, the ABA named him to their "All-Time" team, the Suns retired his number, and he's in the HOF. Those of you who survived the Seventies might remember

Connie on *SNL* when he played Paul Simon in a 1-on-1 game played to the tune of "Me & Julio Down by the Schoolyard" – with Hawkins taking a beatdown at the expense of 5'3" Simon.

264. **C – Boston College**. You know Henry Hill and Jimmy Burke (aka Jimmy the Gent) if you ever saw the movie *Goodfellas*, which documented Hill's life as a member of the Lucchese family. The BC Eagles' center, Rick Kuhn, was the first touch point in the scam. He worked with the mobsters to pick the games where he could influence the outcome and make sure that BC came up short. And for a bad night's work, he would get $2,500. Kuhn (purportedly) brought in teammate – and team captain – Jim Sweeney (more on him later), and they decided to test out the scheme in a game against Providence. Unfortunately, when you don't have everyone on-board, things can go screwy, and they did, with BC winning by 18. They did a reset and got things right the next few games, but decided to mix things up a bit with various overs/unders/pushes to keep them off the radar. Still, there were only two BC players in on the plan and they could only control part of their team's action and none of the opposing team's production. Things started to unravel little by little, Boston College went 22-9, and the goodfellas threw in the towel. Everyone was cool for a couple of years until Hill got arrested on drug trafficking charges and sang like a bird to avoid jail time and having his head bashed in by the Luccheses. A grand jury indicted Kuhn (along with the others) and put him away for 10 years (reduced to 28 months). And Sweeney? Never charged or offered

immunity. In fact, he was so squeaky clean that he won the Frances Pomeroy Naismith Award as the top collegiate basketball player under 6'0" tall.

265. **A – Notre Dame with Knute Rockne** (#1 with .881 winning %) and Frank Leahy (#2 with a winning % of .864). Some quick trivial shots since I'm trying to cover two well-respected coaches' lives in one sitting. First, Knute: 1) Rockne was born in Norway as Knut Rokne; 2) He played football @ Notre Dame as an end and was in the first game where a "forward pass" was used throughout the game; 3) He was on the receiving end of the famous "win one for the Gipper" line when one of his players, George Gipp, was on his death bed suffering from pneumonia; 4) Studebaker developed and sold a car called "The Rockne" from 1931-33; 5) He posted 105 victories, 12 losses, 5 ties and 3 national championships, including 5 undefeated seasons; 6) He died in an airplane crash in Kansas while on his way to film part of the movie *The Spirit of Notre Dame*. Now, Leahy's turn: 1) Frank was the original author of the quote, "When the going gets tough, let the tough get going;" 2) While @ Notre Dame, he produced four Heisman winners (Bertelli, Lujack, Hart, Lattner) and recruited another (Hornung); 3) He had seven undefeated seasons – one at Boston College and six at Notre Dame, four national championship teams, and an unbeaten string of 39 games (37-0-2) in the late 1940s; 5) When he was an assistant at Fordham, one of the guards he mentored was a kid named Vince Lombardi; 6) He was the first GM of the NFL Chargers and, supposedly, picked the team name after going to a

Dodger's game and hearing fans yell "Charge!"
after the notorious bugle call.

266. **D – The Case for the 12-foot Basket**. It came
on the heels of BIG men popping up like daisies in
U.S. basketball. The argument that coaches and
rulemakers were trying to get across was that there
wasn't much left to try to slow down the impact of
the tall timber. They had put a time limit on hangin'
around in the foul lane (1936), eliminated the
center jump after every basket (1937), outlawed
goal-tending (1944), widened the foul lane
(1956), and even banned dunking [damn them]
(1966). The coaches in favor of the 12' idea were
convinced the big guys would (quoting from the *SI*
article) "have to learn the real skills of the game –
shooting, dribbling, passing and defense. More
important, it would bring the talented little man
back to a position of relative value on a par with
his skills. Fewer of his shots would be blocked
because he would be shooting with a higher arc to
reach the goal. He would have a better chance at
rebounds because many of them would bounce
farther away from the rim. Given time to adjust to
the new height, today's good shooters would still
be superior to the others – and the little men are
often the best on the team." In an effort to cut out
any unresearched bias, *Sports Illustrated* got Ray
Mears, then coach at Tennessee, to test out the 12'
basket in his annual Orange-White inter-squad
game. Mears split the teams as height-equal as
possible with 7' Tom Boerwinkle on one team and
the next tallest guy, 6'10" Bobby Croft on the
other. Everyone got 40 minutes to practice on the
higher rims, but that's all and it showed. Both

teams missed their first 10 or so shots and Boerwinkle was having a b**ch of a time. Normally, when a shot rims off a 10' basket, the taller boys have good access, but when they rim off a 12' basket, the carom goes further out or takes longer to come down, giving more players a chance at grabbing the rebound. Boerwinkle didn't swat away one single shot, didn't score a tip-in, and got only one of his 16 shots in the bucket. Not your typical big man performance. On the converse, just like *SI* predicted, the little guys liked the higher rim because it favored jump shots from 15'-25' and, since big guys couldn't lay it in as easily as they could at 10', the ball wound up in the guards' hands more often. The bottom line? Finesse and agility beat out height in the test, but that's as far as the concept got. Seems like we all have a jones for a good poster'ized, windmill dunk over finessed two-hand set shots.

267. **B – Gorodki**. Now, I have to admit, the game sounds like some pee'd-off Duke fan throwing beer bottles at the TV while the Blue Devils are losing their wheels against the Tar Heels, but it ain't. What happens is that wooden dowels are lined up in a variety of shapes – like an arrow, fork, star, lobster, crankshaft, etc. – and dudes come up to "bat," like baseball and throw a bat at the dowel sets. I know... dumb, right?

268. **B – "El Pato,"** or for the Hispanically unwashed, "The Duck." Cabrera was the first Argentine to win The Masters or the U.S. Open.

269. **A – Rocky Marciano**, who went 49-0. Rocky was a man's man back in the day when there really were men's men. Dig this: As a youngster, he made his own weight equipment, including stuffing a mailbag with clothes to make it a heavy bag... he worked as a ditch digger, a chute man on a coal truck, a railroad layer, and a shoemaker... he served in WWII, ferrying supplies across the English Channel to Normandy... even played three weeks in the Chicago Cubs farm system. And he carried that yeoman's work ethic into the ring where he defended his title six times, had a knockout percentage of 87.75%, and beat Joe Louis in Louis' very last time in the ring – a bout where Rocky was a 13-10 underdog. In 1969, right before he died, Marciano and Ali went at it. Well, not exactly. In *The Superfight: Marciano vs. Ali*, they were filmed sparring, then the film edited to line up with a computer simulation of an imaginary fight between them when they were in their prime. One version had Marciano winning and another version had Ali winning. When someone asked Ali his opinion of the result, in typical Ali fashion, he rejected the results as racist, quipping, "That computer must've been made in Mississippi." It's on YouTube if you wanna see it...

270. **D – High Jumping**. Dick Fosbury would be the person behind the Flop. Back in the day, all the high jumpers were taught the "straddle" method – the one where you went over the high jump bar facing down, and lift your legs individually over the bar. Fosbury saw a crease in the rules, which dictates that as long as the jumper jumps off one foot at take-off and gets over the bar, it doesn't

matter *how* they do it. One experiment lead to another until he found the sweet spot in sprinting diagonally towards the bar, then curving and leaping backwards over the bar, which gave him a much lower center of mass in flight than the other techniques jumpers were using. Dick's coming-out party, so to speak, was the '68 Olympics in Mexico City where he won Gold and broke all U.S. records. By the time the next Olympics rolled around, 28 of the 40 high-jumpin' entrants were floppin' like Fosbury, and still are today.

271.   **A – Penn**. It came in '79 and the Quakers shot through Iona, UNC, Syracuse, and St. John's until they got to the Final Four where they had to face Magic Johnson and Michigan State. And, like most unforeseen rocket rides, Penn's coach – Bob Weinhauer – got a better job out of the team's success, landing the head coaching gig at Arizona State where his rocket eventually fizzled out. What ASU should've done was hire Chuck Daly (yeah, the Pistons guy) because *he* was the previous coach who recruited all the players that Weinhauer won with!

272.   **B – Byron Nelson**. Year? 1945. Byron was a house on fire – a stroke average of 67.86 during his 11-win streak – a stroke average that only Tiger's bettered (67.79). Nelson and Woods are also linked when it comes to consecutive cut streaks. Tiger's ran up 142 and Byron 113. Nelson quit the game at the age of 34 because he had made enough money to buy a ranch and that's all he needed. But his legend lived on – a legend so great that the PGA created the Byron Nelson Championship, the first tournament to be named

after a golfer, and *Golf Digest* named him the 5th greatest golfer of all-time (behind Nicklaus, Hogan, Snead, and Bobby Jones).

273. **C – Deion Sanders**. It happened during the 1989 season when Neon Deion was doin' double-duty for the Yankees and the Falcons. Later, when he moved to the Braves, he became the only person to ever play in both the World Series and the Super Bowl, too.

274. **D – Western Oregon**. You don't think you know anything about the Western Oregon Wolves, but I'm bettin' you do. Remember that ESPY for "Best Moment" of 2008 where the girl softball player injured her knee rounding first after she smacked a home run and two girls from the opposing team carried her around the rest of the bases to home plate? Well, the homer hitter was with Western Oregon. Now you know...

275. **B – Brown Stockings**. We sure have had a lot of teams named after socks, haven't we? The National Association was, debatably, the first professional baseball league at a time when baseball was loaded with sock'age: *three* Red Stockings (Boston, St. Louis, and Cincy), *two* White Stockings (Chicago and Philly), the Mutual Green Stockings, etc., but it wasn't the ugly sock color that did St. Louis in – it was game-fixing. However, the remains of the team were clever and they found a super fan in Chris Van der Ahe. Chris owned a grocery/ saloon and was able to buy out the assets of the Brown Stockings for $1,800. He, then, hired future White Sox owner Charles Comiskey to play

first and manage the team. Van der Ahe was like the first Bill Veeck and started selling tickets for a quarter, figuring the Germans in St. Louie would drop even more on beer and something called a "hot dog." And, they did. So much, in fact, that he made a half-mil on the team and had to expand the stadium to hold all the imbibers. But, as egos go, his eccentricity got the best of him and after he built a bigger ballpark, he tacked on an amusement park with a horse track, beer garden, and a lake. Well, that was a dumb idea, and he had to start selling off his players. One by one, Ahe lost money until he lost the team and was reduced to, once again, selling beer in a saloon where he died from cirrhosis of the liver. After he lost the team, it became the Perfectos in 1899, then the Cardinals in 1900. Short of blowing his wad on the idea of showboating that many future owners would copy, Chris' most positive, lasting memory is that he (according to some) coined the term "fan".

276. **A – Gordie Howe**, who owned most goals, most assists, and most points until The Great One took 'em all for himself. Still, Gretzky left Gordie with the records for games played (1,767)... games played with one team (1,687)... (tied for) most NHL seasons (26)... most NHL regular season goals by a right winger (801)... most NHL regular season points by a right winger (1,850)... most consecutive NHL 20-goal seasons (20)... oldest player to play in the NHL (and only one who played past 50)... most NHL All-Star game appearances (23)... and about a half-dozen more. Did you know that there's such a thing as a "Gordie Howe Hat Trick"? Yep, it's where a player

1) scores a goal; 2) records an assist; and 3) gets in a fight. The bottom line is that you gotta be a badass if you want to be counted among those who've pulled off that trilogy and, of all who've slid in the puck and pulled off their gloves, Brendan Shanahan leads with 17 Gordie Howe Hat Tricks and the only player in NHL history with over 600 goals and 2,000 penalty minutes.

277. **A – Johnny Vander Meer**. He did it in 1938 as a Cincinnati Red – first against the Boston Braves, then four days later against the Brooklyn Dodgers (in the very first night game at Ebbets Field). Fourteen years later when he had been sent down to the minors and working for Tulsa, he pulled off another no-hitter at age 40. Along with Tim Lincecum (2008–10), Randy Johnson (1999–2002), Warren Spahn (1949–52), and Dizzy Dean (1932–35), Vander Meer is one of only four NL pitchers since 1931 to lead the league in strikeouts in three straight seasons (1941–43).

278. **B – Lacrosse**. The sport's American invasion started in western New York a decade earlier, but it never reached an organized level until the NYU Violets and Manhattan Jaspers got out the sticks. The first intercollegiate lacrosse *tournament* was held in 1881, with Harvard beating Princeton, 3-0, in the championship game. About 10 years later, lacrosse started its migration out of the northeast corridor, first moving to Baltimore and that's probably why schools in the Maryland and New York areas (Johns Hopkins, Maryland, Cornell, Syracuse) still remain the kings of the sport.

279. **A – Jim "Catfish" Hunter**, albeit in a technicality. He was the first athlete in a major sport to earn at least a mil in a season as part of his *salary*. However, he wasn't the first athlete to sign a *multimillion-dollar contract*. Hockey star Bobby Hull got that accolade when, in 1972, he signed a 10-year deal worth $2.5 mil. The first athlete to *hit a billion*? Well, Forbes says who else but Michael Jordan. Forbes lists him as the highest-paid retired athlete, too, with $100 mil a year comin' in thanks to his Nike deal ($90 mil) and his 89% stake in the Hornets.

280. **D – St. Louis and Boston** (as of 2016). St. Louis Cardinals vs. Boston Red Sox (1946, 1967, 2004, 2013); St. Louis Rams vs. New England Patriots (2002); St. Louis Blues vs. Boston Bruins (1970); and St. Louis Hawks vs. Boston Celtics (1957, 1958, 1960, 1961).

281. **D – Center**. So, how did we come to have the term "english" as in "he put some english on the ball"? It goes back to the early 1800s when a leather tip was added to the cue, which allowed players to add some "side spin" to their shots. By 1860, the French were referring to said spin as "angle" – a clever play on words since anglé meant angled and anglais meant English. That expression caught on with other pool players, and when someone put spin on a ball, it was said that they were playing a ball that was anglé/anglais which, literally translated, becomes "english." And, yesserie, "english" is supposed to be lowercase.

282. **A – Roger Bannister**, one determined dude! Two years before he hit the sub-4:00 mile, he set a British record at the Helsinki Olympics, but only finished fourth overall. That basically flipped the switch on his resolve to break the 4:00 mark and, like the question read, he essentially did it as part of a single day's routine while he was in med school. Forty-six days later, though, Aussie John Landy broke Bannister's record by going the distance in 3:57.9. As luck would have it, in August of that year, the British Empire and Commonwealth Games put those two head-to-head. Bannister won in 3:58.8. Bannister, then, ran one more race where he broke the *metric* mile record, then took his track shoes off to focus on becoming a neurologist and never ran again. What he achieved was impressive enough that *Sports Illustrated* made him their first "Sportsman of the Year." Still, Bannister sort of poo-poos it all. He claims that beating 4:00 was somewhat mythical since it was a round number only slightly better (by 1.4 seconds) than than the world record that held for nine years. And if there hadn't been a world war interrupting athletic progress in the nations affected by the war, 4:00 would've probably been broken organically.

283. **C – Kentucky**, with Adolph Rupp, Joe B. Hall, Rick Pitino, Tubby Smith, and John Calipari. Some trivia? Ok – here's this about Rupp: In Adolph's last game as the Kentucky coach, UK lost to a Florida State team that was coached by a Kentuckian (Hugh Durham) and led in scoring by a Kentuckian (Ron King). Now, Joe B. Hall: Joe's thought to be true Blue through and through, right?

He started his collegiate career at UK, but transferred to Sewanee where he sacrificed graduating so he could tour with the Harlem Globetrotters. Next, Rick Pitino: Most think Pitino got his first head coaching gig at Boston U. or Providence, but it was the U. of Hawaii when he was named the interim head coach after they fired Bruce O'Neill in the wake of going 9-12 in 1976. Tubby Smith? He got the name "Tubby" as a kid because he was fond of staying in the galvanized washtub where the Smith kids took their baths. And, finally, John Calipari: Cal gets the credit for the "dribble drive" offense, but it was developed by a guy named Vance Walberg who designed it when he as the coach at Fresno City College. It was originally called "AASAA" (attack, attack, skip, attack, attack). Calipari loved the idea so much he hired Walberg as an assistant at U. Mass and the offense scheme flowered on from there.

284. **B – Collis & Garrett Temple**. Collis (the dad) was the first African-American at LSU where he as All-SEC. He played with the Spurs for a season ('74-75). Garrett (the son) also played at LSU, and was also All-SEC. And, just like his pa, he did a season in San Antone (2010). As of 2016, he was with the Washington Wizards where someone on WikiPedia had to dig deplorably deep to come up with this piece of trivia: "(Collis was) the first NBA player to score at least 20 in three straight games after not reaching that level for his first 250 contests."

285. **B – Mandingo**. It was a muy awful movie, trust me, but Mr. Norton must've liked the limelight. He

came back to do the sequel *Drum*, a year later, then *Knight Rider* and *The A-Team* TV shows. There's an interesting connection between Norton and Sylvester Stallone. Sly was an uncredited extra in *Mandingo*, then offered Norton the part of "Apollo Creed" in *Rocky*. Norton originally gave the thumbs-up, then pulled out.

286. **B – Doug did *not* play with his brother Darren on the Toronto Argonauts**. Both of the Fluties went to BC (Darren didn't graduate), both played ball in the CFL, and they're both on the CFL's All-Time Top 50 players (Doug was #1). But you probably want more minutiae about Doug than Darren, so here goes: Doug wasn't selected until the 11th round of the 1985 NFL draft (selection #285), making him the lowest-drafted Heisman winner among those who were drafted. Lucky for him, the USFL was throwin' a lot of money around and Donald Trump threw 7 million (over 5 years) at him to get him to sign with the NJ Generals. At the time, it was a deal that made him the highest-paid pro football player and highest-paid rookie in any sport.

287. **A – Seton Hall**. ONIONS! I have to admit that I'm a Raftery fan (SEND IT IN, BIG FELLA!), so indulge me to rap on about who most of the world thinks is just a loosey-goosey color commentator. Coach grew up in Jersey where he became the state's all-time leading scorer (a record that held for 35 years), then on to LaSalle where he scored the most points as a frosh. After college, he was drafted by the Knicks, but didn't make the final cut, so he moved on to the head coaching gigs @

Fairleigh Dickinson and Seton Hall where he moved the Pirates from an independent to the New Jersey-New York 7 Conference (a conference that lasted only three years and included Rutgers, Seton Hall, Columbia, Princeton, Fordham, Manhattan, and St. John's) and, then, to the Big East. After walking the sidelines, he started working for CBS, FOX, ESPN, et al doing college b-ball analysis and he's worked the mic and left "a little lingerie on the deck" for more than 35 years.

288. **D – UNC - Chapel Hill**. And what's the Tar Heel's mascot? Actually, there's two, both named "Rameses." There's one with a person stuffed inside an anthropomorphic costume, plus there's a live Horned Dorset sheep who shows up only at UNC football games, resplendent with Carolina Blue-painted horns.

289. **A – Mildred "Babe" Didrikson Zaharias** who, as of 2016, is the first and only lady golfer to pull off that feat. It happened in 1945 @ the Los Angeles Open, then she continued her streak at the Phoenix Open and the Tucson Open. In '48, she *attempted* to qualify for the U.S. Open, but they rejected her application because she was a woman. Shameful. Most people don't give her the time of day, but ESPN named her as the 10th Greatest Athlete of the 20th Century. Why, you say? On top of her golf superlatives, she excelled in swimming, baseball, diving, and bowling; she was an All-American in basketball, co-founder of the LPGA, won Olympic Gold in javelin and the 80m hurdles and a Silver in the high-jump; then, she won five events in the 1932 AAU

championships. In 1953, she was diagnosed with cancer and doctors told her she'd never play golf again. Bull-crap, Babe said, and she came back to win the US Women's Open with a colostomy bag strapped to her side. If you're more of a "fine arts" person, it'll please you to know that Babe also sang and played some fine harmonica. She had a number of single releases on Mercury Records, her biggest hit being "I Felt a Little Teardrop."

290. **A – Danny Wuerffel, Charles Woodson, Ricky Williams, Ron Dayne**. Which of these stud muffins performed the best after they carried the Heisman home? The stats say Woodson lasted 17 years in the NFL spread over three teams. He's sixth on the all-time interceptions list and tied for the most defensive touchdowns of all-time. One of the more interesting pieces of trivia I've seen comes from when Woodson intercepted Cam Newton during the 2011 season, it was the fourth time Woodson had intercepted a fellow Heisman winner. The other three he picked off? Vinny Testaverde, Carson Palmer, and Matt Leinart. Did you know that Woodson is an oenophile? I'll just put that out there and let you go look it up. ;-}

291. **A – Contract bridge**. The first baseball'er to hit a Grand Slam was Roger Connor back in 1881 when he was playing first base for the Troy Trojans. Rog' was a big dude for the day – 6'3" – and when he moved on to the NY Gothams, the fans started referring to the team as the "Giants" because of his size – a reference that eventually turned into a real team name. He was the original "sultan of swat" – batting .317, hitting 233 triples,

and launching 138 home runs – an effort that gave him the "career home run champ" crown to wear for 18 years until Babe Ruth took over that slot.

292. **B – The first "modern" World Series was a best-of-nine** tussle with the Boston Americans (with Cy Young) digging their way out of a three games to one deficit to beat the Pittsburgh Pirates (with Honus Wagner) five games to three. Here's two tidbits from the Series... 1) Overflow crowds at Pittsburgh's Exposition Park forced the grounds keepers to rope off the outfield to hold the spectators back. If a batted ball rolled under that rope, a "ground-rule triple" was scored. Seventeen ground-rule triples were hit in the four games played at the stadium. 2) Boston's rowdy fan club, the "Royal Rooters," traveled to Pittsburgh to hassle the Pirates, mostly from singing the song "Tessie" ad nauseam with special lyrics directed at Honus Wagner: "Honus, why do you hit so badly? Take a back seat and sit down. Honus, at bat you look so sadly. Hey, why don't you get out of town?" Must've worked – Wagner was gawd awful, going 6 for 27 and committing six errors.

293. **A – Portland Trailblazers**. Portland paid $3.7 mil to join the NBA and their first-ever draft pick was Geoff Petrie who went on to become the league's Rookie of the Year (and was the first NBA player to switch shoes to Nike [from Converse]). However, the Trail Blazers don't have such a good record with their picks. Proof? Well, there's Sam Bowie over Michael Jordan (and Charles Barkley and John Stockton), Mychal Thompson over Larry

Bird, Greg Oden over Kevin Durant, and LaRue Martin over Bob McAdoo.

294. **C – Boston**. The team started as the "Braves". Mostly, I assume, because they played in the same stadium as the Boston Braves baseball team and could qualify as the football version of the baseball Braves. But when they moved to Fenway Park, home of the Red Sox, and hired William "Lone Star" Dietz, who was *supposedly* part Sioux, as the team's head coach, they became the Redskins. Dietz had some cred – he had been head coach at Washington State, Purdue, Wyoming, Louisiana Tech – but he may have been trying to pull off a scam as a real American Indian. Sadly, we'll probably never know. In 1918, the FBI investigated his authenticity, but the first trial ended in a hung jury and the re-indictment wound up with Dietz claiming "no contest" and serving 30 days in the slammer. The issue sat moot for another 70 years until 1988 when the National Congress of American Indians wanted to sit down and discuss the issue with the 'Skins owner, Jack Kent Cooke, but Cooke wouldn't meet. Then in 2004, the *Indian Country Today Media Network* ran a series exposing Dietz as a white man masquerading as an Indian but even that didn't deter Dan Snyder, the new owner of the Redskins, who fully buys Dietz as an "Indian athlete."

295. **A – Lee Elder**. He didn't make the cut, but at least, he got on the course and getting that far was anything but a cakewalk. Leading up to his appearance at Augusta National, Elder was getting one piece of hate mail after another. That

made Lee a little fearful, and during the week of the tournament, he rented two houses in Augusta and would move back 'n forth, plus kept a few people with him when he went out to eat. How bad was racism in golf back in those days? Well, when Elder played the Monsanto Open in '68, the clubhouse wouldn't allow black players, so he and the others had to change clothes in the parking lot. In another instance at a Memphis tourney, it seems a fan picked up Elder's ball and pitched it into a hedge. Not nice, Memphis.

296. **A – Terry Forster**. I'll let Dan Epstein at Fox-Sports.com tell you the story... "Though he was never an All-Star, never won any awards, Terry Forster had a pretty interesting big-league career. In addition to leading the American League in saves with the '74 White Sox, winning a championship ring with the '81 Dodgers, and making 614 appearances (most of them in relief) over the course of 16 years in the majors, the left-hander was also the last A.L. pitcher to steal a base in a regular-season game before the introduction of interleague play, and his .397 career batting average (31 hits in 78 at-bats) remains the highest of any player with 50 or more at-bats and/or at least 15 years of major-league experience. Not a bad legacy, especially for a player who people, er, largely remember today for being dubbed a "fat tub of goo" by David Letterman."

297. **A – Samaki Ijuma Walker**. In Swahili, "samaki" means "fish" and "Ijuma" means "beautiful river". Drafted ninth by the Mavs in 1996, Samaki became not only the youngest player to

ever appear in a Mavericks game but, as a Laker, his halftime heave in a Western Conference finals game is why we have instant replays. The refs counted the shot, but TV replays showed that he released the ball after the buzzer. The very next year, the NBA instituted instant replays to review situations like that. Now, you know…

298. **B – University of Evansville** and its basketball Purple Aces. The crash killed everybody on board – the team, radio announcer, head coach, every single person. However, not all the players made the trip. The lone one who didn't – David Furr – died in an auto accident two weeks later.

299. **A – Hana Mandlíková** (which is an anagram for "Honk – a naval maid!") who, interestingly enough, defeated both Chris and Martina on consecutive days to accomplish that feat at the 1985 U.S. Open. Since becoming the third female player to pull off that grass/clay/hard court hat trick, three others joined that elite group – Steffie Graf, Serena Williams, and Maria Sharapova. Hana put away her racquet in 1990, and went on to coach Jana Novotna to the 1998 Wimbledon singles title.

300. **D – Mike Vrabel**. Bill Belichick likes guys who can do it all and Vrabel fits that mold like a hand-in-glove. On top of his regular gig as a linebacker, he would also pop up on the field sometimes as an eligible receiver on offense, lining up as a tight end. It came down like this in Super Bowl XXXVIII, Pats vs. Panthers: It was the 4th quarter. Tom Brady threw a 1-yard TD pass to Vrabel, who then joined

'Fridge Perry in that elite group of defensive Super Bowl scorers. Vrabel also became the first player — since the official recording of sacks began in 1982 — to have two touchdown catches and a sack in the same game.

301. **B – Water polo**. Johnny W. was like the Michael Phelps of his time. He won 52 U.S. National Championships and set more than 50 world records. It's also purported, but unverified, that he went undefeated in official competition for his entire competitive career. What's the connection between Weissmuller and swimming? Johnny had polio as a child and took up the sport to help battle the disease.

302. **A – It wasn't Dr. J who never fouled out of a game, but Wilt the Stilt!** I'm not going to waste a tree on Wilt or the Doctor, but I will wax a little about that little punk Eddie Shore. The Bostonians among you should know his name well since he led the Bruins to two Stanley Cups, but it was rowdiness that shaped his persona, not holding trophies above his head. During the 1925–26 hockey season, Montreal shipped Billy Coutu and Sprague Cleghorn off to the Bruins. In their first practice session in Beantown, Shore sashayed back and forth in front of his new teammates to a point of pee'ing off Coutu beyond repair. Coutu body-slammed, head-butted, elbowed – anything he could do – to annoy Shore. Next thing Shore knew, Coutu had picked up a puck and made a mad rush at him. Gloves flew, tempers flared, and the two players tore into the other. One thing led to another and Shore's ear was almost ripped off.

And Coutu? Out like a light and out of commission for a week. Shore went doctor to doctor about his little ear issue, but everyone he saw wanted to give him one of those Vincent Van Gogh subtractions. Eventually, he found one who sewed it back on and, being a real man, Shore refused an anesthetic, instead using a mirror so he could watch the doctor sew his ear back on. Adding insult to injury, Shore claimed Coutu used his hockey stick to try and cut off his ear, and Coutu was fined $50. Shore felt bad about his little fib and eventually retracted his claim and Coutu got his money back. Another unusual incident involving Shore happened in 1930 when he was challenged to a boxing match by White Sox player Art Shires. Even though NHL president Frank Calder said it was up to Bruins' manager Art Ross whether or not Shore could fight, baseball commissioner Judge Kenesaw Mountain Landis ixnay'ed Shires' participation. Fast-forward next to 1933 and we find Shore ending the career of Toronto Maple Leafs star Ace Bailey when he cold-cocked Bailey from behind. In cinematic fashion, Bailey's head hit the ice, knocking him unconscious, sending him into convulsions and, then, off to the hospital. As payback, Leafs' ruffian Red Horner punched Shore and Shore's head hit the ice, knocking him out and requiring seven stitches.

303. **C – The 6'11" Bowling Green Falcons' star Chuck Share**. From that point in 1950, when Boston passed on picking Bob Cousy and, instead, blowing that #1 pick on Share, to now (2016), the Celtics have never had another #1 pick. And Share? He never suited up in green. Instead, he

was traded to the Ft. Wayne Pistons, then to the Hawks where he led the NBA in disqualifications during the 1954-55 season and later played center on their 1958 NBA championship team who beat the Celtics for the title. For you purists, there was a league draft that preceded the NBA's. It was the BAA's (Basketball Association of America which eventually became the NBA) and their first draft happened in 1947 when Clifton McNeely from Texas Wesleyan University was that league's very first pick. McNeely never played a lick of pro ball, opting instead for a high school coaching career in Texas. And one last draft pick tidbit: Gene Melchiorre, a 2x All-American at Bradley, is the only #1 NBA pick to never play in the league at all. He was one of 31 players who were arrested for the infamous college basketball point-shaving scandal in 1951 and, as a result, Melchiorre was barred for life from the NBA.

304. **D – The Rams**, who were first in Cleveland (starting in 1936) where they won the 1945 NFL crown and promptly moved to Los Angeles (1946) where they became the only NFL champion to play the following season in another city. In L.A., they won the NFL title in 1951. Then in 1995, they became the St. Louis Rams where they won Super Bowl XXXIV.

305. **A – There's a limit of 12 innings** (during the regular season) in Japan professional baseball. Other diffs? A different strike zone (the strike zone in Japanese baseball is larger, higher and narrower inside than outside the batter)... a smaller playing field in Japan... the Japanese baseball is

more tightly wound and, therefore, harder... and you can have a tie game (at the end of 12 innings or at the 3'30" mark after the first pitch which, then, becomes the final inning). Although not a "rule," players who hit a home run are handed a stuffed animal when they cross home plate.

306. **D – Syracuse**. Next time you have a chance, search for "John Mackey, Super Bowl" on YouTube and you'll understand why football historians consider him one of the greatest tight ends of all time. Off the field, Mackey impacted life in other ways: 1) As the first president of the NFLPA, he organized a strike which resulted in extra benefits for the players; then, as the lead plaintiff in a case against the NFL, helped overturn the "Rozelle Rule" which limited a player's ability to act as a free agent. 2) Years later, John began suffering from the symptoms of dementia and had to be put in an assisted living center. While he had some pension money rolling in from the NFL, it was insufficient to take care of the costs. His wife, Sylvia, reached out to the NFL and commish Tagliabue who, along with NFLPA president Gene Upshaw, came up with the "88 Plan" (Mackey's jersey number) which provided $88k/yr. for nursing home care and $50k/yr. for adult day care for any NFL alum who had dementia or Alzheimer's.

307. **D – William & Mary**, who may be good at educatin' the kiddos, but can't make up their dang mind as to what they want to be called! They started out as the "Orange & White" because those were their colors, then became the "Orange & Black" because they changed those colors, then

the Indians, and in 1978 became the Tribe. When the NCAA was making noise about schools with Native American names, W&M's president got nervous and removed two tribal feathers from the school's logo, then changed the mascot to a griffin ("one-third eagle, one-third lion and, according to this mythical creature, one third amazing"). I'm not entirely sure what the mascot-naming committee was drinkin', but the mascot finalists they came up with were Griffin, the King and Queen (which is understandable), the Phoenix, a Pug, and a Wren.

308. **D – Touchdown**. If you want a backstory about rules, it ain't happenin' here. They is what they is.

309. **D – Red clay**. There's only two types of clay courts – red and green ("rubico") – and they aren't really clay, meaning you can't make a coffee mug for your daddy's birthday present. Nearly all of the red clay courts are crushed brick that's packed to make the court. Green clay is made from crushed basalt rather than brick, making the surface slightly harder and faster.

310. **B – Bill Russell**, who was not just a coach, but the Celtics' player-coach and the guy who took over for Red Auerbach. Russell wasn't Red's first choice, however. He offered the gig to Frank Ramsey, but Frank wasn't gonna walk away from all the money he was making with his little nursing home chain (yes, really). Russell wasn't Red's second choice, either. That was Bob Cousy, but Bob didn't want to coach his former teammates. Russell wasn't even Red's third choice! That would've been Tommy Heinsohn, but Heinsohn

didn't think he could handle the testy Russell. Heinsohn, though, was the one who suggested Russell as player-coach and Red and Bill both bought into it.

311. **C – Skyline**. Based in NYC with schools like Sarah Lawrence, Mt. Saint Mary, Yeshiva (home of the fightin' Maccabees [leaders of a Jewish rebel army that took control of Judea]).

312. **D – Tony Franklin**. In an ESPN.com on the subject, Chuck Klosterman evoked the spirit of Einstein and theorized that there are two schools of thought when it comes to placekicking barefoot. One being that the lack of a shoe provided the kicker with a better "feel" for the ball and greater control over its trajectory. The second theory is that shoes and socks absorbed kinetic energy, and kicking flesh-to-leather created more torque. I'm not sure which applies to Franklin, but whichever it was, it worked like a charm. Tony set 18 NCAA records while he was at Texas A&M – most FGs, most kicking points, longest average FG (39.5 yds.), etc. He set the record for the longest field goal in NCAA Div. 1 history when he nailed a 65-yard FG against Baylor in 1976. However, records are meant to be broken and Tony's has given way to several 67-yarders. If you remove all the levels and leagues, the record for a FG at any level is 69 yards off the foot of Abilene Christian's Ove Johansson in a 1976 game against East Texas State just a matter of hours after Franklin set his record.

313. **A – Pittsburgh Pirates**. Those old-fashioned, striped "pill box" caps were introduced during the

Pirates championship – "We Are Family" – season of 1979. And a little like the buckeye stickers Woody Hayes introduced at Ohio State, Pittsburgh's Willie Shargell would hand out gold "Stargell Stars" to his teammates to acknowledge their on-field performances. Then, it was up to the player whether to sew their star between the stripes on the cap or on the cap's bill. When Willie passed on to the great ballpark in the sky, the Pirates dressed up the front of their jersey with a "Stargell Star" in memory of "Pops."

314. **A – The AFL's "official" football was slightly longer and narrower** (by a quarter-inch), not to mention a little tackier for a better grip.

315. **B – Houston Colt .45s.** Until MLB gave Houston a pro franchise, the city got its baseball fix from the minor league Houston Buffaloes starting back in 1888. The "Colt .45s" came out of a name-the-team contest and meant to tie into the pistol of the same name – "the gun that won the West." They only kept the name for three years, switching to the Astros when they moved out of Colt Stadium and into the Astrodome.

316. **D – Butterbean**. Bob "Butterbean" Love, the basketball player, had a great ride in ChiTown and was the second jersey the Bulls retired (behind Jerry Sloan's). Sadly, after his playing days faded away, he had a hard time finding a job because of a severe stuttering problem. At one point, he was down to working as a busboy making $4.45/hr. The owner of the restaurant knew there was

untapped potential and paid for speech therapy classes to try and help Love into a better situation. The therapy worked and Love returned to the Bulls as their director of community relations, a gig where he regularly speaks to school children and gives motivational speeches.

317. **A – Victor Espinoza** who, at age 43, became the oldest (and first Hispanic) to win racing's Triple Crown. But, it wasn't like he hadn't tried! Vic had three Kentucky Derby victories, three Preakness wins, and was the first jockey to enter the Belmont with a third opportunity to win the Triple Crown, which he finally did in 2015 aboard American Pharoah. If you're into multiple superlatives, raise a banner for Eddie Arcaro. He's the only jockey to win more than one Triple Crown (up to 2016, anyway) with two victories.

318. **A – Akron**. Poor Gerry Faust. He was this off-the-hook high school coach in Cincinnati @ Moeller High, where he ran up a mark of 178-23-2, including seven unbeaten seasons, a kajillion Ohio state titles, and four high school national championships. But, HE WANTED TO BE IRRRRRISSSSSSH! And that yearn went back a long way. When Ger' was a high school QB, Notre Dame offered him a *partial* scholarship, but there weren't enough Benjamins in that deal to pay for bed, board, *and* biology, so he opted for a better ROI at U. Dayton where he got to play under former Notre Dame coach Hugh Devore, so he got to live a *semi*-Irish dream. After Dayton, he went to Moeller and built a program from scratch into the most impressive high school gridiron

program in the country (if you count having future Speaker of the House John Boehner as one of your linebackers). When Dan Devine had enuff of playing Notre Dame coach, the holy water bearers put all their money on Faust and, for a Catholic boy, that's a tough offer to pass up. However, I think the rush to his head was a bit much. For one thing, he started messin' with ND's home jersey colors, then after seeing the Irish' schedule, he had the (prophetic) nerve to say "I hope my lifelong dream doesn't end in a nightmare." After his first game – a win against LSU – vaulted Notre Dame to #1 in the polls, things rolled badly downhill. First was Notre Dame's first losing season in 17 years, then four straight losses to Air Force, and never in the hunt for a national title. Still, he upset #1-ranked Pitt (w/ Dan Marino), routed Penn State, Purdue, and beat Michigan, and that was enough for Notre Dame to hang on to until his contract came to a natural end right after a pathetic 58–7 loss to Jimmy Johnson's U. Miami in the Orange Bowl, the second-highest point total ever given up in one game by the Irish.

319. **D – Baseball**, at least at North Carolina State. When he transferred to Wisconsin, he put baseball aside at the collegiate level but continued to play minor league ball. The Orioles felt Wilson actually had some potential in the sport and drafted him straight out of high school in the 41st round (1,222nd overall). Baltimore thought they were lucky to find him still available and offered a signing bonus to the tune of $350,000 – the third largest bonus any draftee was given that year – if Russell would give up college. He wouldn't, but he

continued to toy with the idea by playing in the minors (Gastonia, Tri-Cities, etc.), then came back for another swing at the draft, moving up about 1,000 places to 140th overall, picked by the Rockies who sent him down to Asheville to play for the Tourists. Before the next season started, Russell told the Rockies he was going to do the NFL thing instead and wasn't coming to spring training. But, the boy just couldn't give baseball up altogether and a couple of years later, he was picked up by the Texas Rangers (via the "Rule 5" draft*) and did spring training with them for two years. Make up your mind, son! *The Rule 5 draft aims to prevent teams from stockpiling too many young players on their minor league affiliate teams when other teams would be willing to have them play in the majors.

320. **D – Minnesota Timberwolves**. It's not that Jonny wasn't better than Seth at the time, but playing for Syracuse where he eclipsed Carmelo Anthony's most points in his freshman debut and led the Orange in the six-overtime game against UConn in the Big East tournament got him more media attention than Curry got playing at Davidson. Jonny started off well for the 'Wolves, but he got hurt, got traded, got traded again, then got waived. Hopefully, he hung on to some of the $9.5 mil he made in his three years in the NBA.

321. **C – Dean Cain** didn't play basketball @ Dartmouth. However, he did play football at Princeton where he set a national record for interceptions in a single season.

322. **C – The Seahawks** do indeed pay the Aggies $5k/yr. for the right to use the phrase "12th Man."

(the deal was renewed in 2016 at an undisclosed sum). And you don't wanna mess with the Aggies, either. The Indy Colts started using "12th Man" and A&M filed a federal infringement case in 2015 asking for a piece of the action using that term on tickets and merch might bring the Colts. You say the other things are a little hard to swallow? Yeah, but they're all the real deal. The only one you might be able to get me to give you a little of your money back on would be the "Steagles" one. Thanks to depleted rosters during WW II, the Eagles and Steelers combined forces for a year. The NFL record book called the team the "Phil-Pitt Combine," but fans and sportswriters called 'em the "Steagles" and that's what they became to be known as.

323. **A – Major League Soccer**, where there's 30 allowable players on a roster. The others are MLB – 25, NHL – 23, and the NBA – 12. Baseball fans may cry "foul" and say "WTF" about the "40-man" roster, but the 40-man squad is composed of all the players in a Major League club's organization who are signed to a major-league contract and include players who can be called up to the 25-man roster at any given time.

324. **A – Getty Oil.** Getty bought their share of ESPN for $15 million and, then, turned around and sold it to ABC for $188 million. Actually, it was Texaco who made that much because they had acquired Getty but didn't want to be in the broadcasting biz. ABC held the right of first refusal should Getty decide to sell its cable business and, as the saying

goes, they made Texaco an offer they couldn't refuse.

325. **B – Earle Bruce.** You know that old axiom about "you can't replace a legend"? Well, Earle was thrust into that position when Woody Hayes retired as Ohio State's football coach. Bruce had it ok his first year – with Woody's players – going 11-1 and losing the Rose Bowl (and, therefore, the national championship), but never contended for a title afterward. OSU's president fired him before his very last game – against Michigan, no less – but let him coach it, anyway. Earle was able to cop a win in Ann Arbor, something the Buckeyes wouldn't do again for another 14 years. After the game, Bo Schembechler told Bruce, "I always mind losing to Ohio State but I didn't mind so much today."

326. **C – Utah Jazz**. And, thanks to SI.com, here are eight facts you probably don't know about Shaq: 1) He has a doctorate (not a honorary one, either) in Education; 2) He scored the same number of 3-pt. shots as Kareem – one; 3) He recorded the highest maximum vertical reach ever measured in pre-draft workouts – 12 ft. 5 in. from a standing position; 4) Only Wilt Chamberlain missed more free throws (5,805) than Shaq (5,317); 5) He challenged Hakeem Olajuwon to a game of one-on-one with a typewritten and signed note shortly after losing to the Rockets in the 1995 NBA Finals. The idea gathered steam, with Taco Bell even signing on to sponsor it as a pay-per-view event, but it never came to fruition; 6) During the Screen Actors Guild strike of 2000, he was fined by the union for crossing the picket line to perform in a

Disney "I'm going to Disneyland!" spot after winning his first NBA title; 7) He was supposed to be with Biggie Smalls the night the rapper was killed. The two had recorded a song together in 1993; 8) He's a Mason – became a member of Widow's Son Lodge No. 28 when he was playing for the Celtics.

327. **D – Futsal.** The name's origin is Spanish: fútbol sala or fútbol de salón , which can be translated as "room football." There's five to a side and the ball is smaller than a soccer ball and doesn't bounce as high. The Brazilians are very good at the game. So are the Spaniards and the Russians. The U.S. team wasn't even in the top 25 the last time I looked.

328. **D – Billiards**. Ewa is striking in 1) a beautiful way; and 2) in a 9-ball way where she's won the U.S., European and World 9-ball championships. You may have seen her on ESPN where she does color commentary for 9-ball telecasts or in commercials for No Nonsense pantyhose.

329. **C – Earl Lloyd**, but with some "howevers." Let me explain: Lloyd's entrance into the pro ranks came in the 1950-51 season, along with three other African-Americans – Chuck Cooper, Nathaniel Clifton, and Hank DeZonie. The reason Earl was the "first" was only because of the order in which the teams' season openers happened on the calendar. Chuck Cooper, however, was the first African-American to get *drafted* into the NBA – second round by the Celtics. On April 26, 1950, Harold Hunter signed with the Washington Capitols, becoming the first African-American to

sign a contract with an NBA team, however Hunter was cut from the team during training camp and did not play professionally. Sticking with the ethnicity theme, Wataru Misaka debuted in 1947 as the first non-white and Asian-American player in the league (Knicks). In 1978, Puerto Rican Butch Lee became the first Latino in the league (Hawks). Then, Wang Zhizhi became the first Chinese player in 2001 (Mavs).

330. **A – Sprinting and wrestling**. Keep in mind, I used the word "suggest" and the paintings were found in France, ok? After that, it took another 10,000 years until cave paintings in Mongolia showed a wrestling match.

331. **D – At least 4**. Yeah, country boy, I know that it's only three years for mares who don't run races, but it's age four in the racing game. Did you know mares carry their young for almost 11 months? Or that a mare isn't sexually receptive during the colder months because of something called an "anestrus period" which prevents her from conceiving and producing a foal during the harshest time of the year?

332. **B – Under Armour**. Curry wore Nike growing up and his godfather, Greg Brink, even worked for the brand, but Nike's periscope didn't foretell Curry's ascendancy and they shot themselves in their endorsement foot in a number of ways: They gave Kyrie Irving and Anthony Davis a camp, but not Steph... in their PowerPoint pitch to Steph, they forgot to change out Kevin Durant's name and put Curry's in... and their pitchman even

mispronounced Steph's name, calling him "Steph-on" (like Urkel's alter ego on *Family Matters*) rather than "*Steph*-on"... there's also a rumor that Curry refused to sign with Nike because the company wouldn't allow him to put Bible verses on his sneaks, but that's unfounded at the moment. Nonetheless, Curry wasn't impressed with Nike and decided to go indie with Under Armour – a move that, according to an analyst at Morgan-Stanley, placed Curry's foot armour worth to the shoemaker a whopping $14+ billion.

333. **A – Carry around buckets of sand** and build a pile of sand before each shot. This, however, became time-consuming and messy, causing a long line of creative golfers to ponder a solution to the problem. The first patented tee rested on the ground and had little prongs to hold the ball up (1889) and the first known tee to pierce the ground was a rubber-topped peg called the "Perfectum" (1892). Whether it was habit or poor marketing, neither one of those caught on and it wasn't until 1920 when New Jersey dentist Dr. William Lowell, Sr. came up with the type tees we use today – something Dr. Lowell called "Reddy Tee." The first ones were stained green, but soon changed to red to make them more distinctive. To market his tee, Dr. Lowell paid golfing great Walter Hagan and his exhibition partner Joe Kirkwood $1,500 to use the "Reddy Tee" and leave them behind as they played. By 1925, he was selling more than $100,000 worth of tees a year and had changed from wood to celluloid. Of course, widespread success brings copycats and before long he was spending more time and money defending his

THE GREATEST SPORTS TRIVIA THROWDOWN OF ALL-TIME

patent and chasing infringers than he was enjoying the profits of his idea, so he sold his company to Red Devil, Inc., the company that makes/sells caulk, adhesives, paint tools, and the like. Quick side note: Dr. Lowell's son, Wm. Lowell, Jr., was pretty creative, too. He's the guy who came up with the "six pack" carton.

334. **A – Darko Milicic**, aka "The Human Victory Cigar." Or you could call him the $52,323,642 mistake that six NBA teams tried to turn into something positive. The Pistons drafted him as an 18-year old after a decent performance with Yugoslavia's U16 team at the 2001 U16 EuroBasket where he won a Gold medal, but he never averaged more than 1.8 PPG in the Motor City and they started the domino effect by trading him to Orlando, who traded him to Memphis, who traded him to the Knicks, who traded him to the T-Wolves, who said he was "like manna from heaven" but still wound up waiving him, then the Celts decided to give him a shot, but waived him after one game. So, he tucked tail and went home to Serbia where he ticked off his homies by making tasteless remarks about the referees and their families after an OT loss to Greece in the 2007 EuroBasket finals. He never got invited to play for Serbia's national team, again. Undeterred, he decided to take up kickboxing, but lost his first match and put the kibosh on that sport, too.

335. **A – Keith Jackson**. Or, at least, that's our perception since Keith's the one who popularized it. If you ask Keith, though, he'll tell you that he picked up the expression from Los Angeles

broadcaster Dick Lane who used it during his play-by-play of roller derby matches. However, Jackson can claim some expressions as being all his – like nicknaming the Rose Bowl as "The Granddaddy of them All" and the University of Michigan Stadium as "The Big House."

336. **A – Holing of a ball** directly from a (green-side) bunker. It's a term that's called a "funny" in golf. Other "funnies" include a "Sandy/Sandie": If you hole out for par (or less) after having been in a bunker at some point during the hole. Then, there's "plonker": If a man's drive fails to reach the ladies' tee, which is typically only a short distance in front of the men's tee. And, also "sister-in-law": A shot that finishes in a far better position than it really should have.

337. **D – Wee Willie Keeler**, whose mindset was "Keep your eye clear, and hit 'em where they ain't." Willie balled from 1892-1910 for the Baltimore Orioles, New York Highlanders, and Brooklyn Superbas (dang, that's a cool name!) with a lifetime batting average of .385. He had a 44-game *regular season* hitting streak in 1897 (one that Pete Rose tied), but he hit safely in his last game the season before, which gave him a 45-game streak that DiMaggio broke in 1941. Keeler also had eight consecutive seasons with 200 hits or more, a record broken by Ichiro Suzuki in 2009.

338. **D – Hal Greer**. Hal shot exactly 80.1% from the charity stripe. A 2011 *New York Times* piece says the origins of the jump shot go back to the Thirties and John Miller Cooper. Cooper was a high

schooler at Corydon* H.S. in Kentucky when the
University of Chicago's basketball team passed
through town and asked if they could practice at
Corydon's gym. There, Cooper saw one of the
Chicago kids catch a ball off the backboard, then
jump and shoot it in mid-air. Cooper mastered the
technique, and then took the shot with him to
Mizzou where he was all-conference. But, like
many good backstories, there's peeps – like the
ones at the Basketball Hall of Fame – who credit
someone else. In the HOF's case, Kenny Sailors
who, by all accounts, didn't take a jump shot until
he was in the pros in '46, about 16 years after
Cooper hoisted his. *Corydon KY is the birthplace of NBA
HOF'er Frank Ramsey and former baseball commissioner
Happy Chandler.

339. **B – Claret Jug**, whose proper name is the "Golf
Champion Trophy." However, the jug wasn't always what the winner got. Originally (1860), it
was a silver-buckled leather belt called the "Challenge Belt." In 1872, the Claret Jug took over and
the first name etched on it was Tom Morris, Jr. who
had won The Open at age 17 – the youngest
Open Championship winner to date – on his way
to an unmatched four consecutive Open Championship victories by the ripe 'ol age of 21. Take
that, Mr. Tiger Woods!

340. **D – 42**, Jackie Robinson's uniform number. 'Nuff
said? Well, there is one thing I'd like to add – do
you what New York Yankee was the last major
league baseball player allowed to wear #42 full-
time? Mariano Rivera.

341. **A – Indy 500**. The Indy race started in 1911, then the 24 Hours of LeMans in 1923, followed by the Monaco Grand Prix in 1929. Brit Graham Hill is the only driver to win the Triple Crown. And, he and his boy, Damon, are the only dad-and-son pair to both win the Formula One World Championship.

342. **A – Milwaukee**, the place where the team first became the Hawks. Before that, they were the Tri-Cities Blackhawks – the three cities being Moline, Rock Island, and Davenport. In 1949, the Blackhawks became one of the NBA's original 17 teams and made the playoffs in their first year in the league. Who coached them that far? The Celtics' legendary helmsman Red Auerbach! Red took the gig because the owner gave him carte blanche to rebuild the team, and Red was hell-bent for leather, too. He traded more than two-dozen players in his first six weeks on the job.

343. **B – Horse racing**. Its original reference was about a thoroughbred jockey who won a race without having to whip his horse or pull back on the reins.

344. **C – Jim Ryun**, the youngest dude to qualify for the Olympics – 1964 – thanks to being the first high school athlete to run a mile in under four minutes. His 3:55.3 mile was a high school best that stood for 36 years. Sticking with age and the Olympics, I bring you these young'uns: The youngest confirmed Olympic medalist is Greek gymnast Dimitrios Loundras who won a Bronze (in a team event) when he was only 10 years, 218 days old. The youngest ever winner in an individual

Olympic event was Inge Sørensen of Denmark, who was 12 years, 24 days old when she won a Bronze medal in the 200m Breaststroke in 1936.

345. **D – Central Michigan**. In 2005, the NCAA put Central Michigan on its watch list of 19 schools with "hostile or abusive" nicknames, but the school successfully appealed the decision, with the helpful support of the Saginaw Chippewa tribe. There were a handful of other schools that also got support from American Indian nations (Mississippi College, Catawba College, Utah) and others (Illinois Fighting Illini, Bradley Braves, Alcorn State Braves) were allowed to keep their nicknames as long as they promised not to use them to represent Native Americans.

346. **A – Football**, at an average clip of 11 minutes of real action per game, followed by baseball at 17:58, then basketball at about 48:00, soccer at 57 minutes, and hockey with the most at 60 minutes ('coz that puck's in play allllll the time).

347. **D – Jim Abbott**. You've seen this guy I'm sure, and if you're anything like me, you're flat-out amazed with the magic he conjures with just one hand. Think about all Abbott had to do: When he was setting up to pitch, he would rest his mitt on the end of his right forearm... then pitch... then slip his hand into the mitt, ready to field any ball that came his way... then, if a ball did come his way, he would secure the mitt between his right forearm and torso, slip his hand out of the mitt, and remove the ball from the mitt so he could throw out the runner at first. The boy could hit, too! Although he

spent most of his time in the AL where there was usually a DH, he tripled once in a spring training game and his Yankees teammate Mariano Rivera swears on a stack of rosin bags that he saw Abbott hitting home runs during batting practice.

348. **A – Clean and press**. The original objective for lifters was to perform the move in "military style" – meaning the lifter faces forward with their body straight as a steel pole, heels together, and relying on only the muscles in their arms and shoulders. But that was darn near impossible, so the lifters started playing out the gray areas (ok, cheating) by developing larger muscle groups like the lower torso, the hips, and legs – anything they could do to win. Since everyone was doing it and it was win-at-all-cost, the judges apparently had nowhere to go but along. Little by little, the clean and press was closer to a quick lift and no longer how it was originally created. Eventually, the International Weightlifting Federation had enough and completely canned the entire event.

349. **A – Tom Zachary**. Not sure if it was done as appreciation or not, but the year after Tom gave up that home run to the Babe, the Yankees hired him and he helped them win the 1928 World Series. A year later, he went 12–0 for the Yankees, which is still the major league record for most pitching wins without a loss in a season.

350. **A – The last helmetless player in the NHL**. The NHL started mandating players to wear headgear in 1979, but the new rule allowed anyone who was playing before '79 the option of

continuing to use their noggin as a helmet if they wanted to. And center Craig MacTavish did! When he hung up his skates from the St. Louis Blues in 1997, he became the glorious footnote as the last helmetless player to bid farewell to hockey. The other answers? Answer "b"? Paul Azinger used the longest putter I could find – 54 inches – that he pressed to his sternum to win the Sony Open in 2000. Answer "c"? Aurele "Al" Couture knocked out Ralph Walton in 10.5 seconds back in 1946. Methinks it qualifies as a sucker punch since Walton had been distracted by his cornerman and Couture took advantage of the moment. Answer "d"? Russell Erxleben would be the highest-drafted kicker in NFL history, going 11th to the Saints in '79 and he was a b-u-s-t BUST, kicking only four FGs before Nawlins moved him to punter. Russ was a sham on and off the field. He was convicted of securities fraud not once, but twice, and spent nearly 13 unlucky years in the federal pen.

351. **D – Chucky Brown**, who – as well as Joe Smith, Jim Jackson, and Tony Massenburg – played for 12 different franchises. And there's a connection between Smith, Jackson, and Massenburg, too – all three of them played college ball for coach Gary Williams (either at Ohio State or Maryland).

352. **A – China**. Knowing how competitive we think China is, it may be hard to believe, but it's true. They've kicked butt since '84, winning more than 500 medals with nearly half of that total coming out of just six sports – table tennis, badminton, diving, gymnastics, weightlifting, and shooting.

353. **A – Barry Switzer**, with a .714 playoff winning percentage. Noll's was .667; Johnson .692; Gibbs .708. Switzer's % ties Bill Walsh's and even eclipses Bill Belichick's (Bill's was .697 as of 2016).

354. **B – Notre Dame**, under the guidance of Digger Phelps, who shares (with Gary Williams) the NCAA record for most upsets over a #1 team at seven. Only 19 days before Notre Dame knocked off UCLA, the Irish defeated Bear Bryant's top-ranked Alabama 24-23 to win the football national championship and finish the season ranked #1. With the win over UCLA, the Irish also moved into #1 in men's basketball, marking the first time in college history where the same school was ranked number one in both football and basketball.

355. **D – Joe Frazier**. It was billed as the "Fight of the Century" and both fighters came into the ring undefeated – the first time two undefeated boxers fought each other for the heavyweight title. Ringside seats were $150 a pop and celebs were crawling over each other to get a good seat. Heck, Sinatra couldn't find anything in the front row, so he cut a deal with *LIFE* magazine to be their photographer just so he could be upfront with his posse. And even though he had never uttered a sports-oriented syllable into a microphone before, Burt Lancaster was a color commentator for the closed-circuit broadcast.

356. **A – NFL playoff game**, dating back to 1932. The Masters started in 1934, the NIT in 1938, and the NCAA in 1939. In case you're interested... the first NFL playoff (actually a championship) was

supposed to be played at Wrigley Field but there was a blizzard goin' on, so they moved it indoors to Chicago Stadium where they played on mulch instead of grass ... the Masters was originally called the "Augusta National Tournament" ... the first NIT tourney had six teams and the first NCAA men's roundball tourney had eight teams.

357. **C – Rutgers**. It was back in the day before there was a Big East and the Scarlet Knights were an independent, so they could frontload their schedule and it was pretty much a cakewalk lined with pansies. They walked into the NCAA tourney undefeated and didn't have any problems with Princeton, UConn, or VMI, but then they got to the Final Four and had to face Michigan (BOOM!), then UCLA in the consolation game (BOOM, again), so they finished up their season 31-2. Rutgers was coached by Tom Young who went on to serve as an assistant coach for the Washington Wizards under head coach Eddie Jordan, who was the starting point guard on that 1976 Rutgers team.

358. **B – The 7th-ranked Kentucky Wildcats**, a team coached by Bear Bryant. The 'Cats beat the Numero Uno-ranked Sooners coached by Bud Wilkinson, 13-7. Oklahoma averaged 34.5 points per game and only one team had scored more than twice in a game against Kentucky that season. Even though UK won, the final Associated Press poll came out *before* the bowl games, and Oklahoma was able to claim and hold onto a national championship. However, because of what happened with Kentucky vs. Oklahoma and other post-final poll bowl games that year, there are *four*

teams that lay claim to the 1950 title, according to the official NCAA record book. They tried to sort things out by asking the ranking gurus and six went with Oklahoma (final record 10-1), six voted for Tennessee (11-1), two picked Princeton (9-0) and one – the Sagarin Ratings – named Kentucky (11-1) as the national champ.

359. **C – North Carolina State**. The sanctions came out of the Wolfpack's recruitment of David Thompson, who, along with 7'2" Tom Burleson and 5'7" Monte Towe, led the team to an undefeated season (27-0) in 1973-74, and then led the Wolfpack to a 30-1 record the next year, which was capped off with a trip to the Final Four where they avenged their only loss of the season by defeating reigning national champions, UCLA, and then thumped Marquette in the championship game. Their coach needs some props, don'cha think? It was Norm Sloan, whose overall win-loss record at NC State was 266–127 in 14 seasons. Norm came from the Florida Gators and brought with him the nickname of "Stormin' Norman" not to mention a rather loud red-and-white plaid sports coat. After a salary dispute, Norm went back to Florida where he rebuilt the program on the backs of guard Vernon Maxwell and center Dwayne Schintzius. Under Sloan, the Gators won 20+ games and made the NCAA Tournament in each of his last three seasons — the school's first NCAA Tournament appearances ever.

360. **D – St. Louis Cardinals**. Back in 1964, the NFL and AFL were really goin' at each other. So much that they even held their drafts on the same day (in

November before the college season was over!) and waged a bidding war for certain players. In Broadway Joe's case, the Jets drafted him as the very first pick while the Cards picked him twelfth. The Jets offered Namath a record salary of $427,000 over three years. Joe didn't blink and St. Louis never got to the negotiating table. Oh, who was the NFL's first pick that year? Some guy named Tucker Fredrickson from Auburn – ahead of HOF'ers Dick Butkus (the third pick) and Gale Sayers (fourth). It's interesting to note that if Sayers and Butkus had gone with their AFL drafters instead of their NFL ones, Sayers would've wound up as a Chief and Butkus a Bronco.

361. **A – Mashie niblick**. Niblick? Yep. Scotland's Archibald Barrie came up with the name. How and why? Well, I found someone named Tony Cooper on an English usage site that explains it this way: *Barrie was a Scotsman with a pronounced overbite. When he brought the first prototype of his niblick to the course, he was eating a coronet of ice cream. His playing partner, noticing the new club, asked Barrie what it was. Barrie replied "It's a nibble lick" thinking that the partner was asking about his peculiar style of consuming the ice cream.* So, how did mashies and cleeks and jiggers become numbered irons? You can thank Spalding Sporting Goods for coming up with that.

362. **C –The first woman to found a major league baseball team**. Now, Joan was a trustifarian (er, a kid with a ginormus trust fund) who liked two things: art and sports. She was one of the owners of the New York (baseball) Giants

and not very happy that the rest of the owners wanted to move the team to San Francisco, so she sold her stock and started looking around for a replacement team to fill the hole that bite put in the Big Apple. Along with Donald Grant, the only other Giants owner who opposed the move, she put together a group of like-minded folks and came up with a New York franchise in the startup Continental League whose goal was to elbow its way into becoming the third major league. The Continental owners – in particular, their negotiator Bill Shea – were aggressive enough to get MLB to blink and, without the Continental League ever playing a single game, Major League Baseball agreed to accept a minimum of eight new teams. And, that's how the Mets were born and how Joanie became the first woman to own a MLB team. Wait! I can tell one of you has a question about the expansion teams. Of the eight proposed Continental League cities, all but one eventually was granted expansion or relocated. First was Minneapolis–St. Paul in 1961, then Houston and New York in 1962, followed by Atlanta in 1966, Dallas/Ft. Worth in 1972, Toronto in 1977, and Denver in 1993. The one who didn't make it? Buffalo. Despite building Pilot Field in the early 1990s, the city didn't offer much of a lure compared to the sun and sexiness of Florida, and the Marlins wound up as the last expansion team.

363. **B – Herschel Walker**. And on top of pigskins, MMA, and bobsled, Walker also has a fifth-degree black belt in tae kwon do, has danced with the Ft. Worth Ballet, and was on the SEC champion 4 × 100m relay squad when he was at Georgia. Off

the playing field, Herschel has some unorthodox habits, too. He says he sleeps five hours a night and eats only one meal a day (dinner), mainly soup, bread, and salads. And, instead of pumping iron, his exercise routine consists of 750-1,500 push-ups and 2,000 sit-ups. Maybe that's why he only has five hours to sleep, 'ya think?

364. **A – At Florida State** with future acting star Burt Reynolds. We probably don't give Corso the credit he's due, but he does deserve some. He was a two-sport stud in high school and even offered a $5,000 bonus to sign with the Brooklyn Dodgers as a shortstop. However, he chose football over baseball and went on to become a Seminole where he roomed with Burt and future University of Miami baseball coach Ron Fraser. While at Florida State, his speed on the football field earned him the nickname "Sunshine Scooter" and as a defensive player, he set the school record for most career interceptions, a record that stood for more than two decades until it was broken by Monk Bonasorte. Interestingly enough, Corso was the starting QB for the South in the 1956 Blue-Gray Game, but his squad lost to the Len Dawson-led North team, 14–zip.

365. **B – Gary Gilmore**, the famous spree-killer who demanded that his death sentence be carried out (1977). Right before the firing squad let loose with the bullets, he uttered "Let's do it". Nike's ad agency (Weiden+Kennedy) were the culprits behind the phrase becoming Nike's signature line.

366. **A – William Howard Taft**. Taft started the U.S. tradition in 1910 at an Opening Day Senators game, but the notion actually started in Japan two years before when Japanese Prime Minister Ōkuma Shigenobu tossed one out at a game in Koshien Stadium. Originally, first pitches were thrown from wherever the honoree was sitting, but Ronnie Reagan changed that when he showed up, albeit not on Opening Day, at an Orioles game and heaved his from the playing field.

367. **C – Chris Weinke**, winning the Heisman as well as the national championship at Florida State. And what goes up must go down, right? After Weinke won the Heisman, he was drafted by the Panthers in the fourth round of the NFL draft where he went on to amass the second longest losing streak in NFL history at 17 behind Dan Pastorini's 21.

368. **D – None of the above**. I can hear the f-bombs dropping because many of you, I'm sure, said Pat Riley. According to the Oxford English Dictionary, the first published use of the portmanteau "three peat" came out of the mouth of Lincoln (IL) H.S. Tiger basketball player Sharif Ford whose team had just completed a "three-peat" of state championships. Pat Riley does indeed own the registered trademark "Three-peat," which he credits the origin of to one of his former players, Byron Scott. What U.S.A. teams had the first "three-peats"? In professional sports, it was the 1929-31 Green Bay Packers; in collegiate sports, the 1934-36 University of Minnesota football Gophers.

THE GREATEST SPORTS TRIVIA THROWDOWN OF ALL-TIME

369. **C – John Tesh**. The genesis of the song was actually during Tesh's coverage of the Tour de France and heard that NBC was looking for a theme for its NBA coverage. Kind of like when Keith Richards come up with the hook for "(I Can't No) Satisfaction," the melody for "Roundball Rock" hit Tesh in the middle of the night and he called his answering machine back home and hummed the tune into the recorder. When he got back, he shined up his idea and submitted it to NBC in a nom de plume. The network brass dug what they heard and made it part of anything and everything they did with a basketball from 1990-2002 until the NBA moved over to ABC.

370. **D – North Texas**, which – best as I could find – is *maybe* the only college team named after a person. However, I said *maybe*. There's two or three different backstories about where "Hoosiers" (as in chair-throwing Bobby Knight and Indiana University) came from and one involves a Louisvillian named "Samuel Hoosier." Sam was a contractor in the excavation of the Louisville & Portland Canal in the Ohio River. As the story goes, Hoosier preferred the work ethic of Indiana workers over the Kentucky ones and his men became known as "Hoosier's Men," then just plain "Hoosiers." Indiana's governor Birch Bayh and senator Vance Hartke bought into the story so much that they convinced the U.S. Congress to make it part of the *Congressional Record* in 1975.

371. **B – Underwater baseball**. The other three really do exist. There's even a world championship in underwater rugby and underwater hockey.

372. **C** –According to SportsGrid.com, in the olden days of baseball, fields were built so that the home plate corner of the diamond pointed west, which kept the afternoon sun out of the batters' eyes. So hitters would face east, with home plate, which means the pitchers were facing west making the left hand/paw on the south side of his body.

373. **A – Chad Henne**, who was drafted 57th overall. Brady was picked 199th, Grbac 219th, and Griese 91st. While Brady kicked his fellow Wolverines' tails in the NFL, Henne is (as of 2016) Michigan's all-time passing yardage leader with 9,715.

374. **C – Pole Vault**. Yelena is considered the undisputable female pole vaulter since Eve (yeah, that girl in the Bible). Two Olympic Golds... she set an astonishing 28 world records... and one of only nine athletes to win world championships at the youth, junior, and senior levels of an athletic event.

375. **D – Knicks**, for their coach Red Holzman and his 613 lifetime wins as the Knicks coach. Holzman was one of very few individuals to have won an NBA championship as both player and coach. His pro ball life started with being named "Rookie of the Year" back in 1944-45 playing for the Rochester Royals who also won the championship that year. After lackluster stints in Milwaukee and St. Louis as player/coach or coach, he beat the streets for 10 years as a Knicks scout and, then, took over the head coach gig in 1967. In 1969, Holzman coached the Knicks to a then single-season NBA record 18-game win streak, breaking the 17-game record first set back in '46. Holzman

was named the NBA's 1970 Coach of the Year as a nod to leading the Knicks to a championship. Red was also one of the rare Jewish NBA players. That short list includes three other Knicks coaches or players – Larry Brown, Ernie Grunfield, and Art Heyman – as well as Jordan Farmar, Rudy LaRusso, Dolph and Danny Schayes, Dukie Jon Scheyer, and Nat Holman, the only coach to win both the NCAA and NIT titles (at CCNY in 1950).

376. **A – Olga Korbut**. When you see all those exuberant, petite girls in the Olympic gymnastics events, you – and they – have Olga to thank for carving out that possibility. Prior to Olga's heroics in 1972, most Olympic athletes were predominantly older and the emphasis was less on acrobatics than it was on grace and style. After Korbut's epic win in Munich – at 4'11" and 82 pounds – the emphasis started to reverse and we saw a steady stream of young girls signing up for gymnastics lessons. After the Munich Olympics, Olga met President Nixon at the White House where he told her that her "performance in Munich did more for reducing the political tension during the Cold War between our two countries than the embassies were able to do in five years." What did Olga do after her Olympics fame faded? Married a Russian rock star, had a baby, moved to New Jersey, taught gymnastics, then off to Georgia where she got a divorce, then west to Scottsdale where she become head coach at Scottsdale Gymnastics and Cheerleading.

377. **A – Association Football** which morphed into "Soccer." Back in the mid-1800s, there were lots of

foot-and-ball sports and most had similar rules. In an attempt to standardize things, a group of English teams decided on a set of rules for what they called "Association Football," with "Association" meant to separate it from other football sports. Brit boys of the day liked to tag everything with a nickname – many by adding an "er". Rugby, for example, was called "rugger" and "Association Football" evolved into "Asoccer," then "Socca," then "Socker," then "Soccer." An Oxford student, Charles Wredford Brown, gets the nod as the nickname's originator. The saga goes that shortly after Association Football was set up, Chaz had some chums who asked him if he'd come play a game of "Rugger", to which he replied he preferred "Soccer".

378. **B – Western Kentucky vs. Middle Tennessee**. That jaunted joust between Murfreesboro and Bowling Green goes back to 1914.

379. **A – Pittsburgh**, where the Pirates, the Steelers, and the Penguins all wear black and gold which is the color scheme of the official flag of Pittsburgh. Prior to 1948, the Pirates' colors were red, white, and blue. While the Pirates weren't the first baseball team to do a color switch, they were one of the first to do this permanently and, along with the San Francisco Giants, one of two pre-expansion National League squads that completely changed their colors.

380. **C – Skeet shooting**, back in the 1920s. Disc golf came into being in 1965; racquetball in 1950; Grand Prix motorcycle racing in 1949). A fervent

grouse hunter by the name of Charles Davis up in Andover, Massachusetts came up with the original idea and called it Clock Shooting. That name came from the circular layout of the course with its circumference marked off like a clock face and a trap set at 12 o'clock. However, that around-the-clock idea didn't last long because someone built a chicken farm next door. The game continued to evolve with a little help from one of the shooters, William Harnden Foster, who plopped down a second trap at the 6 o'clock position and cut the course in half. Little by little, lots of men lined up to shoot things out of the sky and Foster decided to try and make it a national sport. The February 1926 issue of *National Sportsman and Hunting and Fishing* magazine introduced the sport to the masses and offered a $100 prize to some creative so 'n so who came up with a name for the new sport. Gertrude Hurlbutt entered the name "skeet" (I guess "hurl butt" wouldn't have worked). Supposedly "skeet" is derived from the Norwegian word for "shoot" (skyte).

381. **B – Eastern Washington**, who has a red turf field. However, they and Boise State aren't the only ones with colored turfs. There's Central Arkansas (purple and gray alternating every five yards), Lindenwood (red and gray alternating every five yards), New Haven (blue), Eastern Michigan (gray), and Coastal Carolina (teal). Boise State does hold all the cards when it comes to colored turf, though. They had the first college stadium field to be any color other than traditional green, as well as the only college to have a non-green field for 22 years (1986–2008). Back in

2011, the other members of the the Mountain West Conference had an atomic wedgie and got the commissioner to ban Boise State from wearing their all-blue uniforms during home conference games, saying it was an unfair advantage. Two years later, Boise State was invited to join the Big East and the Mountain West laid down, rolled over, and removed the uniform restrictions if they would stay. The Broncos' upper hand didn't end there, either. Boise State holds a trademark on any non-green field, not just blue and has licensed the right to use blue fields to several high schools as well as the University of New Haven.

382.   **C – Corkball**. And how does one play corkball? Well, the equipment is pretty simple – a ball that's stitched like a baseball but about a third of the weight, and a bat that's close to the specs of a fungo bat. Fielders may wear baseball gloves but are not required to, however the catcher must wear a catcher's mask while behind the plate. The pitching rubber and home plate are the same as used in baseball. Teams have to have at least two players (pitcher and catcher) and no more than five players on the field at a time. Measurements can be modified based on available space, but generally batters have to hit the ball at least 15 feet in order to register a hit. Then, any hit between 15 and 150 feet is called a single; 150 up to 200 feet a double; from 200 up to 250 feet it's a triple; and beyond 250 feet a home run. There's zero base-*running* because the scoring is all measured-based. "Runners" advance as many bases as the batter gets on the hit. If a runner is on first and the batter hits a double, then the resulting runners will be on

second and third. If a runner is on first and the batter hits a single, then it will be first and second.

383. **A – Minnesota Vikings'** "Ragnar" who's based
on the legendary Viking ruler Ragnar Lodbrok, a
royal thorn in the side of France and England in the
9th century and the father of many renowned sons,
including Ivar the Boneless, Björn Ironside, Sigurd
Snake-in-the-Eye, and Ubba. Ragnar became the
Vikes mascot when some guy dressed as a Viking
was accidently let onto the field by security at
Super Bowl IV.

384. **D – Four down linemen and three
linebackers**. The 4-3 defense evolved as a result
of the liberalized rules on passing. Before that,
most teams had lined up 7-2 and, as time
progressed, moved to 6-2, then 5-3, and 5-4. After
Paul Brown developed the timed, vertical spread-
out offense at Cleveland and won three AFC
championships in a row, defenses were at a loss as
to how to stop 'em. Giants' head coach Steve
Owen came up with an umbrella defense which
showed a 6–1–4 alignment before the snap but
had the built-in option to flex (drop back) its two
defensive ends into pass protection. His defensive
scheme was a success and the only two losses by
the Browns in 1950 came at the hands of the
Giants. While the concept belonged to Owen, his
newly acquired defensive back, Tom Landry,
explained and taught the defense. From there, it
evolved into the traditional 4–3 defense and the
precursor of the 4–3–4 defense of today.

385. **C – Baseball's** where it started – back in 1922. Prior to that, the winning teams got pocket watches or fob'y things (like medals). The very first team to have a ring? The New York Giants following their Series win over the rival Yanks. A couple of quick side notes: 1) The NFL limits teams to spend around $7,000 per ring and pays for the first 150 rings. 2) In 2005, it was reported that Russian president Vladimir Putin stole a Super Bowl ring from Pats' owner Robert Kraft. Kraft quickly issued a statement saying that he had given Putin the ring out of "respect and admiration" he had for the Russian people and Putin's leadership, but did a 180 later and said his earlier statement was a falsehood – that he'd been under pressure from the White House to put it out there like that and that Putin really did pilfer the ring. Wanna know who has the most Super Bowl rings? Well, it's a guy named Neil Dahlen with seven rings – all as an admin person. Yep. Player personnel guy with the Forty-Niners and GM of the Broncos. The player with the most rings is Charles Haley (Cowboys and Niners) who has five sittin' in his jewelry box.

386. **D – Jim Tressel**. Sadly, Jim's Buckeye boys found their inner dumbass button and started trading jerseys, championship rings, and other assorted football stuff for tattoos at Fine Line Ink, and the NCAA violations poured in. Tressel's "deny, deny, deny" responses eventually came undone, so he had no other choice but to resign. However... before he stepped down, he did some fairly remarkable things at OSU: became the only Buckeye coach to beat Michigan seven times in a

row; and, rung up the first 14–0 season record in major college football since 1897 Penn Quakers. So, what did Tressel do after that debacle? He became a game-day/replay consultant for the Indianapolis Colts, then back to U. Akron as Veep of Student Success, then back to Youngstown State as its President.

387. **A – Hank Greenberg, Ryan Howard, Jimmy Foxx**. Greenberg's 58 came in 1938; Howard's in 2006; and Jimmy Foxx' in 1932.

388. **C – NFL**. That question was probably too easy, wasn't it? Hmm. Even though the NFL draft goes waaaay back to 1936, it wasn't until 1976 that some unlucky dude was officially dubbed "Mr. Irrelevant" and that was Kelvin Kirk, pick number 487 in the draft. Kelvin never made it in the NFL, but there were some "Mr. Irrelevants" who did, like: a) Special teams guy Marty Moore who became the first Mr. Irrelevant to play in a Super Bowl (as a Patriot in Super Bowl XXXI); b) Jim Finn was a fullback for the New York Giants on their victory in Super Bowl XLII; c) 2008 winner David Vobora was a starting linebacker for the St. Louis Rams during the 2009 season; d) 2009 winner Ryan Succop was the Kansas City Chiefs starting kicker, and even went on to tie the NFL record for highest field goal percentage by a rookie in a season with 86.2%. He also passed NFL Hall of Famer Jan Stenerud for most field goals made by a rookie in Chiefs history.

389. **C – Fuzzy Zoeller**, who became the first golfer since 1935 to win The Masters in his first

appearance in the event. The only two other golfers to have won The Masters in their debut at Augusta were the winners of the first two Masters tournaments Horton Smith and Gene Sarazen, in 1934 and 1935 respectively.

390. **A – Stephen Martin**, as a baseball player at Tulane. I can hear you now – and you're screaming at this book "Tulane is <u>not</u> an SEC school, you idiot!" And, you're right – they're not, but they <u>were</u>! A charter member, in fact, and they competed in the league until 1966. Martin played on Tulane's baseball team their last year in the league. Why, pray tell, would any school in their right mind, split from a major conference like the SEC? Well, their excuse at the time was so the football team could broaden its schedule and play more inter-sectional games. The Green Wave isn't the only school to leave the SEC. Sewanee left in 1940 and Georgia Tech said sayonara in 1965, it's said because Tech's football coach Bobby Dodd was ticked off at how well Bear Bryant was doing at Alabama, and the reprehensible means Bear was employing to get, ahem, "student athletes" to come to 'Bama.

391. **D – Overall length of a bowling lane** – 62 feet 10 3/16 inches, measuring from foul line to pit. The distance from home plate to the pitcher's box is 60' 6". The distance from the NBA's three-point goal line to the basket is 22 feet. And the distance between soccer goal posts is 8 yards.

392. **B – NY Giants**. And, man oh man, could Fran SCRAMBLE! So much that he's #4 on the NFL's all-

time career rushing yards for QBs behind Randall Cunningham, Steve Young, and Michael Vick. When Tarkenton left football, he got into some other business games early – like motivational books and tapes (you may remember his "Think and Grow Rich" TV infomercial). Then, he became a software pioneer which landed him (and his partner) a $74 million check when they sold their company in 1994.

393. **A – First female fighter to step into the octagon**. And, know what? She was a tough fighter – <u>had</u> to be – from the moment she was born. Ronda came out of the womb with the umbilical cord wrapped around her neck and, for the first six years of her life, suffered from apraxia and couldn't form an intelligible sentence. At age 11, she started judo training with her mom, and by age 17, she qualified for the 2004 Olympics in Athens, becoming the youngest "judoka" in the games. She medaled at the '08 games and, with that victory, became the first American to win an Olympic medal in women's judo since its inception as an Olympic sport in 1992. She retired from judo at age 21, went into the MMA and the rest, as they say, is history.

394. **B – Louisiana State University**. Pettit's rise to roundball fame started with a couple of hiccups. He got cut from his Baton Rouge high school team as a freshman and a sophomore. However, he had a growth spurt and an additional five inches got him on the team and the team its first state championship in 20 years. He could've gone anywhere to college, but decided to stay at home

and go to LSU where he led the SEC in scoring for three years running and carrying the Tigers to their first Final Four. And Bob's pro career? He signed a contract with the Milwaukee Hawks for $11,000 – an all-time high for an NBA rookie. "I had only $100 in the bank when I graduated from college," Pettit recalled later, "and $11,000 looked like all the money in the world to me." Three years later, the Hawks were world champions and Pettit was on his way to becoming the first NBA player to break the 20,000-point barrier. He averaged 26.4 career points per game which is good for 8th on the all-time list.

395. **D – Ryukyu** (and ryukyu to you, too!). Ryukyu is what we know now as Okinawa (uh, 7,189 miles from Chicago) and it's there during WWII that American servicemen learned about karate and brought it back with them to the States. The World Karate Federation claims there are 100 million practitioners around the world versus 70 million for Taekwondo.

396. **A – Oregon's Autzen Stadium**, a place you've seen before, but probably didn't know it – the scene in *National Lampoon's Animal House* where it served as Faber College's stadium. Autzen's supposedly a real head trip of a place to place in. In 2007, during a 24–17 victory against USC, a record crowd of 59,277 fans was recorded at 127.2 decibels. When they played Michigan, one of the Wolverine's pressers wrote, "Autzen's 59,000 strong makes the Big House sound like a pathetic whimper. It's louder than any place I've ever been, and that includes The Swamp at Florida,

The Shoe in Columbus, and Death Valley at Louisiana State. Autzen Stadium is where great teams go to die." Dittos from *Sporting News* who named Autzen the most intimidating college football stadium in the nation and Lee Corso of ESPN College Gameday who frequently says, "Per person Autzen Stadium is the loudest stadium that I have ever been in my entire life!", and longtime ABC sportscaster Keith Jackson called Autzen "Per square yard, the loudest stadium in the history of the planet."

397. **D – Nolan Ryan**, who is also the only pitcher in baseball history to reach 5,000 strikeouts (he finished his career with 5,714)... the only pitcher to throw the "immaculate inning"(a nine-pitch/three-strikeout half-inning) in both leagues... the only player other than Jackie Robinson who has his number retired by three different teams... and, with his son, a rare father-son duo who were GMs of two separate MLB clubs. There's more "Nolan *is* and you're *not*," but we'll stop there for the sake of saving a tree.

398. **A – Jimmy Johnson**, who was coming off four straight 10+ win seasons and a national championship at the University of Miami. Jimmy and Jerry and been buds since they were roomies at Arkansas, but Jer' must've wondered what the heck he was thinking when Jimmy went 1-15 in his first year as Dallas. But, Jimmy turned things around and got Jerry back-to-back Super Bowl rings. By the way, Johnson was the first and one of only three football coaches to lead teams to both a major college

football championship and a Super Bowl (the other two being Barry Switzer and Pete Carroll).

399. **D – The Kentucky Derby** was the brainchild of Meriwether Lewis Clark Jr., grandson of William Clark (of Lewis and Clark fame). "Lutie" (as he was called) was also the guy who brought pari-mutuel betting machines to the U.S., an idea he picked up on when he was living in France. Where did Churchill Downs get its name? Clark's mom was a Churchill and the track was built on her family's land. The Jordan-got-cut-from-his-high-school-team story? Pure myth. He simply didn't make the varsity team when he was a sophomore and stayed on the JV team.

400. **A – Kentucky Colonels and St. Louis Spirits** (the Virginia Squires had already disbanded about a month earlier). Colonels owner John Y. Brown took his $3 million sorry-about-your-luck check and bought his own NBA team, but it was the Silna brothers (Ozzie & Daniel), polyester moguls and owners of the St. Louis team that made out like bandits. Instead of taking the full $3 mil, they took $2.2 mil and opted to take the rest as one-seventh of the yearly TV revenue from the four ABA teams that jumped to the NBA (Spurs, Pacers, Nets, and Nuggets) – a deal that was to be paid "in perpetuity" (like forever and a day). Their patience proved their idea a genius one and, over the course of the time, they cashed checks amounting to more than $300 million without ever having to lift a finger. The NBA got tired of writing those checks and offered the Silnas a lump sum of $500

mil to bring a close to their lifetime deal and the Silnas took it.

401. **B – Archie Manning at Ole Miss**, who sported #18 for the Rebels. In spite of the incredible job he did raisin' two Super Bowl MVPs, his pro career didn't pan out like his collegiate one did. In fact, he was the first QB to *lose* 100 games in the NFL, finishing with a 35-101-3 record (and, ouch, 340 sacks as a Saint alone!). The golden nugget in Archie's trivia box is this one: Archie was selected in the Major League Baseball draft four times: first by the Braves, twice by the White Sox, and finally by the Royals.

402. **C – 40-49**. The NFL's numbering scheme is based on a player's *primary* position and goes like this ...
   - 1-9: quarterbacks, kickers, and punters
   - 10-19: quarterbacks, kickers, punters, and wide receivers
   - 20–39: running backs and defensive backs
   - 40–49: running backs, defensive backs, linebackers, and tight ends.
   - 50–59: linebackers and centers, defensive linemen
   - 60–79: offensive linemen and defensive linemen
   - 80–89: wide receivers and tight ends
   - 90–99: linebackers and defensive linemen

Two football jersey number odds & ends: 1) 0 and 00 are no longer allowed, but they were before '73 when the NFL put their numbering system into place. 2) If you've noticed, pro football teams don't "retire" many jerseys. Even though the NFL allows it, they poo-poo it because they're paranoid a team will run out of numbers.

403. **A – Syracuse**. The three mack daddy football players? Jim Brown (who set an NCAA single-game record of 43 points against Colgate in a 61-6 Orange romp), Ernie Davis (the first African-American to win the Heisman. He signed with Cleveland to be part of the backfield with Jim Brown, but died of leukemia before ever suiting up for a game), and Floyd Little (averaged 199 running yards a game).

404. **A – Sheryl Swoopes** and her Nike "Air Swoopes." But shoes don't pay the bills, do they, Sheryl? Madam Swoopes made nearly $50 mil and lost it *all*. She blamed herself for the impressive mismanagement of cash and even had to sell her Olympic medals and Naismith trophy to shut up the creditors. And if losin' your lot ain't enuff? In 2013, Sher' became head coach of the Loyola Chicago women's b-ball team only to get fired a few years later for alleged mistreatment of players after the school newspaper reported that 10 of the team's players had either transferred or asked for a release from their scholarships. She's a bad mama jama...

405. **B – Virginia Tech**. Steph's pop, Dell, was a four-year starter for the Hokies basketball squad (second on the all-time points list, but that was before the 3-point'er), then went on to become the Charlotte Hornets' all-time leader in points and three-point field goals made. Dell also played baseball @ Va Tech and got drafted by the Orioles.

406. **C – Aroldis Chapman**, who threw some serious heat at 105.1 mph on that date. Six years later (2016), he matched that speed in an outing against the Orioles. Chapman's got another record, too – in July, 2014, he broke Bruce Sutter's record for the most consecutive relief appearances with a strikeout – that being 40. Chapman topped that by going for 49 consecutive appearances.

407. **B – Shot clock violation**. While it has nothing to do with the answer, but something to do with referees, I'll entertain your paycheck fantasies with this: Entry-level refs in the NBA start out at $150,000/yr. If you're a Senior-level ref, crank that up to $550,000+/yr. College basketball refs make in the neighborhood of $3,000/game in major conferences (plus travel expenses).

408. **D – Horace Fogel**. Baseball people don't get banned as much as they used to. To date, Rob Manfred's only banned one (Jenrry Majia)... Bud Selig only banned one (Marge Schott)... Fay Vincent sent only Steve Howe and George Steinbrenner to extended time in the showers. But, Judge Kennesaw Landis put the ban on 20, mostly related to gambling/game-fixing. Lip Pike – famous for becoming baseball's first professional player when the Philadelphia Athletics agreed to pay him $20 a week in 1866, also became the very first player banned. Pike got a brief call-up in 1881 to play for the Worcester Ruby Legs, but the 36-year-old Pike could no longer play effectively, hitting .111 and not managing a single extra base hit in 18 at-bats over 5 games. His play was so poor as

to arouse suspicions, and Pike found himself
banned from the National League that September.

409. **A – Jim Thorpe**, who's claimed by Jim Thorpe,
Pennsylvania (the county seat of Carbon County).
When Thorpe passed away in 1953, his widow,
Patricia, was incensed that Jim's home state of
Oklahoma wouldn't erect a memorial to honor him.
When she heard that the boroughs of Mauch
Chunk and East Mauch Chunk, Pennsylvania were
anxiously looking for a way to attract business, she
turned her dead husband's remains into a
commodity and made a deal with civic officials
where the boroughs would merge and name the
new municipality in Thorpe's honor. By the way,
Thorpe's not the only athlete to have a town
named after him. Milo, Maine is named after Milo
of Croton, a 6th-century BC wrestler from the
Magna Graecian city of Croton, Greece.

410. **B – Cardinals**. You said Packers, didn't you?
Well, the Green Bay Packers were an independent
team until they joined the NFL in 1921. Sorry. The
Cardinals were established in 1898 in Chi-town
and became a charter member of the NFL in 1920.
If someone tries to lay some jive on you that the
Cardinals have never won a championship, here's
some ammo to put 'em their place. The franchise
has actually won two NFL championships, both
while based in Chicago. The first came in 1925
and their second – and the first to be won in a
championship game – came in 1947, nearly two
decades before the first Super Bowl.

411. **A – John Havlicek**. Havlicek was drafted by
both the Celtics and the NFL's Cleveland Browns in
1962. He came to Ohio State as a high school All-
State star in three sports – basketball, football, and
baseball. And he was very good at all three. As a
QB, he could throw the ball 80 yards, but he never
set foot on the Buckeye gridiron. He did suit up for
OSU in baseball, though, and hit over .400 as a
freshman before he turned all his energies to
basketball where he helped lead the team to a 78-
6 record and a national championship. Still, the
Browns like Hondo's 6'5" 210lb build and thought
they'd use a draft pick on their idea. Havlicek
competed against future All-Pro Gary Collins as a
wide receiver. He played in a few exhibition
games, but Collins was a much better prospect and
Cleveland cut Havlicek, much to the Celtics delight.

412. **D – University of Houston**, who are the
Cougars. And why are they the Cougars? Because
when John Bender, the head football coach of the
Washington State Cougars, took the Houston gig,
he was so enamored with the Cougars moniker that
he decided to slap it on Houston, too. Bender also
qualifies as another trivia question. When he was
head coach at St. Louis University, local newspaper
reporters commented that Bender looked like a
charm doll called a Billiken, which was a fad at the
time. Hence, his squad became known as
"Bender's Billikens," which puts him squarely at the
genesis of SLU's sports nickname.

413. **C – Joe Pepitone**. Joe was his own closet of
anecdotes. One of those can be found in Jim
Bouton's *Ball Four*, where Bouton wrote that

Pepitone went nowhere without a bag of hair products for his rapidly balding head. Supposedly, Pepitone had two toupees, one for general wear and one for under his baseball cap, which he called his "game piece." In one story, Bouton tells about how Joe's "game piece" came loose one day when Pepitone took off his cap for the national anthem.

414. **A – Bill Russell**. In 1957, Russell set the then-record for rebounds in a game (49) and the still-standing record for rebounds in a half (32). Then, in 1960, Bill was the first to grab 50 rebs in a game, which Wilt matched about 10 months later. Between the two of them, they hold down 36 of the top 40 "most rebounds in a game" list.

415. **A – Hakeem Olajuwon**. "Mr. O, how do you describe this move of yours?" Mr. O replies, "The Dream Shake was actually one of my soccer moves which I translated to basketball. It would accomplish one of three things: one, to misdirect the opponent and make him go the opposite way; two, to freeze the opponent and leave him devastated in his tracks; three, to shake off the opponent and giving him no chance to contest the shot. The Dream Shake is you dribble and then you jump; now you don't have a pivot foot. When I dribble I move it so when I come here, I jump. By jumping, I don't have a pivot foot now. I dribble so now I can use either foot. I can go this way or this way. So he's frozen, he doesn't know which way I'm going to go. That is the shake. You put him in the mix and you jump stop and now you have choice of pivot foot. He doesn't know where you're gonna turn and when."

416. **A – The Olympics** and it happened at the
second modern Games in Paris (1900). The
winners actually received valuable paintings and
works of art rather than Gold medals. Then, four
years later in St. Louis, the first instance of Gold,
Silver, and Bronze medals going to the top three
finishers. By the way, they stopped giving away
solid-gold medals to champions after the 1912
Olympics in Stockholm. The ones we see today are
mostly silver and gilt with six grams of gold.

417. **D – Daniel Ruettiger**. If you're into fact
checking, there's a lot less to do on *Rudy* than
there would be on Donnie Trump. Ruetigger says
that the movie was "98% true," but things like
where Dan Devine is given a hostile role in the film
not so much. In real life Devine was one of
Ruetigger's biggest motivators to return to the team
and it was Devine's idea to dress Rudy for the last
game. Rudy's also stated that there was never a
"Rudy" chant during that final game. Rudy's stat
line at Notre Dame? Simple: On the final play of a
game against Georgia Tech, he sacked the
Yellowjacket's QB. Ruettiger is one of only two
players in Notre Dame history to be carried off the
field by his teammates. The other is Marc Edwards,
Irish middle linebacker, who got a hero's ride after
his team's upset win over the #5-ranked Southern
California in 1995.

418. **B – Oakland Oaks** in the '68-69 season. The
Oaks pulled off a historic turnaround, going from
worst to first and capturing their only ABA crown.
The team featured Larry Brown, Doug Moe, Rick
Barry (who moved across the bridge after the

Warriors ticked him off), and someone we seldom think of, Wichita State's Warren Jabali, the ABA's Rookie of the Year and playoff MVP. Didja know that Pat Boone was one of the Oaks' three owners?

419.	**A – "The opera ain't over until the fat lady sings,"** and it was recorded like this in the *Dallas Morning News*: "Despite his obvious allegiance to the Red Raiders, Texas Tech sports information director Ralph Carpenter was the picture of professional objectivity when the Aggies rallied for a 72–72 tie late in the SWC tournament finals. "Hey, Ralph," said Bill Morgan, "this… is going to be a tight one after all." "Right", said Ralph, "the opera ain't over until the fat lady sings." For you etymologists, the roots of this phrase date back to 1872, when a saying about the length of church services was being used analogically. A report in a Cincinnati newspaper discussed incomplete polling data for a U.S. Presidential election and told readers that the fate of candidate Horace Greeley was still uncertain. The line used was, "As long as the organ is playing church is not out. With Indiana and New York Greeley can spare Ohio and Pennsylvania. We see no reason whatever to despair of Greeley's election."

420.	**B – The name Secretariat's owners first applied for**. Actually, it took six tries before the owners ever got a name they wanted approved. After Sceptre, they asked for Royal Line and got denied. Then, Something Special, Games of Chance, Deo Volonti (God Willing), and, finally, Secretariat, which was the idea of the stable's secretary based on her previous job associated with the secretariat of the League of Nations.

421. **B – Lauren Haeger**, who actually may be better than the Babe. Dig... Although Ruth is known as a two-way player, he was a good pitcher first, then started hitting homers after he gave up his time on the mound. Out of the 714 homers Ruth swatted, just 14 of those round-trippers came in a game where he was the pitcher. Now, to Haeger... Keep in mind that pitchers don't usually hit in college softball (they're usually replaced by designated hitters), so that makes Haeger her own designated hitter and the combination of 70 wins as a domineering pitching ace and 70 HRs as a sultan'esque hitter might make her qualitatively and quantitatively better than the Babe. *Might...*

422. **A – Marion Jones**. It wasn't just the doping* that did her in, but she was also found guilty of taking part in a multi-million dollar check-counterfeiting scheme. *She claimed she thought she was taking flaxseed oil supplements. Uh, yeah...

423. **D – New Jersey Institute of Technology** (not to be confused with the Sam Houston Institute of Technology). NJIT became an independent school on July 1, 2013 after the Great West Conference, NJIT's former conference home, dissolved due to all other conference members leaving for more established conferences.

424. **B – Indiana**. After Coach K's college days were over at Army (he avg'ed 6.9 PPG his senior year) and post-grad five-year service in the United States

Army, he joined his old Army coach Bob Knight at IU during their 31-1 '74-75 season. Other assistants on Knight's staff were Bob Weltlich (head coach @ Texas and Ole Miss) and Dave Bliss (head coach @ SMU, Oklahoma, New Mexico, and Baylor).

425. **D – A "Detroiter"**. Not sure why the Motor City gets ownership of the move, but maybe you'll figure it out. The move is performed by the man lifting the lady over his head, holding her parallel to the ice while he is in a two-foot spin. The hold is the most dangerous part of the spin because the man is supporting the lady only by her legs. This move is also performed in more dramatic and dangerous fashion with a one-handed hold.

426. **C – George Halas**, with 30 years heading up the Chicago Bears. Lambeau put in 29 with the Packers, Landry 29 with the Cowboys, and Chuck Noll had 23 with the Steelers. That all had their own unique legacies, too. For example, Halas made the Bears the first team to hold daily practice sessions, to analyze film of opponents to find weaknesses and means of attack, place assistant coaches in the press box during games, place tarp on the field, publish a club newspaper, and to broadcast games by radio. Lambeau supposedly pioneered the forward pass in the NFL, implementing pass patterns and flying to road games. Tom Landry was one of the first NFL coaches to search outside the traditional college football pipeline for talent. For example, he recruited soccer players from Latin America, such Rafael Septien, to be the placekicker for the

Cowboys. And Noll? Under Noll, Joe Gilliam became the NFL's first African-American starting quarterback. Noll also had the first Black assistant coach. And let's not forget he was the first to win four Super Bowls.

427. **B – Nick Buoniconti**. You remember Nick, right? He was on that undefeated Dolphins team in '72 – a mountaintop so meaningful to him that he leads a champagne toast every season after the last remaining undefeated team loses for the first time. It's also rumored that Buoniconti sends a Christmas card every year to former Minnesota Vikings defensive end Bob Lurtsema, whose roughing-the-passer violation in an early 1972 game aided the Dolphins' undefeated season. But, Nick has a soulful side, too. You might remember 1985 when his son, Marc, was playing football at The Citadel and suffered a spinal cord injury making a tackle, rendering him a quadriplegic. Nick then became the public face of the group that founded the Miami Project to Cure Paralysis, now one of the world's leading neurological research centers.

428. **A – Brent Musburger**, although he ump'ed minor league baseball in the Fifties. Billy Packer (born Paczkowski) was an two-time All-ACC guard for Wake Forest's basketball squad. Jim Nantz played on the University of Houston's golf team (where he was Fred Couples' roomie). Curt Gowdy played both tennis and basketball at the University of Wyoming.

429. **A – Korea**. The "parenthood" of Taekwondo is Karate and Chinese martial arts along with the

indigenous styles of Taekkyeon, Subak, and Gwonbeop. "Tae" means "to stomp (or) trample," "kwon" means "fist," and "do" means ~~a deer, a female deer~~ "way (or) discipline." Chuck Norris and Jean-Claude Van Damme are both practitioners of the sport. Lots of UFC'ers and MMA'ers are, too, like Conor McGregor who averages more than a million pay-per-view'ers for his UFC bouts, spurred by his herculean romp at UFC 194, where he won by a knockout after 13 seconds in the first round, the fastest victory in UFC title fight history.

430. **D – Reggie Jackson**, who changed the face of baseball (bad pun) in 1972 when he showed up for Spring Training wearing a moustache. The story goes that Charlie Finley told manager Dick Williams to tell Reggie to shave it off. Dick did and Reg told him where to shove it. So, Dick's next move was to go full-out Freud on Reggie. Knowing that Reggie thought (highly) of himself as individualistic, Dick tried out a little reverse psychology and asked his pitchers to grow a moustache, too, hoping that Reggie would say "screw it" and shave his off. But the theory backfired and the A's wound up with Catfish Hunter, Rollie Fingers, et al all sporting moustaches and giving birth to "The Moustache Gang." That, of course, made the A's unique and since Finley always liked being different, he encouraged everyone on the team to grow one. He even told the team that he'd give a $300 bonus to any player who could grow one by Father's Day. Come Dad's Day, everyone on the dang team – even manager Dick Williams — had one. Finley even

offered free admission to the Father's Day game to anyone sporting a moustache. Well, Charlie was on a roll ticking off all the other owners and decided to get one more unique jab in and made the A's uniforms different from the rest of the league by going with a "two-tone uniform" that included a gold & green pullover jersey along with the traditional white pants. And for my etymology friends, this about the origin of "moustache": The word is French, who stole it from the 16th century Italians, who stole it from the 9th century Medieval Greeks, who most likely purloined it from the 300BC Hellenistic Greeks, who had this word "mustax" that meant "upper lip" or "facial hair."

431. **B – Maryland's Lefty Driesell**. However, for something a little more kin to what we think of as "Midnight Madness," these days, history tells us that in 1982, coach Joe B. Hall and the Kentucky Wildcats men's basketball team started officially promoting a celebration dubbed "Midnight Madness" as a school event with entertainment and an invited student audience.

432. **D – Orlando Cepeda**. His father, Pedro, was a superstar professional baseball player in Puerto Rico, where he was known as "The Bull," so Orlando naturally became "Baby Bull." The most interesting piece of trivia about Orlando is that he became the first player to sign a contract to exclusively play as a designated hitter. It was with the Red Sox in 1973 where his first hit with the team was a walk-off home run to beat the New York Yankees.

433. **C – The only pitcher in Major League Baseball history to throw two consecutive no-hitters**. And he threw both within a span of four friggin' days in 1938.

434. **A – Moses Malone**, the "Chairman of the Boards." Moses was a stud as far back as high school where he led his team to back-to-back undefeated seasons, two state titles, and 50 consecutive wins. He signed with Maryland, but the Utah Stars selected him in the third round of the ABA draft so he decided to throw his body around on the pro level. Malone began his professional career with Utah in the 1974–75 season after signing a five-year contract worth $1 million. The *New York Times* called him "the first high schooler in modern basketball to go directly to the pros." He laced up for 10 different teams during his tenure with most of his success coming in Houston where he was the NBA's Most Valuable Player three times. He ended up in San Antonio where he went out with a bang – during the final game of his NBA career, he hit a buzzer-beating three from the opposing free throw line, 80' away from the goal.

435. **C – Jerry Sloan**. When Jerry retired from coaching, his total number of wins was 1,221 (between the Jazz and the Bulls), placing him third all-time in NBA wins at the time of his departure. Jer' was only the fifth coach in NBA history to reach 1,000 victories and is one of two coaches in NBA history to record 1,000 wins with one club (Utah Jazz). Here's something interesting – When Sloan was playing college ball at the University of Evansville, coach McCutchan suggested Sloan

coach at his alma mater. After McCuthan retired in 1976, Sloan took the Evansville job but withdrew after five days. Had he taken the job, it's possible that he would've been on the same ill-fated flight that the Evansville basketball team and coaching staff were on – the one that crashed and killed everyone on board. It happened the very same season that Sloan would've started coaching the Purple Aces.

436. **D – UNC**, Chapel Hill, where she helped the Tar Heels win four NCAA women's championships in five years (she sat out the 1991 season to concentrate on the FIFA Women's World Cup). UNC only lost one game in the 95 she played on the team.

437. **A – New Orleans Saints**. After graduating from Notre Dame, we all know that Paul became a Packer with whom he went on to win four league championships, as well as the very first Super Bowl. However, oddly enough, he was the only Packer on the roster who didn't play in Super Bowl I. A pinched nerve sidelined him, and he chose not to enter the game in the 4th quarter. And the Saints? Well, Hornung was selected in the expansion draft by New Orleans who later traded for Hornung's backfield mate at Green Bay, former LSU All-American Jim Taylor (Taylor & Hornung were lovingly known as "Thunder & Lightning" by Packer fans). Hornung never suited up for the Saints, as a neck injury forced him to retire during training camp. Btw, the Saints picked up another Packer in that expansion draft – Bill Curry, former 'Bama and Kentucky coach, but he never suited up for the

Saints, either. Got traded to the Baltimore Colts, instead, where he won another Super Bowl.

438. **A – University of Tennessee at Martin** (aka UTMB back in the day), where she was an All-American and later co-captained the United States women's national basketball team as a player at the inaugural women's tournament in the 1976 Summer Olympics, winning the Silver medal. Pat was sort of thrown into the head coaching gig @ Tennessee when, just before the '74-75 season, UT's coach suddenly quit and Pat, a graduate assistant, was named the new head coach. Summitt earned $250 monthly and washed the players' uniforms which were purchased the previous year with proceeds from a donut sale. During Summitt's first year as head coach, four of her players were only a year younger than she was. Now, mind you, this was waaaay back in 1980, when women's basketball was a six-person game where offensive and defensive players never crossed mid-court. Eight years after her Olympics appearance as a player, she coached the U.S. women's team to a Gold medal, becoming the first U.S. Olympian to win a basketball medal and coach a medal-winning team. Her net worth was estimated at around $8 million at the time of her passing.

439. **C – Arthur Ashe.** Ashe was the first black player selected to the U.S. Davis Cup team and the only black man ever to win the singles title at Wimbledon, the US Open, or the Australian Open. Ashe was probably the first celebrity-level AIDS-related victim that any of us remember. However, it wasn't related to sexual contact, but rather a transfusion.

The backstory is that, in July 1979 at age 34, Ashe suffered a heart attack at a tennis clinic he was leading. Then, four years later, another. It was during his second heart surgery doctors theorize Arthur contracted toxoplasmosis, a parasitic disease that is commonly found in people infected with HIV, through one of his blood transfusions.

440. **A – Chuck Daly**. He didn't replace Cousy because Cousy was doing a lousy job at Boston College. Quite the opposite – Bob was 114–38 (.750) at B.C. Nonetheless, Daly succeeded Cous' and went 11-13 and 15-11 before he moved on to Penn, then the Sixers (ass't), the Cavs, Pistons, and the '92 Olympic Dream Team. Back to college ball for a sec – most of us don't associate Daly with Duke, but his first coaching gig ('63-69) was as a Dukie assistant under Vic Bubas. During his six-year stint there, the Blue Devils won the ACC and went to the Final Four twice.

441. **D – Fielding Yost**, who spent 25 years roving the Wolverine sidelines, whipping up six national championships and 10 Big Ten titles. From 1901 to 1905, his "Point-a-Minute" squads went 55–1–1, outscoring their opponents by a margin of 2,821 to 42. The 1901 team beat Stanford, 49–0, in the 1902 Rose Bowl, the first college football bowl game ever played (I know, I know – I've made that point elsewhere in this book).

442. **C – Standardbreds**. What's the differences between a Standardbred and a Thoroughbred? Well, it's like this: Standardbreds were developed about 100 years before Thoroughbreds... they

come in fewer colors than a T'bred... generally, they weigh about 50 pounds less... height-wise, they're about the same... they can perform most of the same sporting functions, except hunting which a Standardbred is good for and a Thoroughbred isn't... and, temperamentally, Standardbreds are a lot less "hot" than Thoroughbreds and, thus, probably don't pout when they lose a match.

443. **B – Ryan Lochte**. Despite always finishing second to Michael Phelps and anything but welcome in Brazil, Lochte is due some pool props. Before he was a backstroke and team medley stud at the Athens, Beijing, London, and Rio Olympics, he tore it up in Gainesville. At the University of Florida, Lochte was the NCAA Swimmer of the Year twice, a seven-time NCAA champion, a seven-time SEC champion, and a 24-time All-American. At the 2006 NCAA Men's Swimming and Diving Championships, he won national titles in all three of his individual events, setting U.S. Open and American records in the 200-yard individual medley and 200-yard backstroke. Out of the pool, Ryan's ego and good looks served him well, too. Seth MacFarlane parodied him on *SNL*, he did cameos on *30 Rock* and *90210*, and even had his own show on *E!* called *What Would Ryan Lochte Do?* that scored him a Teen Choice Award nomination (you go, boy!). Trying to capitalize on his celebrity, Lochte even filed an application to trademark his personal catchphrase, "Jeah," with the U.S. Patent & Trademark Office. Sadly, he abandoned the application before it was finalized. And I was looking forward to that becoming part of our vernacular, dammit! Jeah? Juhno.

444. **A – Winners of the LPGA "ANA Inspiration"**
(what used to be the Dinah Shore Classic) **jump
into the lake**. Amy Alcott was the first golfer to
take the plunge (1988), an act that has come to be
known as the "Champion's Leap." The other
answers? Close, but no cigar as far as the truth
goes. For example, the football players at Notre
Dame do slap a sign, but the sign that says "Play
Like a Champion Today" came to life when Lou
Holtz found an old Notre Dame photo that included
the sign. But the Irish may have ripped it off of the
Sooners since OU has had a sign in their locker
room with the exact same phrase since the '40s.
Oklahoma even takes a version of the sign on the
road and, since OU and ND had an annual series in
the '50s, the picture that Holtz saw may have been
one of the Sooners' signs from that era, and not one
belonging to Notre Dame. The one about jersey-
swapping? Dunno of anyone in the U.S. that's done
that, but at a 1931 soccer match where France
upset England, the French players asked the Brits for
their jerseys as a sign of respect and a way to
memorialize their victory. And, it was President Taft,
not Ike, that got up to stretch at a Senators game in
1910. When he rose, all the other fans did, too, in
respect for the Commander-in-Chief.

445. **C – Mariano Rivera**, or **D – Dan Quisenberry**, who both won the award five times.
However, if you look at career saves, Rivera kicks
everyone else's tush with 652. Breaking that down
to seasonal saves, Francisco Rodriguez of the
Angels had 62 in 2008. As far as consecutive saves,
the Dodgers' Eric Gagne had a Superman-like 84 in
a row from 2002-2004. If you turn this award

upside down – meaning *blown* saves – you'd see Goose Gossage at the top of the list with 112.

446. **B – 49ers and Bengals**, a game that the Niners won 28-21. The trivial side of the match-up? Here you go: It was the only Super Bowl (to date) played at the Pontiac Superdome ... Cincinnati head coach Forrest Gregg became the second man to play in a Super Bowl and then be a head coach in a Super Bowl (Gregg played in Super Bowl I and Super Bowl II as a member of the Green Bay Packers. Tom Flores, who played in Super Bowl IV and coached in Super Bowl XV, was the first to hit that trivia lick.) ... and, it was the only Super Bowl to date between two teams who had losing records the previous season.

447. **A – South Carolina**. It happened in 1971 and the Gamecocks' original notion was to carry on as an independent. The ACC kept on keepin' on as a seven-school conference until 1978 when they invited Georgia Tech to join, followed by Florida State in 1991 – both of those schools robbed from the cradle of the Metro Conference. Why oh why is there an ACC, anyway? It's because of ... you guessed it, football! Clemson, Duke, UNC, NC State, Maryland, Wake, South Carolina were in the Southern Conference, but the conference put forth a ban on post-season football and, boom!, they were goners.

448. **D – San Diego Conquistadors**. It was 1973 when the Conquistadors signed Wilt to a three-year, $1.8 million contract as the team's player-coach. The Lakers promptly went to court and won

a ruling that Chamberlain could only *play* pro ball for the Lakers, but the court did allow Wilt to coach the Conquistadors. Wilt wasn't exactly into the gig, though. Since he couldn't play (and didn't have any experience as a coach), he left most of the coaching duties to Stan Albeck. That is, *when* Wilt was actually at the game. He was pre-occupied with promotion of his autobiography *Wilt: Just Like Any Other 7-Foot Black Millionaire Who Lives Next Door* than with coaching. There was even one instance where he skipped a game to sign autographs for the book.

449. **C – Mississippi State**. The story goes like this... Before it was certain that Mississippi State would face Loyola and their four black starters, the racist side of the Mississippi media thought they'd kick up some dust like when the *Jackson Daily News* printed a picture of Loyola's starters to show that four of them were African-Americans. The caption of the picture read "Readers may desire to clip the photo of the Loyola team and mail it today to the board of trustees of the institution of higher learn-ing" to prevent the game from taking place be-cause, at the time, there was a Mississippi state pol-icy that barred college teams at state schools from playing games against racially integrated teams. The editorials were a direct response to the Missis-sippi State President Dean W. Colvard's decision to accept the automatic tourney bid since they were outright SEC champions. MSU's board even met and upheld Colvard's decision. But just a day be-fore the team was scheduled to travel to East Lansing, a couple of state senatorial cronies ob-tained a temporary injunction against the team

leaving the state. Conversely, the team got word that sheriffs were on their way to Starkville to serve the injunction, and put a contingency plan into effect. Before papers could be served, President Colvard left the state for a speaking engagement in Atlanta and Babe McCarthy, the coach and AD, along with his assistant AD, drove to Memphis, and then flew to Nashville. Early the next morning, the team's trainer and a handful of seldom-used reserves drove to a private airport in Starkville. When they saw the path was clear, they called to an assistant coach who was hiding with the varsity players someone on campus and told 'em to high-tail it to the airport. They boarded a plane without incident, made a stop in Nashville to pick up McCarthy and his assistant, then caught a commercial flight to the game at East Lansing, Michigan.

450. **A – The first female reporters ever allowed to enter a men's professional team locker room**. It was at the 1975 N.H.L All-Star Game in Montreal. Yet, it's *Sports Illustrated* reporter Melissa Ludtke who gets more light shining on her than Herman and St. Cyr because she took on Major League Baseball and sued them on the foundation that her 14th amendment rights were violated when she was denied access to the New York Yankees clubhouse while reporting on the 1977 World Series.

451. **A – Hoyt Wilhelm**. Something you've probably never thought about, but because of the physics of the pitch, it's hard to find a catcher that can actually snare a knuckleball. And that was sort of a double-edge sword for Hoyt. While he had some great

years and in the hunt for "best (pick it) of the year" type honors, the stuff he threw also created a lot of "passed balls" – so many (49) that Hoyt's cadre of catchers hold an MLB record for passed balls. One skipper, the Orioles' Paul Richards, even designed a larger catcher's mitt to try and overcome the issue. One little "feel good" for you old folks before we go to another question – the Society for American Baseball Research calls Hoyt the "most famous 'old' player" in baseball history. He didn't make his major league debut until age 29 and held on until he was almost 50. Like the question said, he was the oldest player in Major League Baseball for each of his final seven seasons.

452. **D – War Memorial Stadium in Buffalo**. All of the baseball scenes in *The Natural* were filmed there except for the one scene set at Wrigley Field, which was filmed at Buffalo's All-High Stadium. All-High has been long since demolished, much in part to being deemed unsuitable for National Football League play after the AFL–NFL merger. As part of a deal with Congress clearing the way for the merger, the NFL declared that stadiums seating fewer than 50,000 people were not suitable for league needs. War Memorial could only seat 46,500 people and could not be expanded. This resulted in two things: 1) The Bills almost moved to Seattle so they could get the stadium they needed; then, 2) After that threat, the city got off its butt and built Rich Stadium in suburban Orchard Park.

453. **B – Team handball**, aka Olympic handball, European team handball, European handball, or Borden ball. A seven-meter throw is sort of like a

penalty kick in soccer. I don't think you're too interested in team handball minutiae, so I'll just move on, now.

454. **B – Oklahoma**, who has also eclipsed 150 points twice (but so has Tulsa). Georgia Tech is the only Division I team to record over 200 points in one game, which happened in 1916 when the Yellow Jackets beat Cumberland 222–0.

455. **A – Bill Murray**, whose thrown money at the Charleston RiverDogs, Hudson Valley Renegades, Brockton Rox, Utica Blue Sox, Fort Myers Miracle, Catskill Cougars, and Salt Lake City Trappers. Bill also suited up for the Grays Harbor Loggers in 1978, and appeared in two at-bats with one hit which gives him a lifetime batting average of .500. And his boy? Luke's his name; basketball his game. Assistant coach at Arizona, then at Wagner, Towson, Rhode Island, and Xavier.

456. **D – Pete Rose**, who, upon being traded from the Montreal Expos to the Cincinnati Reds in 1984, was immediately named the Reds' skipper. Rose managed and served as a backup infielder until the end of the 1986 season, when he retired as a player. A quick side note: Major league rules are somewhat different for trips to the mound by the manager if he is a player-manager (with regard to being required to change pitchers), and a player-manager puts himself into or out of the lineup just as he would any other player.

457. **B – CCNY** (City College of New York), but only a year later, they rolled up into a big ball and died a

painful death because of point-shaving. Seven CCNY basketball players wound up being arrested and the scandal led to the decline of CCNY from a national powerhouse in Division I basketball to a lowly member of Division III. Basketball fans might also be interested in knowing that the year CCNY won it all was also the first year that John Wooden led UCLA to the NCAA tourney.

458. **C – Michigan State**, then it was another 40 years before the next team – Penn State – joined. Sparty has the University of Chicago to thank for joining the Big 10. When U. Chicago eliminated varsity football and withdrew from the Western Conference (now the Big Ten) in 1946, Michigan State lobbied to take its place and, despite opposition from the folks in Ann Arbor, the Big Ten admitted the Spartans in 1949.

459. **C – Brett Favre**, who also, at the time of his retirement, was the NFL's all-time leader in passing yards and passing touchdowns. Both records have since been broken by Peyton Manning.

460. **B – Bundesliga**. Yep, it does sound like a disease you'd have been likely to get in your wilder days, but it means "Federal League" in English and it has the largest average attendance of all the soccer (non-U.S. football) leagues. It's an 18-team league that got its start in 1962 and there've been more than 50 teams that have been league members during its history. Last time I checked, Bundesliga averaged 43,527 folks per game or about 10-thou more than the English Premier League. If you add up the average attendance of all the soccer

leagues in the world, you're looking at an average attendance of more than 144,000 fans per game and a total of 53 million fans who go to soccer games a year.

461. **B – Octavio Dotel or C – Shayne Graham** would get you the prize since they both have 13 different teams on their résumé (Graham would have more than that if you count practice squads or offseason duty). Chucky Brown is one of four NBA'ers who've played for 12 teams (the others being Jim Jackson, Tony Massenburg, and Joe Smith). Mike Sillinger also played for 12 NHL teams. If we turn this question on its head and ask what player toiled the longest for one single "major league" team during their career, my research says Alex Delvecchio of the Red Wings holds the record of the greatest number of seasons with 24 in Detroit, then Brooks Robinson and Carl Yastrzemski who both put in 23 years for the Orioles and Red Sox respectively.

462. **A – Bobby Collins**. 'Ol Bob was on a roll, gig-wise – he'd run a 48-30-2 record at Southern Miss and had leveraged his prowess into a 31-4-1 stretch (from '82-84) at SMU coupled with three Top 11 final poll rankings before his world came tumbling down. Although he admitted that he knew that players were being paid, but just not sure who, the NCAA gave him a pass and SMU gave him $850k to keep his mouth shut. Still, the perception of his goose was cooked and he never coached (in any capacity) in the collegiate ranks, again.

463. **A – Memphis** in 2008. KU had been keeping
good tabs on Memphis' free throw percentages
and started tactically fouling the Tigers. Memphis
missed five FTs in a row while the Jayhawks rung
up 12 points in the last two minutes. In retrospect,
John Calipari would probably tell you he screwed
the pooch by not putting the Jayhawks on the foul
line, but he left 'em alone and let fate do its thing.
Had the Tigers won, they would've had to give the
trophy back anyway as they got nailed for Derrick
Rose having a little help on the SAT. That little oops
added to the sour side Memphis' W-L balance
sheet, which now includes 14 tournament victories
and 47 victories overall they've had to cross out.
While that sounds like a lot, it's a far cry from
Michigan who had to wipe out 150 wins thanks to
NCAA sanctions, Syracuse lost 106, and Ohio
State had to forfeit 82 victories.

464. **A – Josh Gibson**. Josh was a catcher, born in
Buena Vista GA, a lifetime batting average of .359
and slugging percentage of .648, 69 round-
trippers in a single season, and almost 800*
homers which would put him at the top of the
career HR list. Even though Gibson never played in
the major leagues because of an unwritten
"gentleman's agreement" policy that prevented
non-white players from participating, he was
thought to be as good as Jackie Robinson, if not
better. Larry Doby, who broke the color barrier in
the American League a few months after Robinson
broke it in the National, said at the time of
Robinson's signing with the Brooklyn Dodgers
organization, "One of the things that was
disappointing and disheartening to a lot of the

black players at the time was that Jackie was not the best player. The best was Josh Gibson." In 1972, he was the second Negro leagues player (after Satchel Paige) to be inducted in the Baseball Hall of Fame. *Josh's stats include playing vs. semi-pro competition and in exhibition games. The "almost 800 HRs" is because there's no exact data on that metric and 800 is the HOF's best estimate.

465. **C – Bocce**. The "jack" is the ball that's thrown to start a match.

466. **B – Tommy Lasorda**. What is they say? "Those who can, do; those who can't, teach"? Tommy could manage his butt off (won 1599 games and two World Series), but in his two years as a pitcher with the Dodgers and one with Kansas City, it wasn't such a pretty picture, going 0-4 with an ERA of 6.49.

467. **A – Houston Oilers**. Oliver went to West Virginy to school where he QB'ed the couch-burning Mountaineers. He was the third quarterback picked in the 1982 draft (behind Art Schlichter and Jim McMahon), spent his first year in Texas on the bench, then became the Oilers' starter, going 2-14. On the heels of that season, the team hired Warren Moon and the writing was pretty much on the wall for Mr. Luck. So, whaddya do at that point? Hmm, how 'bout go to law school. And that he did. He eventually wound up back at WVU as the A.D., and, then, he moved to Indy and the NCAA HQ where he became the Veep of Regulatory Affairs.

468. **D – Glenn Hall**, who is credited the goaltender who developed the butterfly style of goalkeeping

where the goalie guards the lower part of the net by dropping to their knees to block attempts to score. The butterfly style derives its name from the resemblance of the spread goal pads and hands to a butterfly's wings.

469. **A – William Renshaw**, who also won the title a record six times consecutively (1881–86) (Borg and Federer won five consecutive titles). Additionally, Willie won the doubles title five times together with his brother Ernest. Still, he's a fur piece behind Martina Navratilova's 20 Wimbledon titles.

470. **D – Dick LaBeau**. I say "57+" seasons because, as of 2016, Dick's still doin' it. Fourteen of those seasons were with the Lions as a player, then 43 as a coach. Considered a defensive genius, the Dickster created the "zone blitz" when he was defensive coordinator of the Cincinnati Bengals in the late 1980s. He's got two Super Bowl rings as well as a collegiate national championship when he played for THE Ohio State University and Woody Hayes.

471. **A – Southern Conference**. Before the SEC, ACC, etc., there was the Southern Conference. Way back in 1921, 14 schools split from the Southern Intercollegiate Athletic Association to jump to the new Southern Conference. Charter members were Alabama, Auburn, Clemson, Georgia, Georgia Tech, Kentucky, Maryland, Mississippi State, North Carolina, North Carolina State, Tennessee, Virginia, Virginia Tech, and Washington & Lee. In 1922, six more universities – Florida, LSU, Mississippi, South Carolina, Tulane,

and Vanderbilt joined the conference – and, a few years later, Duke, VMI, and Sewanee signed on. I think it's fair to say that the Southern was also the pappy of two other major conferences – the SEC and ACC – when two geo-centric groups of schools broke off to form those conferences. Ok, back to the answer... The SoCon became the first league to hold a post-season basketball tournament to decide a conference champion. The first champ was North Carolina who defeated non-member Mercer in the finals 40-25 back in 1922. The next-oldest tournament overall is the SEC Men's Basketball tourney, which started in 1933, but it was suspended after its 1952 tournament and didn't resume until 1979.

472. **B – University of Nebraska**. Y'all know what it means when we say that a player was "redshirted," right? Ok, then, I'll proceed. The origin of the term was likely from Warren Alfson of the University of Nebraska who, in 1937, asked to practice but not play, so they gave him a red Nebraska jersey without a number to wear.

473. **B – Peanuts**. Starting in 1980, Charles Schulz started incorporating Zambonis into his *Peanuts* comic strip as well as into the 1980 television special *She's a Good Skate, Charlie Brown*. Thanks to Shulz' help, the Zamboni became a lot closer to becoming a household word than it would have any other way.

474. **A – Pommel Horse**. The history of the pommel horse goes way back to Alexander the Great. In the 4th century, Vegetius described Roman soldiers

using wooden horses for practice in his "Overview of the Roman Army". Then, about 13 centuries later, I guess someone found Veg's book at a yard sale and decided to turn that military practice into a sporting activity and, eventually, an Olympic event starting in 1896.

475. **B – In squash, if you hit the "tin," your ball's considered out**. That and squash is 122 years older than racquetball.

476. **B – Table tennis** (ping-pong). Makeshift versions of the game were developed by British military officers in India in around 1860s. They set up a row of books along the center of the table as a net, then used two more books as rackets and the ball was a golf ball. The game had several different names like 'whiff-whaff," but "ping-pong" was the one that stuck British manufacturer J. Jaques & Son Ltd trademarked it in 1901. Snowboarding? 1965 when Sherman Poppen, an engineer in Muskegon, Michigan, invented a toy for his daughters by fastening two skis together and attaching a rope to one end so he would have some control as they stood on the board and glided downhill. Dubbed the "snurfer" (combining snow and surfer), the toy proved so popular among his daughters' friends that Poppen licensed the idea to Brunswick who sold about a million snurfers over the next decade. Midget car racing? It was officially born in 1933 at the Loyola High School Stadium in Los Angeles as a regular weekly program under the control of the first official governing body, the Midget Auto Racing Association (MARA). And, finally, miniature golf: The earliest documented mention of a

geometrically-shaped mini-golf course made of artificial materials (carpet) came in a 1912 edition of *Illustrated London News* which introduced a mini-golf course called "Gofstacle." Glad they got rid of that moniker – sounds a little painful if you know what I mean.

477. **C – Enos Slaughter**. Enos was a gutsy son-of-biscuit-eater and he proved it in what baseball historians call the great "Mad Dash." It came in Game 7 of the 1946 World Series between the Red Sox and Slaughter's Cardinals. Red Sox center fielder Dom DiMaggio drove in two runs in the top of the eighth to knot everything up at 3. But, DiMaggio pulled a hamstring during the play and was forced to leave the game, being replaced by Leon Culberson. When St. Louis got up to bat, Slaughter led off with a single, but neither of the next two batters was able to reach base safely nor advance the runner. That's when things got interesting. Cardinal outfielder Harry Walker stepped to the plate and, after the count reached two balls and one strike, the Cardinals called for a hit-and-run. As the runner (Slaughter) started, Walker lined the ball to left-center field, where Culberson fielded the ball. As he threw a relay to shortstop Johnny Pesky, Slaughter rounded third, disregarded the third base coach's stop sign, and continued for home. No one's sure what was going on in Pesky's head at that moment, but his brain sorta hit the pause button. He either assumed Slaughter would not be running home and checked Walker at first base instead of immediately firing home, or he was completely freaked to see Slaughter on his way to score and simply had a

mental lapse that accounted for the delay. Whatever was going on in Pesky's pumpkin, his little procrastination and a weak throw home allowed Slaughter to score just as Red Sox catcher Roy Partee caught it up the line from home plate. The run put the Cardinals ahead 4-3 and proved to be the winning run of the decisive game 7.

478. **B – Bill Walton** won a couple of championships at UCLA, but son Luke didn't get to cut down the nets during his career at Arizona. Other than the ones listed, the only other father-son duo that can claim a championship between 'em are Henry and Mike Bibby.

479. **A – Because you could sneak up on someone**. The year was 1887 when the *Boston Journal* made reference to "sneakers" as "the name boys give to tennis shoes."

480. **A – Bobby Jones**, whose retirement dream was to build a golf course and nuttin' else. The spot of land where the Augusta National sits, now, used to be an indigo plantation (shrubbery, but not the Monty Python kind ☺) and a plant nursery. But Bobby didn't do the course alone. He hired a chap named Alister MacKenzie who was a famous camoufleur – someone who designs camouflage. MacKenzie thought there was a great similarity between golf course and camouflage design, so he took that slant and was off on his merry Masters-buildin' way.

481. **B – The candlepin ball is smaller <u>but</u>** it doesn't have *any* finger holes.

482. **D – Roque**. Yep, you guessed it – croquet without the "C" and the "T". Played on hard, smooth surface that was walled and beveled so it was kinda like playing billiards on the floor with players banking off the walls like a pool player would bank off the cushions of a pool table. The sport's popularity shrunk over the years and by 2004, the American Roque and Croquet Association suspended tournaments because of the scant number of participants.

483. **B – Buffalo Sabres**. The Sabres' GM at the time, Punch Imlach, thought he'd have a little fun during the 1974 amateur draft and asked his PR guy to come up with a fictional player. The PR guy thought an Asian would be hilarious and remembered the name of an Asian grocery store he used to pass when he drove on Route 16 from Buffalo to St. Bonaventure – the Tsujimoto store. The Sabres felt it would only be polite to ask if they could use the family name and the Tsujimotos gave their blessing without being told the real intent of how the team would use it. The Sabre folk coupled it with a popular first name in Japan and, hence, "Taro Tsujimoto, the star center of the Japanese Hockey League's Tokyo Katanas" was born (Katanas means something akin to "sabres" in Japanese. The NHL made the pick official, and it was even reported by media outlets including *The Hockey News*. Tsujimoto's pick came at a time when the NHL was beginning to expand its reach for players outside Canada and the USA and getting a player from Japan didn't seem to be that much out of the ordinary. The Sabres kept the ruse alive until just before the start of training camp that

year and the NHL eventually changed the pick to an "invalid claim" for its official record-keeping purposes. To this day, Buffalo fans chant "We Want Taro" when games got one-sided. In addition, for many years, banners would be hung from the balcony rail stating "Taro Says..." followed by a witty comment against an opponent. Trading card company Panini America even went as far as adding Tsujimoto to its 2010-11 Score Rookies & Traded box set using a picture of an unidentified Asian man playing hockey for a team wearing blue-and-gold colors similar to the Sabres'.

484. **A – Tampa Bay Buccaneers**. I'm not gonna dwell on the Bucs foibles since the question did a pretty good job, but the biggest hurdle they had to overcome was the age and shape of their players. Back in the day, the NFL expansion draft was made up of mostly aging players and the expansion teams were given zero medical history on the available players. That lack of knowledge bit the Bucs in the butt and, by the time their first season ended, they had 17 players on injured reserve. Their coach was John McKay, who they hired from Southern Cal where he led the Trojans to four national titles. Despite being offered head coaching gigs with the Cleveland Browns, New England Patriots and Los Angeles Rams, it was the Bucs' money that talked the loudest – $2 mil a year, more than five times what he made at USC, so he thought it was worth the gamble. Following one of Tampa's many early losses, McKay was asked what he thought of his team's "execution." He replied, "I'm all for it." After the Buccaneers won their first regular season game against the

New Orleans Saints during the 1977 season, McKay mused, "Three or four plane crashes and we're in the playoffs." And, after receiving harsh criticism from the media about his NFL coaching skills, McKay replies "You guys don't know the difference between a football and a bunch of bananas." In the next interview, members of the media left bananas for McKay. He then replied, "You guys don't know the difference between a football and a Mercedes Benz." Ha!

485. **B – Indiana State Sycamores** (who used to be called the "FiDghting Teachers" when it was "Indiana State Teachers College"). The Missouri Valley Conference goes way back and counts about 50 schools on its past-and-present list, including Kansas, Oklahoma, Louisville, SMU, Houston, Cincy, Missouri, Kansas State, TCU, Iowa, Iowa State, Nebraska, even Vandy (in men's soccer). One thing that the MVC doesn't have as a conference sport is football, so the schools that want to play on the gridiron have to play in a separate conference for that.

486. **C – Polo** with four. Ice hockey, 6... Ultimate Frisbee with 7... Field hockey with 11. And, didja know that women's lacrosse has 12 players on the field at the same time where men's lacrosse only has 10? Or that slow pitch softball has 10 folks on the field simultaneously where fast pitch only has 9?

487. **B – The tradition of cutting down the nets.** The year is correct, but it was North Carolina State coach Everett Case and not IU's coach Branch McCracken. Case wasn't trying to upstage anyone,

mind you. He just was a dude who wanted a little souvenir he could take home when the Wolfpack won the Southern Conference tourney. But, neither Case or the conference higher-ups hat planned for this moment and he had to ask his players to hoist him on their shoulders so he could cut the nets instead of the ladder they use today. Btw, if do any research on this question, you might find a dissenting opinion about Case actually starting this trend at a high school in Indiana rather than NC State, but either way, he was still the guy who popularized the notion.

488. **C – Baseball umpire**. The Phog'er lettered in baseball and basketball at KU, and lucky enough to play basketball under James Naismith, the game's inventor. He also served as the head football coach at Kansas for one season and Jayhawk baseball coach for two seasons, plus served as the university's athletic director from 1919-1937. During his tenure at Kansas, Allen coached Dutch Lonborg, Adolph Rupp, Ralph Miller, and Dean Smith, all future Hall of Fame coaches. Among the Hall of Fame players he coached were Paul Endacott, Bill Johnson, and Clyde Lovellette. He also recruited Wilt Chamberlain to Kansas, and even coached former United States Senate Majority Leader Bob Dole.

489. **D – Spurs**. I, for one, didn't know it, but Tark the Shark was actually offered the head coach gig of the L.A. Lakers back in '77 (taking Jerry West's place), but opted to stay in Vegas doing college ball. The Spurs were able to snag him in 1992, not long after he left UNLV. However, Tark and Spurs'

owner Red McCombs didn't see eye-to-eye over things like an experienced point guard. The Spurs had lost Rod Strickland to free agency and they were stuck without a PG who had noteworthy NBA experience. Instead, the Spurs had signed Vinny Del Negro, a combo-guard from the Italian League, and NBA journeyman Avery Johnson. Tarkanian went on record saying that the team would suck without someone decent at the point, but McCombs disagreed and canned Jer' after only 20 games. Tark walked away with a $1.3 million settlement, which he used to fund a lawsuit against the NCAA.

490. **B – Doc Adams**. Back in baseball's infancy, teams would field anywhere from 8 to 11 players. With 8, there was a defensive player for every base; with 11, there were simply extra outfielders. The baseball they played with was a lot lighter than the one we're familiar with and outfielders had a hard time throwing the ball to the infield because of its light weight. So, Doc came up with the shortstop position which basically served as a connector between the outfield and the infield. As baseballs became better built and could be thrown longer distances, Doc just moved the shortstop into the infield. And, we can thank Doc for building those better balls, too. Clubs had a hard time finding baseballs so Doc started his own ball manufacturing concern. One of the things he found was that stitching the ball tighter created a "livelier" ball which meant longer distances when the ball was hit or thrown. Like the question said, he also had some involvement in the number of players and the number of innings. And his to-do

list didn't stop there, either. Chalk up the following as an additional part of Doc Adams influence: the distance between bases; the distance from home plate to the pitcher's mound; and the elimination of the "bound rule", which allowed for balls caught after one bounce to be recorded as outs. Most of this can be found in a tome that Adams wrote in 1857 called 'The Laws of Base Ball'. Good luck finding a copy, though. An anonymous buyer purchased one in 2016 for $3.26 million, the most a series of baseball documents had ever sold for. The price paid is the third-highest for a piece of sports memorabilia, behind a 1920 Yankees' Babe Ruth jersey for $4.4 million in 2012, followed by the Naismith Rules of Basketball at $4.3 million.

491. **B – The overtime procedure** is sometimes called the "Kansas Plan" or "Kansas Playoff" because that's the state where it began. The rest of those answer options? All true. Really. The one I like most is the "eephus pitch" one. It came out of a hunting accident where Rip Sewell's big toe – the one he used to pitch off of – took two loads of buckshot. With his pitching motion all funked up because of the accident, Rip had to re-engineer how he pitched. The result was a blooper pitch – one where he held onto the seam and flipped it off three fingers to get backspin. Sewell's blooper reached an arc of 25 feet and, needless to say, it freaked the bejesus out of batters. Pittsburgh outfielder Maurice Van Robays named Sewell's blooper pitch the "Eephus pitch", saying, "Eephus ain't nothin' and that's what that ball is." Need clarification on that word, don'cha? "Eephus" may come from the Hebrew word אפס (pronounced

"EFF-ess"), which means "nothing". Oh, that question about the Paralympics? According to the HuffPo peeps, "the medals at the 2016 Paralympics have been filled with small steel balls that make a particular noise when shaken. The balls allow visually impaired athletes to know exactly which medal they have in their hands, as the Bronze, Silver and Gold medals all make different noises."

492. **A – Chicago Cubs**, who owns one incredible list of trivia bits. Among the ones the *Chicago Tribune* lists as "108 Things Every Cubs Fan Should Know," these... From 1921 to 1951 – with just a short break during World War II – the Cubs trained on Catalina Island off the coast of Los Angeles ... Wrigley Field had night lights ready to install for the 1942 season, but instead donated them to the government the day after Pearl Harbor ...the club was originally known as the "White Stockings" from 1876-1894 ... Pearl Jam's Eddie Vedder wrote a song called "All the Way" for the team and the Beach Boys were hired to re-lyric "Barbara Ann" as "Here Comes the Cubs" for the team's 1987 broadcast theme song ... Cubbies' pitcher Ferguson Jenkins played for the Harlem Globetrotters in the off-season ... made one of the dumbest trades in history when they shipped Lou Brock off to St. Louie ... in the early '60s, the team did away with the position of a single manager and went with a rotation of "head coaches" instead ... star Sammy Sosa was once placed on the injured reserve list as a result of a sneeze that caused back spasms ... Cub Hack Wilson (a powerful lad – 5'6", 195 lbs., with an 18" neck

and size 5 ½ size shoes) hit 191 RBIs in 1930, a record that still stands ... and if a batted ball gets stuck in the ivy? Ground rule double.

493. **B – Nile Kinnick**. A quarterback from the University of Iowa, Nile was the Heisman winner in '39. I don't think any of us were around, then, but this boy could flat-out ball! Dig: he threw for 638 yards and 11 touchdowns on a mere 31 passes... ran for 374 yards... involved in 16 of the 19 touchdowns Iowa scored and involved in 107 of the 130 points that Iowa scored his Heisman year... and played 402 of a possible 420 minutes for the season. All told, he set 14 school records, six of which still stand over 65 years later. He died during WW II while serving as a Navy aviator. Kinnick was inducted into the College Football Hall of Fame in 1951, and, in '72, the University of Iowa did right by him and renamed its football stadium Kinnick Stadium in his honor.

494. **A – Bernie Williams**. Of all the sports cats who released records, Bernabé Williams Figueroa Jr. should probably get the most respect. A classically-trained guitarist, he started bending chords during his last three years in MLB. He signed with Paul McCartney's publishing company, pulled in heavyweights like Springsteen and Béla Fleck to play on his records, released two Top 5 Jazz albums, and got nominated for a (Latin Jazz) Grammy. Other athletes who are/were wannabe music start? There's Shaq who released four LPs – one on 'em (*Shaq Diesel*) even went platinum. Kobe wasn't going to be outdone by Shaq, so he inked a deal with Sony, but the label was

underwhelmed and dropped Bryant from the label after his single "K.O.B.E", featuring supermodel Tyra Banks singing the hook, flopped. Neon Deion (Sanders) put out *Prime Time* which you can now buy on Amazon for $3. Boxer Manny Pacquiao decided to get in the music biz, too. He released two albums and even had the cajones to cover Dan Hill's "Sometimes When We Touch." Chris Webber got in the music game and released an album in 1999, but C-Webb's biggest accomplishment in the music industry came when he turned producer and pulled together a track for Nas' 2006 numero uno selling album *Hip Hop is Dead*.

495. **A – Bob Hayes.** Bob was a football stud in high school, and although football is what won him a scholarship to Florida A&M, his success on the track & field team is what made people sit up and take notice. Bob's sprintin' glory days started at the 1964 Olympics when he won Gold in both the 100m and 4x100m relay. The Cowboys had been keeping an eye on Bob and thought it was worth a crapshoot to select him 88th (7th round) in the 1964 NFL draft. Good bet! Bob ran up a thousand yards in his rookie season, plus 46 receptions and 13 touchdowns. He finished his 11-year career with 371 receptions for 7,414 yards and 71 touchdowns, giving him an impressive 20 yards per catch average (both career TDs and yards per catch average remain Cowboy franchise records).

496. **B – Johnny Unitas**, in 1969. By the time he said sayonara to football, Johnny U. had won 118 games (118-64-4 to be exact). Johnny's career stood for nine years until Fran Tarkenton took over

with 119, a title he held for another 18 years when John Elway snatched it away. Then, Favre, Peyton Manning, yadda... just one of those metrics that will probably update itself ad infinitum.

497. **A – Oksana Baiul.** Nancy came close – even won the short program – but lost the free skate to Baiul in a 5-4 decision (sigh). Tonya Harding finished eighth (yay). Do you remember what happened when the medals were about to be handed out? While Kerrigan and Chen Lu (Bronze) waited nearly a half-hour for officials to find a copy of the Ukrainian national anthem ("Oh Bohdan, Bohdan, our great hetman, what for did you give Ukraine to wretched Muscovites?!"), someone spilled the beans to Kerrigan that the delay was because Baiul cried so hard that her make-up came off and she was getting it retouched. Kerrigan, a little fume'y, was caught live on CBS saying "Oh, come on. So she's going to get out here and cry again. What's the difference?" Chill, Nancy. Remember, you only had to put up with Tonya, and Oksana had all those dreaded Muscovites to deal with.

498. **D – Philadelphia**. Since 1900 (including the Athletics' presence in Philly from 1901-1954), the world "Philadelphia" has never appeared across the chest of any Phillies uni. Although in 1992, Wilson Sporting Goods did mock up a version for consideration, but it never saw the light of day. In doing my homework on this, I found that the Orioles omitted "Baltimore" from their jerseys from 1973-2008 in an effort to attract fans from the Washington, D.C. area. The idea worked, too, with the O's attendance ranking doing one of those

worst-to-first reversals. When the Nationals started up in D.C., however, "Baltimore" went back on the Orioles' road unis.

499. **A and C** are the true ones. "B"? What used to be the Gator Bowl is now the Taxslayer Bowl. And "C"? What started out as Joe Robbie Stadium in Miami has carried seven different names.

500. **C – Incubation of fantasy football**. Fantasy football as we know it today goes back to 1962 and Wilfred Winkenbach. Wilfred was a limited partner of the Oakland Raiders, and on a trip with the team to the Big Apple he, Raiders PR guy Bill Tunnel, and *Oakland Tribune* sports reporter Scotty Stirling, cultivated a system of organization and a rulebook in Wilfred's hotel room. When they got back to Oakland and Winkenbach's rumpus room, they came up with a league – GOPPPL (Greater Oakland Professional Pigskin Prognosticators League) – and a player draft, all the basis of modern fantasy football. Camden Yards? Opened in 1992. The first WrestleMania? 1985. Nabors singing at the Indy 500? He started in 1972.

501. **B – Jennifer Capriati**. Before I get to the reason why, let me say that Jennifer's not the only athlete whose ways and means created a rule. There was Lew Alcindor ("no dunking"), Wayne Gretzky (neither team losing a player when coincidental penalties were called), Ricky Williams (prevented a player under suspension in the NFL from signing with a CFL club), et al. Now to Capriati – Jennifer turned pro at age 13 and in her first year became the youngest ever to reach the finals of a

tournament, youngest ever to reach the semifinals of the French Open, and the youngest seed ever at Wimbledon. She also broke into the top 10 rankings at age 14 and won Olympic Gold at 16. By 17, she was burned out and took a two-year break. However, when she came back, she wasn't her old self and her losing performances sent her rankings plummeting. Nonetheless, she finally regained her mojo, won her third Grand Slam, and retired with a Top 10 ranking. Still, the emotional and physical stress of going pro at age 13 was more than a young teen should endure and the WTA enacted a minimum age of 15 and limited the number of tour appearances one could make until turning 18. That new regulation was commonly referred to as the "Capriati Rule."

502. **A – Ben Franklin**. Say what? I always trust the truth mongers at MentalFloss.com and here's what they had to say: "As a youngster, Ben learned to swim in Philadelphia's Schuylkill River and became somewhat of an expert. On a Thames River boating trip, a 19-year-old Franklin jumped into the river and swam from Chelsea to Blackfriars (around 3.5 miles), performing all sorts of water tricks along the way that surprised and pleased those to whom they were novelties. Of course, he also invented his own swim fins. Franklin's Phelpsian feats earned him an honorary induction into the International Swimming Hall of Fame in 1968."

— THE END —

Why 502 questions? 'Coz it's the area code for Louisville KY and the author is a bit of a home'r.

Sources

ALLABOUTBASKETBALL.US
ALLDAY.COM
ALLIGATORARMY.COM
BASEBALLHALLOFFAME.ORG
BLEACHERREPORT.COM
BOWLINGBALL.COM
BUSTER OLNEY'S 'DYNASTY'
CHEATSHEET.COM
CHICAGOTRIBUNE.COM
CLEVELAND.COM
COLLEGEFOOTBALL.AP.ORG
COMPLEX.COM
DEADSPIN.COM
ETYMONLINE.COM
FACTMONSTER.COM
FOOTBALLPERSPECTIVE.COM
FTW.USATODAY.COM
FUNWHILEITLASTED.NET
HARDBALLTIMES.COM
HEALTHYLIVING.COM
HUFFINGTONPOST.COM
KIDZWORLD.COM
KINESIOLOGY.MSSTATE.EDU
LEADERBOARD.COM
LISTVERSE.COM
MASCOTDB.COM
MENTALFLOSS.COM
MYLOSINGSEASON.NET
NEALROZENDAAL.COM
NFL.COM

NJ.COM
NOTABLEBIOGRAPHIES.COM
NYTIMES.COM
PBA.COM
QUOTEINVESTIGATOR.COM
RAIDERS.COM
REALCLEARSPORTS.COM
REDDIT.COM
RUNNING.COMPETITOR.COM
SABR.ORG
SBNATION.COM
SEEDYKSPORTS.COM
SLATE.COM
SNOPES.COM
SPORTS ILLUSTRATED.COM
SPORTS-REFERENCE.COM
SPORTSGRID.COM
STACKEXCHANGE.COM
SUREPAYROLL.COM
TELEGRAPH.CO.UK
THEINDYCHANNEL.COM
THEOPEN.COM
THESPORTSDESIGNBLOG.COM
TODAYIFOUNDOUT.COM
TOPENDSPORTS.COM
UNI-WATCH.COM
US NEWS AND WORLD REPORT
VICE.COM
WIKIPEDIA.ORG
WILSON.COM

Making a Game Out of the Book

Most people will probably use this book to self-challenge their sports trivia knowledge, but there's a way you can use this as a multi-player game with three or more players.

The game will be played similar to how you'd play a baseball game. Here's our suggestions:

- On a piece of paper, sketch out nine innings (boxes). I've created a scoresheet you can download and print out if you like. It's available by e-mailing garyworld@gmail.com.

- If you want to play with the option of a cash prize for the winner, you could have every player pony up a certain amount at the beginning of the game and, then, the winner-takes-all.

- The person who owns the book (and has probably soaked up enough answers to slay the others) will be the "ump."

- Decide who'll be "up to bat" first, second, third, etc. Play will be in that order going clockwise starting with the first player to the ump's left.

- For each "inning," players choose a number between 1 and 500 and the "ump" asks that numbered question from the book, then marks that number off of the number list so that question isn't asked again.

- If the player gets the question correct, they get a "run" (point). When a player answers incorrectly, the "ump" gets the run/point (see below).

- When a player gets a run/point, they have the option of trying to answer another question and getting more runs/points or letting the next player play. A player can continue answering up to three questions until they a) decide they want to stop, or b) answer a question incorrectly.

- When a player answers a question incorrectly, they lose all the points/runs during that turn and the "ump" is awarded those runs/points. Example: Player 2 answers the first question correctly and decides to try another and they get that one correct as well. That gives them 2 runs/points. They decide to try a third question, but they get that one wrong, so the 2 points that they won go to the ump and the player gets zero runs/points for that round/inning.

- At the end of 9 innings/rounds, the player (or the ump) who has amassed the most runs/points wins the game. If there's a tie between players, those players play up to 3 extra innings/rounds or until one player outscores the other at the end of an inning/round. If there's no winner after 12 innings, the game is a "tie". If there's a prize involved, the prize is split equally between the players who tied with the highest score.

About the Author

Gary Guthrie is like most Baby Boomer guys who live down the street from you – someone who eats at Subway, has an occasional beer, drives a Honda, prefers college ball over pro, gets a little misty when he thinks about the special moments he had playing pitch-and-catch with his dad, loves his daughter (lots), enjoys the greatest kiss on the planet (one that took him 54 years to find), can sing along to "Aqualung" and "Stand by Your Man" and, most of all, just wants to be happy.

He's had a long career in radio (you may have read about his pioneering of the Classic Rock format or heard about his escapades with Streisand & Diamond's "You Don't Bring Me Flowers"), and keeps happy by following creative blisses of art, music, and trivia on the side.

Gary's favorite sports teams? The Mantle-era Yankees, Denny Crum's/Louisville's Doctors of Dunk and Rick Pitino's '13 NCAA champs, all of Scott Davenport's Bellarmine Knights squads, Howard Schnellenberger's U of L 1991 Fiesta Bowl champs, Ed Diddle's Western Kentucky teams, Murray State with Virden & Blondet, and those smooth-as-silk teams Adolph Rupp put on the floor at Kentucky.

If you'd like to check out Gary's other works, there's g.org's *A New Kind of Blue* – the 45th Anniversary tribute to the Miles Davis classic; a self-help oriented quotes book called *Stuck in a Moment*; and Gary's music trivia book *Rock and Roll Heaven Entrance Exam*.

To contact Gary with high-fives, Bronx cheers, corrections, or Q&A ideas (that you'll get credit for in future editions) you can e-mail him at garyworld@gmail.com.

Made in the USA
Columbia, SC
16 December 2020